Can we know anything for certain? There are those who think we can (traditionally labelled the 'dogmatists') and those who think we cannot (traditionally labelled the 'sceptics'). The theory of knowledge, or epistemology, is a great debate between the two. Some dogmatists have sought certainty in the deliverances of the senses. Sceptics objected that the senses are neither a secure nor an adequate basis for certain knowledge. Other dogmatists have sought certainty in the deliverances of pure reason. Sceptics objected that rational self-evidence is no guarantee of truth.

Common Sense, Science and Scepticism is an introductory and historically based survey of the debate. It sides for the most part with the sceptics, showing how the desire to vanquish scepticism has often led philosophers into doctrines of an idealist or anti-realist nature. Scepticism joins with common sense and science in opposing such doctrines.

The book develops out of scepticism a third view, fallibilism or critical rationalism. Although we can have little or no certain knowledge, as the sceptics maintain, we can and do have plenty of conjectural knowledge. This third view incorporates an uncompromising realism about perception, about science and about the nature of truth.

COMMON SENSE, SCIENCE AND SCEPTICISM

COMMON SENSE, SCIENCE AND SCEPTICISM

A historical introduction to the theory of knowledge

ALAN MUSGRAVE

Professor of Philosophy, University of Otago

CAMBRIDGE
UNIVERSITY PRESS

Published by the Press Syndicate of the University of Cambridge
The Pitt Building, Trumpington Street, Cambridge CB2 IRP
40 West 20th Street, New York, NY 10011–4211, USA
10 Stamford Road, Oakleigh, Victoria 3166, Australia

First published 1993

Printed in Great Britain at the University Press, Cambridge

A catalogue record for this book is available from the British Library

Library of Congress cataloguing in publication data

Musgrave, Alan.
Common Sense, Science and Scepticism: a historical introduction to the theory of
knowledge – Alan Musgrave.
p.   cm.
Includes bibliographical references.
ISBN 0 521 43040 2 (hardback) – ISBN 0 521 43625 7 (paperback)
1   Knowledge, Theory of. 1. Title
BD161.M89 1993
121 – dc20   92-12657   CIP

ISBN 0 521 43040 2 hardback
ISBN 0 521 43625 7 paperback

To Sir Karl Popper

Contents

Preface

This book has grown out of introductory lecture courses in the theory of knowledge which I have given at the University of Otago most years since 1970. It is unusual in several ways which need to be noted here. Although it is an introductory book it does not seek to be even-handed in the way many such books do. Rather, it is a sustained argument for a particular epistemological stance, fallibilist or critical realism. Although it is historical it does not seek completeness, either overall or even in the treatment of the historical figures who are discussed. Some historical figures are singled out for discussion, and some aspects of their thought emphasised, because I think that they have made lasting contributions to the evolution of our ideas on the problems with which the book is concerned. Some of my interpretations of the historical figures may be controversial: where I know them to be so, I say so, but I seldom canvass rival interpretations. Throughout, the historical discussions are subservient to the needs of the sustained argument of the book as a whole. This is not, therefore, an orthodox book in the history of philosophy. (In lecturing on these matters, one of my hopes was that students would become interested in finding out more about the philosophers I mention, and would study them further in more orthodox historical courses. The hope was sometimes fulfilled. When it was, students would come to tell me that my treatment of Descartes or Hume had been incomplete, lop-sided, even plain wrong. I count such occasions as successes, and hope that the book may have similar ones.)

My chief pedagogic debt is to those generations of New Zealand students whose questions and objections and quizzical looks have given it whatever clarity and coherence it possesses. My chief intellectual debt is to Sir Karl Popper, to whom the book is dedicated. As will be apparent to anyone familiar with his ideas, this is a 'Popperian' book – which is not to say that Popper himself would necessarily agree with everything said in it, not even with everything said in it about him. Several colleagues and friends have read the manuscript and I have profited from their suggestions, especially those of Hans Albert, Colin Cheyne, John Watkins, and an anonymous reviewer. Finally, I am grateful to Anita Wells for her patient and ever-cheerful secretarial work.

A word about 'gender-inclusive language'. All of the philosophers discussed in the book are men, making frequent use of masculine pronouns a grammatical necessity. However, an anonymous sceptic looms large in the book, who is always 'she'. When, late in the piece, she turns into a critical rationalist, she does not change sex also. Thus the hero of the book is, in fact, a heroine.

Acknowledgements

I am indebted to Oxford University Press for permission to reproduce (as Figure 4 on p. 63) a diagram from Sir Karl Popper's *Objective Knowledge* (1972), and to Collins Publishers for permission to reproduce (as Figure 6 on p. 76) a diagram from N. Tinbergen's *The Herring Gull's World* (1953).

CHAPTER I

The problem of knowledge

The problem which will concern us can be stated very simply, as can most important philosophical problems:

Can we know anything?
If so, what sort of things can we know?
And how can we come to know them?

As with most important philosophical problems, the first difficulty is to see that there is any real problem at all.

It is natural to suppose that the answer to our first question is obvious. Of course we know lots of things. After all, it is our ability to know things which sets us apart from the other animals and which makes us the most powerful and successful animal of all. Some animals can run faster than us, but we construct cars which enable us to go faster than any animal. Some animals see better than we do, but no animal sees better than a human being armed with a telescope or microscope. Birds can fly and we cannot, but we have built aeroplanes which fly faster and further than any bird. In all these cases it is human knowledge which makes the difference, the knowledge which enables us to construct the cars and the telescopes and the aeroplanes. Knowledge is power, and it is human knowledge which has made human beings the most powerful creatures of all. The answer to our first question is, then, perfectly obvious. Anyone who denies that we can know things must be just crazy.

But we should not give up our first question so easily. In order to see that there might be a genuine issue here, let us ask exactly what is involved in knowing something. Once we have become a little clearer about this, we will return to the question.

KNOWLEDGE AS JUSTIFIED TRUE BELIEF

Suppose I say that I know that there is someone standing outside the door. What must be the case for this claim of mine to be correct? The orthodox answer to this question goes like this.

First of all, I must believe or think that someone is outside the door. I must not, for example, be telling a lie. For if, in saying 'There is someone outside the door', I am telling a lie, then I do not believe it and cannot be said to know it. (This holds even if, by chance, there does happen to be someone outside the door, so that my statement happens to be true. I still told a lie, said something I did not believe to be true, and so did not know that someone was outside the door.) So the first condition for the truth of a statement of the form '*A* knows that *P*' (where *A* is a person and *P* a proposition) is that *A* genuinely believes that *P*. But clearly belief is not enough: I may genuinely believe that someone is outside the door, but if in fact there is no one there I will not be said to know it. Belief is, as the philosophers say, a necessary condition for knowledge but not a sufficient condition. What else is required?

The second condition is obvious enough. If I am to know that there is someone outside the door, then there really must be someone outside the door. Before the belief is entitled to be called 'knowledge', what is believed must be true. If I say 'I know that *P*' and then find out that *P* is false, I will withdraw my claim to knowledge: I will say that I thought I knew that *P* but did not really know it. So now we have two conditions for the truth of a statement of the form '*A* knows that *P*': *A* must believe *P*, and *P* must be true. Is anything else required?

Most philosophers say that it is. They defend this view by asking us to imagine cases in which a person believes something, the belief happens to be true, but the person has no good reason to suppose that it is true so that the true belief is just a lucky accident. The uninformed punter may believe that Philosopher King will win the 3.30 and place his bet accordingly. Philosopher King may romp home, showing the belief to be true. Even so, it is argued, the punter did not know that Philosopher

King would win, his true belief was merely a lucky guess. (Remember that he is an uninformed punter who is supposed to know nothing about the field for the 3.30 or about horse-racing in general, but is supposed to believe that Philosopher King will win. It is an interesting question whether people do have completely uninformed beliefs such as this. Uninformed punters there are, who place bets at race meetings. But whether they actually believe that their horse will win, or even believe it to the degree indicated by the odds, I rather doubt. Perhaps a better example is the person who believes something which happens to be true because of a dream or 'premonition'. But let us set aside these questions and proceed.)

A third condition for knowledge will be apparent in what has already been said. For me to know something it is not enough that I believe it and that it happens to be true; I must also be able to give reasons for my belief, or justify it, or show that it is true, or prove it. Only if I can justify my claim and show that it was not a lucky guess, will I be said to know it.

So we now have three conditions for knowledge. For a statement of the form '*A* knows that *P*' to be correct, it must be the case that:

(1) *A* believes that *P*
(2) *P* is true
(3) *A* can justify his belief that *P*.

We have now arrived at the traditional philosophical distinction between genuine knowledge and mere belief or opinion: genuine knowledge is justified true belief.

As we will see, it is the third condition for knowledge which gives rise to most of the special problems of the theory of knowledge. So far we have formulated this condition in a pretty vague way: the knower must be able to justify his belief, give reasons for it, perhaps even establish it or prove it. It may be objected that there is a world of difference between giving a reason for a belief and establishing or proving it. I might cite the *Guinness Book of Records* as my reason for believing that Everest is the tallest mountain, but be reluctant to say that the statement in the book proves that Everest is the tallest mountain, for after all, books contain mistakes. There are reasons which are not conclusive reasons, and when we cite such reasons we are not claiming to prove things. Quite so. However, many philosophers have given our third condition for knowledge a very strong interpretation, whereby to justify a belief is to give conclusive reasons for it, reasons which do establish or prove it. Such philosophers say that the only genuine knowledge consists of beliefs which we can prove or establish. For them the only genuine knowledge is certain knowledge; the phrase 'uncertain knowledge' is a contradiction in terms. They reject the idea that a belief might be justified, and hence entitled to be called 'knowledge', by reasons which are less than conclusive. The Greeks called this absolutely certain knowledge *episteme* and contrasted it with *doxa* or mere opinion. And it is *episteme* which gives the theory of knowledge its fancy name, 'epistemology'.

The philosophers who identify knowledge with certain knowledge also see the problem of knowledge in a special way. For them, the problem of knowledge is really the problem of certainty:

Can we know anything for certain?
If so, what sort of things can we know for certain?
And how can we come to be certain about them?

For a while we are going to accept, for the sake of the argument, the identification of knowledge with certain knowledge. Only after we have seen the difficulties which beset this view, will we consider whether a less demanding conception of knowledge should be considered.

The three conditions for knowledge which are incorporated into the traditional view (belief, truth and justification) are meant to be severally necessary and jointly sufficient conditions: each of the conditions must hold for there to be a case of knowledge, and when they all hold together then a case of knowledge results. But this traditional account has not gone unchallenged, and in the next section we mention a few objections to it.

SOME OBJECTIONS TO THE JUSTIFIED TRUE BELIEF ACCOUNT

The main objections to the justified true belief account fall naturally into two groups: first, there are those who argue that our three conditions are not sufficient for knowledge; second, there are those who argue that our three conditions are not necessary for knowledge.

The first objection is associated chiefly with Edmund Gettier who devised pretty bizarre cases where a person has a justified true belief (so that all the conditions hold) but where we would not, intuitively at any rate, want to say the person knew the proposition in question. One of these examples will give the flavour of all of them.

Smith has a friend, Jones, who he knows has in the past always owned a Ford and who has just offered Smith a lift in a Ford. Smith justifiably believes (a) Jones owns a Ford. Smith has another friend, Brown, of whose whereabouts he is totally ignorant. However, Smith deduces from 'Jones owns a Ford' the proposition (b) 'Either Jones owns a Ford or Brown is in Barcelona', and so comes to believe this proposition too. Now suppose that Jones does not in fact own a Ford (the car he is driving is a rental car), but that by lucky chance Brown is in fact in Barcelona. Does Smith know (b)? Intuitively not. Yet he believes (b), (b) is true, and he is justified in believing (b) since he deduced it from (a) which he justifiably believes (see Gettier 1963).

Defenders of the justified true belief account of knowledge must either bite the bullet and say that, contrary to intuition, Smith does know (b), or argue that he does not because one of the three conditions for knowledge is not satisfied after all. The only plausible candidate for the unsatisfied condition is the third: Smith is not, after all, justified in believing (b). But why not?

Alternatively, we can accept the counterexample as a genuine one and require a fourth condition for a justified true belief to count as knowledge, a condition which will prevent Smith's justified true belief in (b) from counting as knowledge. But what shall this fourth condition be? This is still a hotly debated question, but we shall not enter into those debates here.

The second objection, that justified true belief is not necessary for knowledge, rests upon the cases of knowledge or types of knowledge which simply do not fit the definition. I know my next-door neighbour, the smell of pineapples and the Eiffel Tower. But there do not seem to be any statements or propositions involved here which I believe, which are true and which I can justify. This is knowledge of things rather than knowledge of propositions. Bertrand Russell called it 'knowledge by acquaintance'. Again, I know how to ride a bicycle and how to play chess. Here, too, there do not seem to be any statements or propositions involved. Gilbert Ryle called this 'knowledge-how' as opposed to knowledge-that or propositional knowledge. So there seem to be, on the face of it, three different kinds of knowledge:

(1) knowledge of things or objects (knowing-of or knowledge by acquaintance);
(2) knowledge of how to do things (knowing-how);
(3) knowledge of statements or propositions (knowing-that or propositional knowledge).

And the objection we have to consider states that the justified true belief account really only applies to the third kind of knowledge.

There seems to be a good deal in this objection. There are philosophers who have tried to discount it by arguing that propositional knowledge is fundamental and that, despite appearances, the other kinds of knowledge can be reduced to it or exhibited as special cases of it. They first reduce knowledge by acquaintance to know-how: knowing my next-door neighbour is merely knowing how to recognise him, pick him out from a crowd and so on. And then, these philosophers say, know-how can be reduced to knowledge-that. Knowing how to ride a bicycle is knowing that you must keep the momentum going, lean into the corners and so forth. Knowing how to play chess is knowing that the bishop moves diagonally, that the object is to capture the opponent's king and so forth.

The thesis that all knowledge is, at bottom, propositional knowledge raises some interesting and difficult questions. There are obviously cases where a person knows how to do something but cannot articulate the propositional knowledge which may be involved and may never have been explicitly aware of those propositions at all. We can all speak English, but how many of us can articulate the grammatical rules governing the production of correct English sentences? Fish are good swimmers but are not much good at hydrodynamics. The grammarian and the expert on hydrodynamics may know the propositions which the English speaker or the swimmer does not. But are we to say that the English speaker and the swimmer subconsciously or unconsciously know them too, merely because they can talk and swim? Matters are even more complicated, for there are cases of special skills where nobody knows the propositional knowledge which might be involved. The case of chicken-sexing is a famous one. Large-scale producers of battery hens have an obvious financial interest in rearing only hens, and like to sort out the day-old chicks into females and males. This is not an easy thing to do, for they look very much alike, and careful anatomical inspections by a vet would be too time-consuming and costly. But it turns out that certain people (most of them, apparently, women) can tell at a glance which is which, and they are employed to do just that. Nobody knows how they do it, not even themselves, but that they can do it is shown pretty convincingly by trials that have been conducted. This is a special piece of know-how: the possessor of it cannot articulate it in propositional terms (that is not so unusual), and nobody has so far been able to articulate it in propositional terms.

There is a related question here, the question of animal knowledge. We ordinarily assume that animals can know things: 'Puss knows that her dinner is in the fridge', we say of the cat sniffing at the refrigerator door. Yet it can be argued that animals cannot possess propositional knowledge. The argument runs like this. We first claim that in order to believe any proposition, let alone to justify any proposition, it is necessary to possess a language in which that proposition and its justification can be stated. We next claim that animals do not possess languages which would enable them to formulate beliefs or their justifications. From these two assumptions it follows that animals cannot possess any propositional knowledge or knowledge-that. If we accept this argument, and if we further accept that all knowledge is propositional knowledge, then we are committed to the view that animals possess no knowledge of any kind.

The last conclusion is certainly counter-intuitive. We might avoid it by questioning the assumption that propositional knowledge requires language, or by questioning the assumption that animals do not possess language of the required kind. And we might also avoid it by questioning the reducibility of all knowledge to propositional knowledge. The last course would enable us to maintain that animals can have knowledge by acquaintance (the dog knows his master) and knowledge-how (puss knows how to get us to feed her), while reserving propositional knowledge for possessors of fully fledged languages. (And if it should turn out, as some maintain, that animals do possess fully fledged languages, then it may also turn out that they have propositional knowledge too.)

Rather than trying to defend the reducibility of all knowledge to propositional knowledge, I think it better to admit that the justified true belief account really applies only to one kind of knowledge. For in restricting ourselves for the most part to propositional knowledge, we will still have a great variety of kinds of knowledge (or of knowledge-claims) to consider. There is practical knowledge, such as the claim that the best way to kill a chicken is to wring its neck. There is scientific knowledge, such as the claim that water consists of hydrogen and oxygen, or the claim that humans and the apes evolved from a common ancestor. There is mathematical knowledge, such as the claim that the square on the hypotenuse of a right-angled triangle is equal to the sum of the squares on the other two sides (Pythagoras' theorem), or the claim that there are infinitely many prime numbers. There is moral knowledge, such as the claim that eating people is wrong. There is aesthetic knowledge, such as the claim that Beethoven is better than the Beatles.

There is religious knowledge, such as the claim that God exists and Jesus is His son.

People have claimed to have propositional knowledge of many different kinds. The first question before us is whether any of these claims is correct: can we really know any of these things for certain? A further question which will concern us is whether we acquire these different types of knowledge in the same way. So we see that confining ourselves to knowledge as justified true belief, and hence to propositional knowledge, still leaves us plenty to discuss.

Another objection to the justified true belief account raises an interesting issue. The objection is that our second condition is redundant once the third condition is stated: if a belief is justified then it follows automatically that it is true, so that we need not state this as a separate condition. Now if 'justify' is interpreted strongly, to mean 'give conclusive reasons for' or 'prove', then there seems to be some justice in this complaint. Can one give conclusive reasons for or prove a falsehood? But if 'justify' is interpreted more weakly, to mean 'give a reason for', then matters are not so clear-cut: we can give reasons, even good reasons, for propositions which turn out to be mistaken. With 'justify' interpreted weakly, we may have justified beliefs in false propositions. But we would not want to say that we knew false propositions. Hence the condition that the belief be true as well as justified is necessary in this case. Now we do not want to beg the question in favour of the strong interpretation of the justification condition, and therefore it is better to state the truth condition separately.

A final comment on the justified true belief account: according to this account, all knowledge requires a knower, all knowledge is possessed by some person or other. The same proposition may be known by one person and only believed by a second, if the first person can justify her belief while the second cannot. As we will see, this has important repercussions for the question of whether we can acquire knowledge from other people, by hearing them talk or reading what they write. The emphasis upon personal knowledge, knowledge which requires a knower, contrasts with various impersonal uses of the term 'knowledge'. We say things like 'Scientific knowledge made great advances in the seventeenth century' or 'Chemical knowledge is now so vast that no single person can grasp it all' or 'There is more knowledge stored in the University Library than in people's heads'. In such statements there is no mention of any knower. It can be argued, however, that these impersonal uses of the term 'knowledge' are very much derivative uses, that the body of scientific or chemical knowledge is built up because individual scientists or chemists came to know things in the fundamental personal sense.

DOGMATISM, SCEPTICISM AND INFINITE REGRESSES

Do we know anything for certain? Can we establish or prove the truth of any of our beliefs? Most philosophers say 'yes', but a few say 'no'. The latter group are called the 'sceptics'. Scepticism first reared its ugly head among the Greek philosophers, and the Greek sceptics labelled their opponents the 'dogmatists'. The label is a bit unfortunate; it should not be taken to mean that the opponents of scepticism were necessarily dogmatic about the matter, for many of them were not. A dogmatist may be very open-minded, willing to take seriously the views and arguments of the sceptics, and hence far from dogmatic about his dogmatism. With this proviso, we will operate with these traditional labels. The theory of knowledge, or epistemology, is actually a long and still unfinished war between dogmatism and scepticism. It is this war, a war of words rather than swords, that we shall be examining.

I suspect that most people, if asked where their sympathies initially lie, would side with the dogmatists: of course we can know things for certain. So I shall not disguise the fact that my own sympathies tend to lie with the sceptics. One of the earliest 'epistemologists' was Xenophanes, who lived around 530 BC and who expressed his scepticism in some rather lovely verses. He writes (the translation is due to Popper 1962: 26):

> As for certain truth, no man has known it,
> Nor will he know it; neither of the gods,

Nor of all the things of which I speak.
And if by chance man were to utter
The final truth, he would not himself know it;
For all is but a woven web of guesses.

It will be objected that it was all very well for Xenophanes to write in this vein, living as he did some two-and-a-half thousand years ago when people did not know very much at all. Can his position be maintained in our day and age, when we know lots of things that the Greeks did not and when sceptical despair of our ability to know things is quite absurd? But is it so absurd?

The Greek sceptics invented an argument which was meant to show that we never really have any justified true belief. The sceptic does not dispute the fact that we have beliefs, nor, more importantly, does she dispute the fact that some of our beliefs might happen to be true. She focuses her attack on the third condition for knowledge, the requirement that our true beliefs be justified. And she claims that the process of justifying beliefs falls prey to a fatal infinite regress.

Consider our simple example. Suppose I claim to know that someone is outside the door. The sceptic will ask me how I know this, will invite me to justify my belief, to prove it or give reasons for it. Suppose I say that I know that there is someone outside the door because I arranged with a friend that he would come to stand there at this time. The sceptic will then ask me how I know that he has kept his promise: perhaps he is unreliable, perhaps his watch stopped and he mistook the time, perhaps he got stuck in the lift on the way down. To this I might respond that my friend always keeps his promises, that his watch is new and Japanese and foolproof, that the lift is pretty reliable, too. To which the sceptic will reply that the fact that my friend has kept his promises *up to now*, or that his watch and the lift have not broken down *up to now*, provides no reason for supposing that these happy states of affairs will continue. (This is a point to which we shall be returning.)

The sceptic's strategy is plain enough. Whenever I try to justify any belief or to give a reason for it, I merely mention some other belief which I happen to hold. But unless this other belief is itself a justified belief, I have got nowhere. If I attempt to justify this second belief in turn, then I merely cite a third. And so on, *ad infinitum*. The project of justifying beliefs in terms of other beliefs is subject to an infinite regress. And the sceptic concludes from this that no belief is ever really justified: our so-called justifications merely shift the question back to other beliefs. Since nobody can actually complete an infinite series of justifications, everybody will rest beliefs upon unjustified assumptions. What rests upon mere opinions consists of mere opinions, and the edifice of knowledge collapses.

Now it is worth noting that this general argument goes through both against the strong conception of justification (give conclusive reasons for or prove) and against the weaker one (give non-conclusive reasons for). There is an infinite regress of reasons as well as an infinite regress of proofs.

Sceptics used the infinite regress of justification to support the apparently absurd view that we are never really justified in believing anything. They discovered a second infinite regress which they used to support the even greater absurdity that we can never really know what it is that we believe in the first place! This second infinite regress was the infinite regress of definitions. The argument goes like this. To know what it is that we believe, we must know the meanings of the words we use to express our belief. To know the meaning of a word is to be able to say what it means or to define it. But in defining a word we employ other words, which must be defined in their turn. What do you mean by 'puppy'? A puppy is a young dog. What do you mean by 'young' and by 'dog'? And so on, *ad infinitum*. Since nobody can actually complete an infinite series of definitions, everybody must use words whose meanings they do not know because they have not defined them. And since all of our beliefs are expressed, in the last analysis, using words we have not defined, we never really know what it is that we believe!

The conclusion is ridiculous, you may think, and so something must be wrong with the argument. But before we try to say what has gone wrong with the argument, and with the preceding one, it is worth dwelling on the infinite regress of definitions for a while, since it has some interesting implications. The first is that the ploy, which one often encounters, of asking an opponent in a discussion to define his terms is a sure-fire winner. You can pick on a word which somebody uses and ask him to define it, then pick on a word in the definition and ask him to define that, and so on. The defining will go on forever and the original topic of the discussion will be completely lost. The English politician Richard Crossman became frustrated at the way politicians often talked at cross-purposes, used words in slightly different senses, and therefore argued endlessly without coming to any agreement. He suggested that debates in the House of Commons would be improved and shortened if politicians were compelled by law to define their terms. But as Popper points out (1945, II: 16–17), the infinite regress of definitions teaches us that such legislation would make the debates infinitely long. Moreover, politicians would never actually get to talk about politics but would be endlessly bogged down in preliminary 'clarifications' of the meaning of words.

A more interesting question raised by the infinite regress of definitions concerns language-learning. Children perform the miraculous feat of learning their native language. How do they do this? Sometimes we teach a child the meaning of a word by employing other words: 'sibling' means brother or sister, we say. But it is perfectly obvious that this procedure will only work if the child already understands certain words whose meaning has not been explained verbally. The enterprise of defining words or explaining their meaning is parasitic upon some prior knowledge of meanings and cannot get off the ground if that prior knowledge does not exist. The child who does not know what 'brother' and 'sister' mean is not going to be enlightened by the explanation of the meaning of 'sibling'.

STOPPING THE REGRESSES: EMPIRICISM AND RATIONALISM

Let us return to the infinite regress of justifications and see how we might respond to it. Dogmatists responded by challenging the view, on which the sceptic's argument depends, that a belief can only be justified by citing another belief. They claimed instead that certain beliefs do not require justification in terms of other beliefs, because their truth can be apprehended directly or immediately. The so-called infinite regress of justifications can be stopped at such beliefs: other beliefs must be justified in terms of them, but they do not require a further justification in turn. So to deal with the infinite regress argument, dogmatists invoke a distinction between two kinds of knowledge:

(1) immediate knowledge of basic propositions or first principles or axioms which do not require further justification;
(2) mediate or derived knowledge of propositions which require justification from the basic propositions or first principles or axioms.

The dogmatist response to the infinite regress of definitions is structurally similar. It challenges the view, on which the sceptic's argument depends, that we know the meaning of a word only if we can define it in terms of other words. Dogmatists claimed instead that the meaning of certain words does not require explanation in terms of other words, because their meaning can be apprehended directly or immediately. The infinite regress of definitions can be stopped at such words: other words must be defined in terms of them, but they do not require definition in turn. So to deal with the second infinite regress argument, dogmatists invoke a distinction between two kinds of words or terms or concepts:

(1*) primitive concepts whose meaning does not require explanation because it is immediately apparent;
(2*) defined concepts whose meaning must be explained or defined in terms of the primitive concepts.

Clearly, this answer to the sceptic stands or falls with the theory of immediate knowledge. What is the source of our immediate knowledge of the truth of certain propositions (and of the meaning of certain terms)? In the history of epistemology there have been two competing answers to this question: the first answer, in a word, is experience; the second answer, again in a word, is reason.

The first answer is intuitively the most natural one. Let us return to our simple example, my futile attempt to convince the sceptic that I know that someone is outside the door by citing various reasons I have for believing that there is somebody there. The whole silly business can be brought to an end by opening the door and looking to see whether anybody is there. If we see somebody standing there, then we know that somebody is there. And it would be silly to ask for a reason for this belief: the fact that we see the person is reason enough. So the natural idea is that by using our senses, our eyes and ears, we can come to know the truth of certain propositions immediately or directly. The propositions in question are statements reporting what we observe or experience, or for short, observation statements. And these are the basic propositions or first principles or axioms in the light of which we can justify other beliefs.

The appeal to sense-experience as a source of immediate knowledge of observation statements is the central idea of a theory of knowledge called 'empiricism'. This theory also appeals to sense-experience to cut short the infinite regress of definitions. The primitive concepts, whose meaning requires no explanation or definition, are observation concepts. These stand for features of the world which are immediately apparent when we experience the world. The usual examples include 'red' and 'blue', 'hot' and 'cold', 'rough' and 'smooth', 'loud' and 'soft', 'sweet' and 'bitter'. The meaning of such words need not be defined, indeed, some empiricists say, cannot be defined: instead, it can be grasped, indeed must be grasped, by having the appropriate experiences and associating them with the words. Other concepts must be defined in terms of these observation concepts.

A further feature of empiricism needs to be mentioned here. Many empiricists claimed not only that experience was a source of immediate knowledge (and meaning), but also that it was the only source. They claimed that everything that we can know consists of observation statements and of what can be justified by appeal to observation statements. An old Latin slogan summed up this strong version of empiricism: 'Nihil in intellectus quod non fit priori in sensu.' Roughly translated, this says: 'Nothing is in the intellect which was not previously in the senses.' Not all empiricists were as imperialistic as this: some insisted that experience was a source of knowledge, but conceded that it might not be the only source.

Now as I already mentioned, the empiricist appeal to sense-experience was not the only response to the sceptic's infinite regress argument. The second response was based upon an appeal to reason or intellectual intuition as a source of immediate knowledge. The infinite regress of justifications was to be cut off at the first principles or axioms which were rationally self-evident or known to be true by intellectual intuition: once a rational person understood these propositions, she could see immediately that they are true; and the truth of other propositions, which might at first sight be very far from obvious or self-evident, could be established on the basis of self-evident axioms. This is the central idea of a theory of knowledge called 'rationalism' or 'intellectualism'.

Rationalism is a far less plausible doctrine than empiricism: what are these rationally self-evident propositions and can anything really interesting be established as true on the basis of them? The best way, indeed the only way, to answer this question is to point out that it was mathematical knowledge, and in particular Euclidean geometry, which was the chief inspiration for rationalism.

We have seen that the empiricists regarded sense-experience not merely as a source of certain knowledge of the truth of observation-statements, but also as a source of meaning for observation concepts. Did the rationalists similarly think that reason or intellectual intuition could make clear the meanings of certain primitive or undefined concepts? The answer is that they did, and that mathematics and in particular Euclidean geometry was the chief inspiration for this doctrine also. We shall elaborate this later, in Chapter 10.

Earlier I mentioned that some empiricists did not confine themselves to the view that sense-experience was a source of immediate knowledge, but also defended the imperialist thesis that it was the only source. The same can be said of certain rationalists. They, too, thought that reason or intellectual intuition was the only source of genuine knowledge, and that what could not be known in this way could not be known at all. Other rationalists were more modest and conceded that other sources of knowledge existed (some even allowed that sense-experience was such a source).

The historical situation is even muddier than this. We have seen that both rationalism and empiricism developed claims about our knowledge of the truth of statements and about our knowledge of the meaning of terms. So we might distinguish empiricism about statements from empiricism about concepts, and rationalism about statements from rationalism about concepts. And then we might note that various hybrid views are possible. One might, for example, be a thoroughgoing empiricist about concepts (claiming that we learn the meaning of all concepts from experience) while being a rationalist about some or perhaps all statements (claiming that when we know the truth of some statements, perhaps of any statement, it is by the use of reason).

Despite these complications, it is still true to say that empiricism and rationalism were often regarded as opposing views. The sceptics liked neither, and as we will see, argued against both the appeal to sense-experience and the appeal to reason. And the sceptics often found ready allies in the two dogmatist camps. Empiricists joined sceptics in denying the power of pure reason to give us certainty. Rationalists joined sceptics in denying the power of sense-experience to give us certainty. The battles become as confusing as any three-cornered fight. Descartes, a chief defender of the rationalist view, plays the sceptic when discussing what sense-experience can achieve. Mill, a chief defender of empiricism, plays the sceptic when discussing what reason can achieve.

I mention these complications only as a warning that it is often misleading to label a thinker simply as an empiricist or a rationalist or a sceptic. But the positions can be clearly defined and are important whether or not any real philosophers have ever occupied them straightforwardly. It can be, and has been, argued that out-and-out scept*ics* are very hard to find: but out-

and-out scept*icism* can be reconstructed by combining ingredients from various sources.

To sum up: we have examined the infinite regress arguments used by the sceptics to show that justified true beliefs are an illusion. We have seen how empiricists and rationalists, in different though structurally similar ways, tried to answer these arguments. The sceptics were not silenced by these dogmatist responses, and attacked both the appeal to experience and the appeal to reason. But they were also attacked themselves, and that will be our next topic.

CHAPTER 2

Scepticism under attack

IS SCEPTICISM CONSISTENT?

Are we really to take scepticism seriously? That many people find it hard to do so is not simply due to any instinctive sympathy with dogmatism that they might possess. For scepticism is, on the face of it, an extremely peculiar position. The out-and-out sceptic claims that nothing can be known. And pointing to the infinite regress of proofs or justifications, she argues that no belief can really be proved or justified. But wait! Does not the sceptic claim to know that nothing can be known? And does she not try to prove that nothing can be proved? You contradict yourself if you claim to know that nothing can be known or claim to have proved that nothing can be proved. Out-and-out scepticism is therefore a self-contradictory position.

This is a very old objection, which was levelled against the earliest Greek sceptics. And if it is correct, then it is a very damaging objection. A self-contradictory position cannot be true, and if out-and-out scepticism cannot be true then we might as well forget about it. The Greek sceptics tried to meet this objection by formulating their position so that it ceased to be self-contradictory. They found two ways to do this.

The first was to formulate scepticism as the view that nothing can be known except the fact that nothing can be known, and nothing can be proved except the fact that nothing can be proved. This version of scepticism came to be called 'academic scepticism', not because it was 'merely academic' but because it was the sort of scepticism said to be taught in Plato's Academy in Athens. It is associated historically with Plato's teacher, Socrates, who claimed that the only thing we can know is that we know nothing else and that it is important to know this.

Academic scepticism looks like a dodge, and in a way it is. But it is important to realise that it is a successful dodge. The objection was that scepticism is self-contradictory, that it cannot be stated consistently. The academic sceptic's dodge shows that this is not so: by a slight reformulation which makes an exception of scepticism itself, we have a position which, whatever else might be said about it, is at least consistent. The obvious question about academic scepticism is that if one thing can somehow be known, then why cannot other things be known in a similar way? But this gets tricky: if anything else can be known, then academic scepticism is false (for it says that only academic scepticism can be known), and being false it cannot be known either (for we cannot know a falsehood). Here we touch upon the peculiarities which result when statements refer, among other things, to themselves.

Other Greek sceptics did not like academic scepticism: they called it 'negative dogmatism' and said that it was not a thoroughgoing form of scepticism at all. They preferred to reformulate scepticism as the view that nothing can be known not even the fact that nothing can be known, and nothing can be proved not even the fact that nothing can be proved. This version of scepticism came to be called 'Pyrrhonian scepticism', after the sceptic Pyrrho who founded it.

Pyrrhonian scepticism also looks like, and is, a dodge. But it, too, is a successful dodge in that it formulates scepticism in a logically consistent way. The objection that scepticism cannot be consistently stated does not seem to be a very decisive one, if we can answer it with slight reformulations which preserve the essence of the position being attacked.

But does Pyrrhonian scepticism preserve the essence of scepticism? If the Pyrrhonian cannot prove that she is right, why should we worry about her and why should we not be dogmatists instead? The traditional sceptic response to questions such as these runs in terms of using the weapons of your opponent to beat your opponent, without believing that these weapons have any special potency. Dogmatists believe that argument has the power to establish things. Sceptics show that arguments (such as the infinite regress argument) can equally well show that nothing can be established. The true sceptic does not prize her arguments over those of the dogmatist, nor does she think that she can establish things while the dogmatist cannot. The true sceptic says simply that if we accept the dogmatist procedures (for the sake of the argument), then scepticism is as sensible a position as dogmatism by dogmatist standards. The true dogmatist, on the other hand, can never accept this point of view.

Pyrrho's follower Sextus Empiricus considered the objection that in trying to prove that nothing can be proved, the sceptic contradicts herself. He answered it by likening the sceptic's use of the dogmatist's method of proof to our using a ladder to reach a high place – having climbed the ladder, you can kick it away:

> Yes, say they, but the argument which deduces that proof does not exist, being probative itself, banishes itself. To which it must be replied that … even if it does banish itself, the existence of proof is not thereby confirmed … the argument against proof, after abolishing every proof, can cancel itself also. And … just as it is not impossible for the man who has ascended to a high place by a ladder to overturn the ladder with his foot after his ascent, so also it is not unlikely that the sceptic after he has arrived at his thesis by means of the argument proving the non-existence of proof, as it were by a step-ladder, should then abolish this very argument. (1933–49, II: 487–9)

David Hume, himself a great sceptic, defended scepticism against this objection in a similar way:

> I … cannot approve of that expeditious way, which some take with the sceptics, to reject at once all their arguments without enquiry or examination. If the sceptical reasoning be strong, say they, 'tis a proof, that reason may have some force and authority: if weak, they can never be sufficient to invalidate all the conclusions of our understanding. This argument is not just; because the sceptical reasonings … wou'd be successively both strong and weak, according to the successive dispositions of the mind. Reason first appears in possession of the throne … Her enemy, therefore, is oblig'd to take shelter under her protection, and by making use of rational arguments … prove the

fallaciousness and imbecility of reason. This...gradually diminishes the force of that governing power [reason], and its own at the same time; till at last they both vanish away into nothing... (*Treatise*, I, iv, 1; 1888: 186–7)

Sextus' analogy of the ladder which you kick away once you have climbed up it was to become quite popular. Fritz Mauthner wrote a book which argued that we must dispense with language if we want to see the world as it really is. In other words, he used language to try to destroy language, and defended the procedure as follows:

If I want to ascend into the critique of language, which is the most important business of thinking mankind, then I must destroy language behind me and in me, step by step, I must destroy every rung of the ladder while climbing upon it. (Cited by Weiler 1958: 80)

Ludwig Wittgenstein, who was influenced somewhat by Mauthner, wrote a famous book called *Tractatus Logico-Philosophicus* to demonstrate the sceptical thesis that philosophy (and in general anything that was not science) was actually nonsense. In other words, he wrote philosophy to show that philosophy was nonsense, and defended the procedure at the end of the book as follows:

My propositions serve as elucidations in the following way: anyone who understands me eventually recognizes them as nonsensical, when he has used them – as steps – to climb up beyond them. (He must, so to speak, throw away the ladder after he has climbed up it.)
He must transcend these propositions, and then he will see the world aright. (1922: 6.54)

The best comment on this view of Wittgenstein's was made by his disciple Frank Ramsey: 'What you can't say, you can't say – and you can't whistle it either' (1931: 238).

Let us leave the metaphor of kicking away the ladder after you have climbed it, and return to the main point. We considered a logical objection to out-and-out scepticism – that it cannot be stated consistently – and saw how the sceptics tried to answer it. Now it may be that the sceptic response fails to convince. This would not matter much because, as I said earlier, there are few, if any, out-and-out sceptics. Most sceptics are sceptical about some particular kind of knowledge, while remaining far from sceptical about other kinds. Out-and-out scepticism is an extreme position which can be put together by combining the more limited scepticisms which have actually been defended. And even if it should turn out that total scepticism can be refuted on logical grounds, we would still have to take seriously the less extreme sceptical views out of which it is compounded.

IS SCEPTICISM IMPRACTICAL?

There is another very old objection to scepticism, which holds that no matter what she says the sceptic cannot herself take her philosophy seriously and live by it. For consider what this would mean. The sceptic claims that we cannot know for sure that the next piece of bread we eat will nourish us while the plate on which the bread lies would not nourish us. So the consistent sceptic, offered sandwiches on plates, ought to bite into the plates as often as she bites into the sandwiches. Similarly, the sceptic wishing to descend from a tall building claims that we cannot know for sure that taking the lift will be safe while chucking herself out of the window will be unhealthy. So we ought to find sceptics regularly throwing themselves out of windows in order to get to the ground!

One of the most consistent sceptics seems to have been Pyrrho. Bertrand Russell tells a nice story about him:

Pyrrho... maintained that we never know enough to be sure that one course of action is wiser than another. In his youth, when he was taking his constitutional one afternoon, he saw Anaxarchus, his teacher in philosophy (from whom he had imbibed his principles) with his head stuck in a ditch, unable to get out. After contemplating him for some time, he walked on, maintaining that there was no sufficient ground for thinking he would do any good by pulling the old man out. Others, less sceptical, affected a rescue, and blamed Pyrrho for his heartlessness. But his teacher, true to his principles, praised him for his consistency. (1935: 11–12. The source of the story is Diogenes Laertius 1853: 403)

Pyrrho is said to have lived an extraordinary life, in which he paid little heed to his comfort or safety. He is also said to have

lived to a ripe old age! The secret of his success lay with his
disciples, who followed him around and saved him from himself,
making sure he ate properly, dressed warmly, did not walk over
cliffs, and so forth. (My favourite story about Pyrrho is that the
government so admired him that they decided to exempt all
philosophers from taxation!)

These stories merely reinforce the objection that one could
not adhere consistently to sceptical principles and live very
long. But the Greek sceptics justified the actions of Pyrrho's
disciples in the following way. Every day all of us must make
countless decisions to act in one way rather than another. In
each society there will be certain customary ways to behave: it
is the custom in our society to eat the sandwich rather than the
plate on which it is offered, to take the lift to get down to the
ground rather than throw yourself out of the window and so
forth. Now there is nothing to stop the sceptic, since she has to
behave somehow, from behaving in the customary ways. And
this is what, in fact, the sceptics do. The difference between the
dogmatist and sceptic lies not in the way that they behave, but
in whether they think the customary ways of behaving can be
shown to be correct. The dogmatist claims to know that the
sandwich will nourish him while the plate will not. The sceptic
eats the sandwich, too, but with no such pretension to
knowledge. One of Pyrrho's followers writes:

We live in accordance with the normal rules of life, undogmatically,
seeing that we cannot remain wholly inactive. And it would seem that
this regulation of life is fourfold, and that one part of it lies in the
guidance of Nature, another in the constraint of the passions, another
in the tradition of laws and customs, another in the instruction of the
arts. Nature's guidance is that by which we are naturally capable of
sensation and thought; constraint of the passions is that whereby
hunger drives us to food and thirst to drink; tradition of customs and
laws, that whereby we regard piety in the conduct of life as good, but
impiety as evil; instruction of the arts, that whereby we are not
inactive in such arts as we adopt. But we make all these statements
undogmatically. (Sextus Empiricus 1933–49, 1: 23–4)

Is this response adequate? If the sceptic is to behave in the
customary ways, to do in Rome as the Romans do, as we say,

then she has to know what the Romans do, what are the customary ways of behaving. But the true sceptic cannot claim to know this either. Quite so. The sceptic will reply, however, that just as she eats the sandwich without claiming to know that it will nourish her, so also she eats the sandwich without claiming to know that this is the done thing.

DOES SCEPTICISM MATTER?

At this point impatience is likely to set in. And impatience leads to a further objection, not so much to scepticism as to the whole enterprise in which we are engaged. If the sceptic and the dogmatist are going to behave in the same way, do the same things in the same situations, then what does it matter who is right? Is not the whole dispute merely academic and un-important?

This is a serious objection. It can be answered on two levels. First, one might quarrel with the implicit assumption that 'merely academic' questions are unimportant and not worth bothering about. People are less likely to take this view about disciplines other than philosophy. For example, cosmologists are interested in the question of whether the universe originated in a so-called 'Big-Bang' long ago or whether it has always existed in a 'Steady State'. (I gather that at the moment the evidence favours the former view.) Now this is a purely academic question, in the sense that which answer is correct makes no difference to the way we behave in the ordinary affairs of life. But one seldom hears it objected that the cosmologists should stop worrying their heads about the question. It is the same, one might say, with the question of dogmatism and scepticism. It would be nice to know whether we can know anything for sure, even if the answer is going to make no difference to the way we behave in the ordinary affairs of life.

But is our problem a 'merely academic' problem which makes no practical difference? This brings me to the second level on which this objection can be met. It does make a difference whether one is a dogmatist or a sceptic. One way to see this is to realise that the customary ways of behaving are not always and everywhere the same. Imagine a society where it is the custom not to eat other people, and where some people think they know that eating people is wrong and that anyone who does it will be eternally punished in the fires of hell. (Perhaps we live in such a society, perhaps not.) Now imagine that a dogmatist and a sceptic from this society visit another one where it is the custom to eat people. How will the two behave in this new setting? The dogmatist, secure in the knowledge that eating people is wrong and has the most dreadful consequences in the afterlife, will certainly try to persuade the people of the error of their ways. And if he happens to be put in charge of the society and has power over its members, he will certainly try to compel them by force to stop eating people in their own best interests. The sceptic, on the other hand, will notice that the customs in the second society are different and, doing in Rome as the Romans do, will start eating other people, too.

The example is far-fetched but the point it illustrates is not. Institutions such as the Inquisition existed to force people, in what were thought to be their own best interests, to adopt certain religious beliefs. Sceptics do not set up inquisitions. The French sceptic Montaigne lived in a town where the local officers of the Inquisition were busy accusing women of being witches, proving that they were by time-honoured methods, and burning them. Montaigne's comment was: 'It is rating our conjectures pretty highly to roast people for them.'

Now it is worth remembering that the notorious Inquisition was not unique. There have been many inquisitions throughout history, and there are still some even today: an inquisition is any institution which persecutes people for believing things in religion or morals or politics which are 'known' to be mistaken and wicked. Only dogmatists set up inquisitions. And we should also remember how many wars in human history were religious wars, fought by people who knew the truth and sought to convince their opponents of the error of their ways.

There is even something like a philosophical justification for persecuting people for beliefs which we regard as erroneous. It is a justification which is only available to dogmatists, and the essence of it is captured in the slogan 'Ignorance is sin'. How could anyone come to suppose that to be ignorant of something or to be mistaken about it is a sin? Well, suppose we think that the truth can be known for sure. Presumably, there will be a method for coming to know the truth for sure. If this method is open to all of us, then all of us can employ it to find out what the truth is. How are we then to explain the fact that some people do not know the truths in question or have mistaken beliefs on the matter? The answer can only be that they have not employed the proper method. Their ignorance or their errors are therefore their own fault, for refusing to employ the proper method. And if our ignorance or our errors are our own fault, then others are justified in punishing us for them.

As we will see later, dogmatists have often embarked on the curious task of explaining how we make mistakes. This 'problem of error' as it is called, is parasitic upon dogmatism: only those who think there is a method for finding the truth are obliged to explain why we do not always find the truth. And the 'theories of error' which are advanced to solve this problem are all what Popper (1963: 7) calls 'conspiracy theories of error', which say that error is the fault of those who fall into it. Sceptics, who do not believe in certain knowledge and who therefore deny that there is a royal road to it, do not have the problem of explaining error at all. These conspiracy theories of error, with their slogan that error and ignorance are a sin, provide the philosophical justification for inquisitions, religious wars and any other practice of persecuting people for their mistakes (or what are thought to be their mistakes).

It can be argued, then, that the dispute between dogmatism and scepticism is not an idle and 'merely academic' dispute which makes no practical difference. Bertrand Russell once wrote a popular essay called 'On the value of scepticism'. The essay opens as follows:

I wish to propose for the reader's favourable consideration a doctrine which may, I fear, appear wildly paradoxical and subversive. The doctrine in question is this: that it is undesirable to believe a proposition when there is no ground whatever for supposing it true. I must, of course, admit that if such an opinion became common it would completely transform our social life and our political system:

since both are at present faultless, this must weigh against it. I am also aware (what is more serious) that it would tend to diminish the incomes of clairvoyants, bookmakers, bishops and others who live on the irrational hopes of those who have done nothing to deserve good fortune here or hereafter. In spite of these grave arguments, I maintain that a case can be made out for my paradox, and I shall try to set it forth.

First of all, I wish to guard myself against being thought to take up an extreme position... The scepticism that I advocate amounts only to this: (1) that when the experts are agreed, the opposite opinion cannot be held to be certain; (2) that when they are not agreed, no opinion can be regarded as certain... and (3) that when they all hold that no sufficient grounds for a positive opinion exist, the ordinary man would do well to suspend his judgement.

These propositions may seem mild, yet, if accepted, they would absolutely revolutionize human life.

The opinions for which people are willing to fight and persecute all belong to one of the three classes which this scepticism condemns. (1935: 11–13)

In the rest of his essay, Russell illustrates his last point: some of the examples he gives are a little dated, but still well worth reading.

It can be argued, then, that a healthy dose of scepticism would make the world a happier place – and sceptics have always argued this. The Greek sceptics went further. They claimed that being sceptical made one a happier person. The sceptic does not chase after the will-o'-the-wisp of certainty and make herself miserable by failing to achieve it, or by seeing that other people do not share her opinions and getting into arguments with them. Instead, the aim of the sceptical arguments is to reach a point where one suspends judgement on all issues (or on all contentious issues, if one is not a total sceptic). And the interesting psychological claim was made that this suspension of judgement brought with it peace of mind and a contented, happy feeling. The Greek sceptics claimed that their philosophy brought this peace of mind (or quietude), whereas dogmatism brought nothing but unhappiness.

I do not know whether the sceptic's psychological claim is

true. (And what business has she anyway in making such claims?) Against it one can argue that if you desperately want to know the right answer to some question, you are not going to be happy suspending judgement on the question. But the issue illustrates another way in which our dispute might make a practical difference.

CHAPTER 3

Scepticism regarding the senses

In the chapter before last we introduced the empiricist view that the senses are a source of immediate knowledge of the truth of observation statements, and that other true beliefs could be established or justified on the basis of these observation statements. The sceptics were far from silenced by this rebuttal of their infinite regress argument. They counter-attacked on two fronts: (1) observation statements do not provide a secure basis for knowledge; (2) observation statements do not provide a sufficiently broad basis for knowledge even if we were to grant that they are secure. We will consider the first objection, and its repercussions, in this and the next four chapters. The second objection will be considered in Chapters 8 and 9.

SEXTUS EMPIRICUS VERSUS EMPIRICISM

The Greek sceptics devoted much of their energy to the demolition of empiricism. Their attempts are preserved for us in the writings of Sextus Empiricus, a disciple of Pyrrho. Sextus lived around AD 160–210, and Pyrrho about five hundred years earlier, around 275 BC. Sextus does not seem to have been a very original thinker or even a very clever one. Most of his views and arguments were probably invented by earlier sceptics, especially by Pyrrho, whose own works are lost, and Sextus does not always do a very good job of preserving them for us. His books are long and repetitious, each of the good arguments is buried among lots of bad ones, and points are illustrated with dozens of examples, most of them silly ones, when one decent example would do. Sextus tries to defend this style: the consistent sceptic has no business selecting the best arguments or examples since she is not supposed to know which are the best – instead she must give them all and in no particular order! The best of Sextus' three books is *Outlines of Pyrrhonism*, which contains the sceptic attack on empiricism. But the titles of the others are worth a mention. The second is *Against the Dogmatists* in three parts: *Against the Logicians*, *Against the Physicists* and *Against the Ethicists*. The third book is *Against the Professors* in six parts: *Against the Grammarians*, *Against the Rhetoricians*, *Against the Geometers*, *Against the Arithmeticians*, *Against the Astrologers* and *Against the Musicians*. As you can see, Sextus was against everybody, especially the professors! (Sextus' writings came to be extremely influential in the sixteenth and seventeenth centuries; see Popkin 1964).

Sextus begins by saying that the sceptic does not dispute the fact that our senses tell us how things appear to be, rather she asks whether the senses tell us how things really are.

And when we question whether the underlying object is such as it appears, we grant the fact that it appears, and our doubt does not concern the appearance itself but the account given of that appearance – and that is a different thing from questioning the appearance itself. For example, honey appears to us to be sweet (and this we grant, for we perceive sweetness through the senses), but whether it is also sweet in its essence is for us a matter of doubt, since this is not an appearance but a judgement regarding the appearance. (1933–49, I: 19–20)

Here the problem of appearance and reality makes its first appearance.

Empiricism claims that by using our senses we can immediately know that certain observation statements are true. And these observation statements tell us how things we can observe really are, not merely how they appear to be. Typical observation statements would be 'The table is brown', 'This honey is sweet', 'The sun is shining', 'The fire is hot', 'Someone is standing outside the door', and so on. The empiricist's claim is that we can be sure of the truth of such statements by using our senses, by verifying them with the senses.

Sextus' basic strategy for refuting this view is to point out that the appearances contradict one another, thus presenting us with the problem (which he thinks insoluble) of deciding which appearance we shall trust to tell us how things really are. Let us see some of the examples that Sextus gives, and also catch the flavour of the whole.

Do our eyes tell us the real shapes and sizes of things? Well, the same tower appears round and small from a distance, and square and large from close-up. Which of the appearances shall we take to tell us how the tower really is? In general, the apparent shape of an object depends upon the position from which we view it: a coin looks round viewed from above but elliptical viewed from the side; the apparent shape of a table-top will be different for everyone who looks at it, since each views it from a different position. The oar appears to be straight when viewed out of the water and bent when viewed half-immersed in the water. If we press our eyeball, what appeared to be the one object will appear double. The eyes of cats are differently shaped than ours, and are likely to reflect the shapes and sizes of things differently, as do differently shaped mirrors. Perhaps puss sees the world as it really is and we do not.

Is snow white? Well, it sometimes appears so, but 'sufferers from jaundice declare that objects which seem to us white are yellow, while those whose eyes are bloodshot call them blood-red' (Sextus Empiricus 1933–49, 1: 29). And we do not have to get jaundice or a hangover to experience such things ourselves: look at a patch of snow, look up at the sun, and then look at the snow again – what originally appeared white will now appear yellow. Shine a red torch on the snow and it will also appear red.

Is sugar sweet? Well, it sometimes appears so, but it might not do so if we are ill. Different substances appear sweet or foul to different peoples, judging by the diversity of substances which these different peoples like to eat. Animals are attracted to things which repel humans, suggesting that those things appear differently to animals and humans.

Here we might support Sextus with a recent discovery. A certain chemical, phenylthiocarbamide (or PTC) has an unpleasant taste for some people and no taste at all for others. And it turns out that this is genetically determined: whether it tastes unpleasant depends upon your parents, and whether it

tasted unpleasant to one or both of them. Sextus would have
asked: is PTC really unpleasant-tasting or not?

Sometimes the same sense will give us conflicting information.
Water which appears hot to one part of the body will appear
only lukewarm to a part of the body which is inflamed – is it
really hot or lukewarm? Take three buckets and fill one with
water that feels hot, the second with water that feels cold, and
the third with water that feels warm; now put your right hand
in the first bucket and your left hand in the second; finally put
them both in the third bucket, which will appear cold to your
right hand and hot to your left hand – is it really hot or cold? Or
as Ogden Nash put it:

> I test my bath before I sit,
> And I'm always moved to wonderment
> That what chills the finger not a bit
> Is so frigid upon the fundament. (*Samson Agonistes*)

Sometimes the information given by one sense conflicts with
that given by another. A surface may appear smooth when we
look at it, and rough when we touch it. Is it really rough or
smooth?

We confidently assume that our senses will tell us what there
is in the world. But perhaps other animals can sense things that
we cannot. (I am told that one of the Beatles records ends with
a tune for dogs, so high-pitched that humans cannot hear it. So
when humans get to the end of what they can hear and say 'The
record is finished', they are wrong.)

We confidently assume, too, that what our senses tell us about
exists in the world. But people have hallucinations, and see
things that are not there at all. Can we ever be sure that we are
not hallucinating on any particular occasion? Also things
appear very differently to us in our dreams from the way they do
in waking life. Can we ever be sure that we are not dreaming on
any particular occasion? Perhaps hallucinators and dreamers
experience the world as it really is, and the sober perceptions of
waking life are the real 'illusion'.

Enough has been said to illustrate Sextus' basic strategy and
to give the flavour of the whole. The basic strategy is to point

out that the senses often give us conflicting information about the world. Which of the conflicting 'appearances' shall we take for reality? We can never, says Sextus, simply assume that the real world is as it appears to be. We can never, that is, simply assume on the basis of our experience that any observation statement is true. So the senses are not a source of immediate knowledge after all.

Some of these arguments have become so important that they have been given special names:

The argument from illusion: (1) When an illusion occurs, things are not really as they appear to be. (2) We can never be sure that we are not having an illusion. (3) Therefore, we can never be sure that things are really as they appear to be.

The argument from hallucination: (1) When a hallucination occurs, things are not really as they appear to be. (2) We can never be sure that we are not having a hallucination. (3) Therefore, we can never be sure that things are really as they appear to be.

The argument from dreams: (1) When we dream, things are not really as they appear to be. (2) We can never be sure that we are not dreaming. (3) Therefore, we can never be sure that things are really as they appear to be.

Notice that these arguments are structurally identical: they lead to the same conclusion, and the premises differ only over whether illusions, hallucinations, or dreams are referred to. These are not the only ways, or even the most usual ways, to formulate these famous sceptical arguments. In the customary formulations, the conclusions are that we might always be the victims of illusion or hallucination, or might always be dreaming. And philosophers have spilled much ink in trying to show that such sceptical conclusions, and the premises from which they follow, are 'incoherent'. I shall not discuss such formulations or the attempts to debunk them. I merely observe that the formulations given above are quite different and do not have the sceptic asserting 'incoherent' (or allegedly 'incoherent') theses. Actually, what we have here are not different formulations of the same argument, but quite different arguments. The customary argument is: 'We sometimes have illusions or hallucinations or dreams. Therefore, it is possible that we always have illusions or hallucinations or dreams.' I think that the mainstream sceptical arguments, and the ones most difficult to rebut, are those that I have given. But I shall not argue the point here. I mention it only to emphasise the importance, in philosophy, of getting the argument we are considering straight.

AN ARISTOTELIAN REPLY

Some of Sextus' arguments and examples look pretty ridiculous. It is tempting to dismiss them by saying that, *of course*, when we are sick or deranged, or the circumstances of our perceiving are otherwise abnormal (like pressing our eyeball while looking at something), we will have peculiar experiences which will not be a reliable picture of how things really are. But if we are normal, healthy people using our senses in normal circumstances, then we do have immediate knowledge of the truth of observation statements. The senses are a source of knowledge after all, but only the senses of normal, healthy people in normal circumstances. A view like this was defended by Aristotle and with it he tried to dispose of arguments based upon the way things appear in dreams, or when we are ill or hallucinating. Is this modified version of the empiricist thesis acceptable?

Sextus Empiricus did not think much of it, and criticised it on several counts. First, he said, the whole normal/abnormal distinction is quite fishy. It is perfectly normal for people with jaundice to see everything tinged with yellow, and for drunkards to have hallucinations. This is just a verbal point. What is not normal, we might reply, is to be ill with jaundice or drunk.

Second, Aristotle simply assumes that the experiences of normal healthy people in normal circumstances (call these 'normal experiences' for short) are a reliable guide to how things really are. How does he know this? Perhaps abnormal experiences are the reliable ones, perhaps only the sick or the drunk or the hallucinating see the world as it really is. (There is nothing new under the sun. What was only a possibility for Sextus, raised for sceptical purposes, has been asserted to be the truth by prophets of the 'drug culture'. They say that one ought to take mescalin or LSD if one wants to experience the world as it really is. A student put a sticker on my office door which reads: 'Reality is an illusion caused by lack of drugs'.) Aristotle proposes a criterion for when 'appearance' and 'reality' match up. Are we to accept this criterion without proof? That is unsatisfactory. How could Aristotle prove it? If he proves it by appealing to normal experiences, he argues in a circle. If he proves it by appealing to some other reason, then we will ask him to prove this other reason in turn, and we are off on an infinite regress. (Here something like the old infinite regress argument turns up again. It will recur again and again in sceptical thought. In its most general form it is used to demonstrate the impossibility of a criterion of truth: see below, pp. 251–2.)

Third, Sextus argues that even if we accept Aristotle's criterion without proof, we have to apply it to particular cases of perception. In other words, before we can trust our senses on any given occasion, we must be sure that we are normal and healthy and that the circumstances are normal. Since we can never be sure of this, Sextus argues, we can never be sure that any particular experience tells us how things really are.

Fourth, Sextus argues that even if we accept Aristotle's criterion and even if we assume that there is no problem about applying it, it still will not deal with all of the contradictions in our experience. In particular, it will not deal with the argument from illusion. You do not have to be sick or hallucinating or dreaming for a stick to appear bent when half-immersed in water. It is quite normal for a stick to appear bent in this case, and we would think something was wrong with a person who did not see it so. Aristotle might reply that the circumstances of the perceiving are not normal, that it is not normal to view a stick partly through water and partly through air. Why say this? Why say that viewing a stick wholly through air is viewing it in normal circumstances, viewing a stick wholly through water is viewing it in normal circumstances, but viewing it partly through air and partly through water is not viewing it in normal circumstances?

HOW BELIEF AND EXPERIENCE INTERACT

The answer to this last question is perfectly obvious, one may think. A straight stick viewed wholly through air looks straight, as it really is; a straight stick viewed wholly through (calm) water also looks straight, as it really is; but a straight stick viewed partly through air and partly through water looks bent though it is not really bent. We know that the stick is straight, and that is why we declare that there is something 'abnormal' about the circumstances of perception in which it does not appear to be as it really is. But this answer is curious: it says that we know what the stick is really like (it is straight) and judge our perceptions of the stick in the light of this knowledge, accepting some as telling us what the stick is really like but discounting others. In short, using a couple of useful terms, we use our knowledge to sort our perceptions into the veridical (truthful) and the non-veridical (mistaken). This is curious because according to empiricism our knowledge was supposed to be based upon our perceptions. The senses are a curious foundation for knowledge, if the knowledge supposedly erected upon that foundation can sometimes overturn it.

Yet this curious position does seem to be the position that we are in. None of us is actually fooled by the illusion of the bent stick (and hence 'illusion' is not such a good word for it). None of us, confronting a stick half-immersed in water, will say 'The stick is bent'. All of us will say 'The stick looks bent (or appears to be bent), but really it is straight'. (It may happen, however, that we are fooled by some less familiar illusions, and actually come to hold false beliefs as a result of such experiences.) In this case we can (somehow) sort appearance from reality and we can (somehow) resolve the contradiction in our sense-experience. The interesting question is not whether we can do this, but how we actually do it.

It is the same with the other 'contradictions' to which Sextus Empiricus points. The tower may appear round from a distance and square from close up, but we know that it is square and discount the former 'appearance'. A coin may look elliptical viewed from the side and round viewed from above, but we know it is round and discount the former 'appearance'. The apparent shape of a table-top may be different for every observer, but the interesting thing is that twenty observers asked what shape the table-top is will all confidently declare that it is rectangular. This is a striking case where we have agreement in perceptual judgement despite an alleged wide diversity of perceptual experience. Macbeth knew that the bloodstained dagger he saw was an hallucination because he could not reach out and touch it:

> Is this a dagger which I see before me,
> The handle toward my hand? Come, let me clutch thee:
> I have thee not, and yet I see thee still.
> Art thou not, fatal vision, sensible
> To feeling as to sight? or art thou but
> A dagger of the mind, a false creation,
> Proceeding from the heat-oppressed brain?
>
> (*Macbeth*, Act II, Scene 1)

The hallucinator who really thinks there are pink rats running up the wall will soon be put straight by his friends or by the family doctor. And however realistic our dreams seem while we are dreaming, we can afterwards tell them from waking life and reassure ourselves that 'it was only a dream'.

Now the interesting question, to repeat, is exactly how we come to resolve the contradictions in our experience. The answer to this question, in a nutshell, is something like this. We perceive the world armed with certain beliefs which we have previously formed or acquired. And we sometimes discount the evidence of the senses, refuse to believe our eyes or ears, because what they tell us conflicts with our prior beliefs. This answer, if correct, raises many interesting questions which we shall have to discuss. But first, let us illustrate how it works with the case of the stick half-immersed in water.

Suppose that we first view a stick out of water and it looks straight, and then we view it half-immersed in water and it looks bent. Why do we discount the latter experience? Why do we say, automatically and without thinking, that the stick in water only looks bent but is not really bent? One might suppose that this is the only thing to say, that there is no alternative. But there are at least two alternatives: we might say that the stick out of water only looks straight but is really bent; and we might say that at first the stick was straight and then it became bent when it was dipped into the water. Why not the latter? Well, if pressed a person would be likely to reply: 'Dipping the stick into water could not bend it.' And if pressed further, he might say: 'It would take quite an effort to bend a stick like that – and if one tried it would probably snap it in two. Certainly the water could not exert enough pressure to make it bend. And sticks do not bend like that of their own accord.'

The details of the story do not matter so much as the general picture. And the general picture is of a person who appeals to beliefs about sticks, what it takes to bend sticks, and water, in order to justify setting aside the evidence of his senses.

Or perhaps something more straightforward might happen. We pick up a stick, it looks straight, and when we run our hand along it, it feels straight, too. But when we dip it in water it looks bent. We declare that it is not really bent, and we confidently predict that if we were to run our hand along it again it would feel straight under water also. We perform the experiment (noticing that as our arm goes in the water it, too, develops a kink!) and feel justified in our original conclusion. Three experiences indicate straightness, only one bentness, and we go with the majority and declare the minority a 'wild' experience. 'Why not favour the minority?' Sextus would no doubt ask. Indeed, why choose at all? Why not accept all the experiences as veridical? The attempt to answer this last question will uncover beliefs like the following: 'We cannot accept all these experiences as veridical because there is a single stick out there in the world with a single shape (straight or bent). We can see the stick as well as touch it. There are not two sticks, the one we see which at first is straight and then bent, and the one we touch which stays straight.'

Enough has been said to indicate the kind of way in which we set about sorting experiences into the veridical and the non-

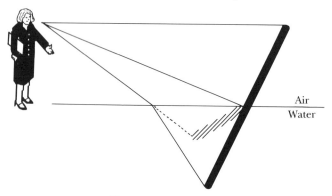

Figure 1. The bent stick

veridical. We do it in the light of our prior beliefs. These may range from very basic beliefs like that in independently existing material objects, like the stick, which are accessible to the senses, to rather primitive bits of science, such as beliefs about water's inability to bend rigid bodies.

Of course, discounting the appearance of the bent stick in water as illusory raises an interesting problem: Why do sticks look bent when immersed in water? Many do not worry about such problems: confident that the stick is straight all along, they get on with the business of life. But the professionally curious, the scientists, have taken up the problem. They have produced an interesting explanation of why the stick looks bent, an explanation which is interesting from a philosophical point of view also. They tell tales about the mechanism of vision: in order to see something, rays of light must be produced by, or reflected from, the thing and enter the eye. And they tell tales about these rays of light: they travel in straight lines, but when they pass from one medium (such as water) into another medium (such as air) they bend or refract at a certain angle (see Figure 1). Armed with these stories, scientists can explain why sticks look bent when half-immersed in water, why round coins viewed from the side look elliptical, why the apparent shape of a table-top changes as the observer changes position and so forth.

These interesting stories of the scientist show us (provided, of course, that we accept them) that we were right all along to discount our experience of the bent stick. For the scientist explains what we instinctively postulated: that the stick is straight but looks bent. And most of us, in the face of the nagging sceptic who says 'But can you prove this postulate of yours?' are likely to reply 'Well, I cannot but the scientists have'. Yet the scientist's story is philosophically interesting. For one thing, we cannot see or touch the 'rays of light' which he postulates (when we popularly say that we can see a torch-beam, what we actually are seeing are lots of things from which the rays of light in the beam are reflected). The scientist tells us we were right to discount the evidence of our eyes because of his nice story about the behaviour of things we cannot see at all! Moreover, the scientist's story raises as many problems as it solves: What is the nature of these rays of light? Why do they bend when they pass from one medium to another? The sceptic will not be impressed. And yet the scientist can point to all kinds of things which can be explained and predicted by his story, things which he will say justify him in accepting the story.

There are many examples of the way in which scientists of one kind or another have been able to explain why certain experiences are non-veridical. Medical scientists can, I suppose, explain why severe jaundice makes people see everything yellow (or rather, with a yellowy tinge). Psychologists can presumably explain why lukewarm water appears cold to a hand that has just been immersed in hot water. In many cases we have, as yet, no scientific explanation of these perceptual anomalies. Doctors know that taking certain drugs will cause you to hallucinate, but so far as I know they do not know why.

Now, although this is not a book on philosophy of science, we shall be returning to some issues that are raised by scientific explanations like the one we have been considering. For the moment let us simply note that science often supports common sense in discounting certain experiences as non-veridical. Common-sense beliefs and scientific beliefs join forces sometimes to discount the evidence of the senses.

Where does this leave naive empiricism? It leaves it, I think, in tatters. Naive empiricists regard sense-experience as a foundation for knowledge: our senses assure us of the truth of observation-statements and our other beliefs must be justified by appeal to sense-experience. But we have seen that our other beliefs may assure us of the falsity of certain observation-statements and lead us to reject them. The relationship between belief and experience cannot be so straightforward as the naive empiricist supposes. There is a curious interplay between belief and experience: experience may lead us to form certain beliefs or to modify and even abandon beliefs we already have; but beliefs may also lead us to abandon certain experiences as non-veridical, and they also, as we shall see, help to form and modify experiences, too.

Several philosophers have tried to sum up this curious interplay between belief and experience, or between knowledge and experience. The poet Goethe (who was also a philosopher) said: 'We do not so much know what we see – rather, we see what we know.' Otto Neurath likens our knowledge to a ship which we must repair and improve as we sail along and in which no particular plank is sacrosanct:

There is no way of taking conclusively established pure [observation-statements] as the starting point of [knowledge] ... We are like sailors who must rebuild their ship on the open sea, never able to dismantle it in dry-dock and to reconstruct it there out of the best materials... *We also allow for the possibility of discarding [observation sentences].* (1959: 201–4)

Karl Popper uses the metaphor of building a house (the house of knowledge) on a swamp:

The empirical basis of [knowledge] has nothing absolute about it. [Knowledge] does not rest upon rock-bottom. The bold structure of our knowledge rises, as it were, above a swamp. It is like a building erected on piles. The piles are driven down from above into the swamp, but not down to any natural or 'given' base; and when we cease our attempt to drive our piles into a deeper layer, it is not because we have reached firm ground. We simply stop when we are satisfied that they are firm enough to carry the structure, at least for the time being. (1959: 111)

We have seen that the empiricist view that the senses are a source of immediate knowledge of the truth of observation-statements cannot be quite correct. For in order to resolve the contradictions in our sense-experience we often discount certain experiences as non-veridical, say that they do not indicate how things really are, and refuse to accept as true the observation-statements they suggest. Confronted with the stick half-immersed in water, we do not declare 'The stick is bent', but say instead that it only appears or seems to be bent but is not really so. And if we ask on what basis we do this, the answer in general terms is that we employ our knowledge or beliefs about the things observed in order to sort our experiences into the veridical and the non-veridical.

Now this answer raises three interesting questions. The first question is how we acquired the beliefs which help us resolve the contradictions in our experience: were they not themselves somehow acquired from experience? This is, properly under-stood, a question of psychology or a factual question. But it is connected with, and has repercussions for, a second question which is more philosophical. The second question is whether, if we rely on prior beliefs to make sense of our experiences, these beliefs cannot lead us to make mistakes. What if we have a false belief and on the basis of it declare a veridical experience non-veridical, or a non-veridical experience veridical? This question leads in turn to our third question. If we rely on prior beliefs to interpret or make sense of our experience, then we can be sure that we have done this correctly only if we can be sure that the beliefs on which we rely are correct. But can we ever be sure of this?

For the moment I shall concentrate on the second question. The first question will occupy us in the next chapter. The third question, which is the most general question of all, will lurk in the background for quite a while yet.

THE PROBLEM OF PERCEPTUAL ERROR

Does it ever happen that we declare a veridical experience non-veridical, or vice versa? And if it happens, does it happen because we rely on false prior beliefs? It certainly happens. It happens, first of all, whenever a person is actually fooled by an illusion. The stick which looks bent when half-immersed in water is so familiar that we are not likely to be fooled by it

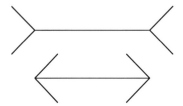

Figure 2. The Mueller illusion

(though I imagine that children can be fooled by it at an early stage of their learning careers). But consider a less familiar illusion such as the Mueller illusion (see Figure 2). The first line seems or appears longer than the second. And anyone unfamiliar with the illusion is quite likely to declare (especially after only a casual glance at the lines) that it actually is longer. Anyone who does so has deemed a non-veridical experience veridical, and as a result has accepted a false observation statement. Illusions are special and puzzling cases. Does it ever happen that prior beliefs can lead us to misinterpret our experience and to accept as true observation-statements which are false, or merely to set aside an experience as illusory or somehow peculiar when it is not? There are countless ways in which this happens; let me mention just a few.

Experiments have been staged to test the reliability of eye-witness testimony in the courts. A mock crime will be staged before an audience: say a masked man bursts through a french window and stabs a man sitting at a desk. The audience are then asked separately to give an account of what they saw. It is notorious that these accounts can vary widely: each eye-witness notices different things and reports them. It is also notorious that the eye-witness reports will often contradict one another on all kinds of points, many of which are difficult to explain. But some of the discrepancies can plausibly be explained by appealing to the beliefs of the witnesses. For example, the racially prejudiced are quite likely to declare that the murderer was not masked at all but was a black man.

A famous example concerns experiments with anomalous playing-cards (Bruner and Postman 1949). Here people are shown a series of playing-cards, each for a short time, and asked to name them, 'six of diamonds', 'four of clubs' and so forth. Each time they name a card, we have an observation-statement. Now, unknown to the subjects of the experiment, there are some anomalous cards: for example, the even-numbered hearts might be coloured black instead of red. Pretty well everybody who participates in such experiments fails to notice the anomalous cards and issues lots of mistaken observation statements: 'Six of spades', 'Ten of spades' and so forth. What they are looking at is not a regular six of spades; it is the wrong colour. Yet, subjects typically overlook this. And the explanation is that they believe the cards come from a perfectly normal pack, indeed are even led to believe this by the experimenter, and therefore discount the evidence of their eyes. It is only when they start to suspect that something might not be in order (perhaps by the experimenter asking whether they are sure that a card is a six of spades and inviting them to look again), that the subjects are able to see what is there to be seen.

Even people trained in the art of very accurate observation can be led by their prior beliefs to make perceptual errors. Before William Harvey discovered the circulation of the blood, the prevailing belief among anatomists required blood to pass directly from one side of the heart to the other, through a muscular wall known as the 'septum'. Anatomists postulated that there were many little channels or pores in the septum through which the blood passed. And several reliable anatomists declared that they had actually seen such pores when dissecting corpses. (When others said that they could not see them, the answer was that they rapidly close up after death and are therefore very difficult to see!) No such pores exist. But otherwise reliable anatomists persuaded themselves that they had seen them, because their belief demanded that they be there to be seen.

Astronomers are trained to make observations of extreme accuracy. One of the best observational astronomers of the nineteenth century was a Frenchman called Lalande. Now, when we observe stars, they do not change their positions relative to one another, but when we observe planets, they do. In 1795 Lalande directed his telescope to a region where he

Figure 3. Perceptual oversight

believed there were no planets (at the time astronomers believed there were only six planets). Lalande actually saw a then unknown planet, now called Neptune, and carefully noted its position. He saw it again and carefully noted its position each time. Then he realised that it had changed its position relative to the stars in that region. Something was wrong: either the astronomers were wrong that there are only six planets, none of them in the region; or Lalande's observations, carefully recorded, were wrong. Lalande chose the latter course, and declared that his earlier observations must have been erroneous. Historians of astronomy talk of 'pre-discovery observations' of planets: Lalande saw Neptune in 1795 but because he stuck to his prior beliefs about the planets he was not able to discover it. It was not discovered until 1848 by Adams and Leverrier – neither of whom saw it when they discovered it. (They discovered it by predicting where it would be seen – but that is another story.)

These are pretty esoteric examples. But more familiar examples where we fail to notice what is there to be noticed, or 'see' what is not there to be seen, are easy to find. Asked to read the sentence in Figure 3, many people will fail to see the second occurrence of the word 'the' or the fact that the letter 'r' in 'springtime' is defective. We know written English, believe or expect a perfectly ordinary sentence, and overlook the peculiarities of the inscription which actually confronts us. Anybody who has had to read proofs to check for printer's errors knows that it is pretty fatal to attend to the meaning of what is written, let alone to get engrossed in it. For then one misses the misprints in the medium in order to get at its message!

It is not merely that our prior beliefs or expectations help us to interpret (and on occasions misinterpret) our experience. They also help determine what it is that we shall experience in the first place. At any moment of our lives the sensory system is constantly being bombarded with all kinds of messages or stimuli from the outside world. But receiving a sensory stimulus is not the same as sensing or having a sensory experience. Most stimuli never reach our conscious awareness at all; most of them are unconsciously filtered out in favour of a few things which we do notice, pay attention to and interpret in various ways. As the psychologist and philosopher William James said (1878: 19):

> Millions of items of the outward order are present to my senses which never properly enter into my experience. Why? Because they have no interest for me. My experience is what I agree to attend to. Only those items which I notice shape my mind – without selective interest, experience is an utter chaos.

Now what determines 'what I agree to attend to' are my interests and my expectations or beliefs. If you have an interest in learning philosophy and are interested in the philosophy lecture, you do not notice the fly buzzing in the window. The hungry spider, whose interests are more mundane, might make it the centre of his attention. Your attention to the philosophy lecture might be diverted, however, by something unexpected. You would certainly pay attention to a giant tortoise, should one lumber through the door, because that would be a surprising and unexpected thing to see in a philosophy lecture. But nothing can be unexpected to a person who has no expectations: it is only because we have other expectations that we find the giant tortoise in the lecture room surprising.

We may be quite unaware of these 'expectations' or beliefs of ours. It may only be when an expectation is disappointed that we become aware that we had it. A person who walks down a flight of stairs and reaches the bottom with a jolt simultaneously becomes aware that he had expected one more step and had adjusted his movements accordingly.

To sum up. We have seen how our interests, and our prior beliefs and expectations, help to determine what sensory stimuli we will pay attention to. We have seen several examples of the way in which prior beliefs or expectations help us to make sense of our experience, to count some of it as veridical and some of it as non-veridical. And we have seen numerous ways in which this can lead us into perceptual error: we accept as true observation-statements which are false, and we fail to accept as true observation-statements which really are true.

The empiricist philosopher who first drew attention to this kind of thing was Francis Bacon (1561–1626). He did not like it; he thought that it arose because we adopt an erroneous attitude or method towards our experience, and he thought it could be overcome by adopting a correct attitude or method. This will be our next topic.

Francis Bacon was a statesman before he was a philosopher, and he rose to be Lord Chancellor of England under King James I. He was dismissed from this position for taking bribes in connection with legal cases which he had to judge. His defence against the charge was interesting: he admitted taking the bribes, but insisted that they had not influenced his decisions in any way! (He ought not to have accepted bribes. But, one feels, having accepted them, he ought to have been influenced by them. A knotty problem for the moral philosopher.)

Bacon's most important book was *Novum Organum* published in 1620. The title, which means 'New Method', was something of a joke. Aristotle's writings on the theory of knowledge had been collected together and were referred to as the *Organon* or 'Method'. So Bacon was saying he was going to improve on Aristotle. But Bacon did not have the last laugh: William Whewell later published his *Novum Organum Renovatum* ('New Method Renovated') to improve upon Bacon.

Bacon was an empiricist: he believed that genuine knowledge could be obtained using the senses. He was also very critical of what passed for knowledge in his day: mistaken views abounded, and uncertainty clouded everything. Bacon thought that all this error and uncertainty arose because we used the wrong method, in particular because we did not employ experience or observation in the proper way. Bacon called this erroneous method the 'anticipation of nature': the mind anticipates what nature will reveal to it through the senses; it jumps to conclusions and allows these premature speculations or preconceptions or prejudgements (prejudices) to distort the message of the senses. Perceptual errors arise, we overlook the true state of affairs, and we cling to our false and uncertain preconceptions or prejudices.

Bacon goes to a great deal of trouble to classify the different kinds of preconceptions or prejudices to which we are prone. He calls them all 'idols of the mind', false gods which we worship instead of the true God, pure and unadulterated sense experience. Here he has many interesting points. He says, for example:

The human understanding is of its own nature prone to suppose the existence of more order and regularity in the world than it finds. (1620: I, aphorism xlv)

Having supposed that some regularity obtains, that is, formed a belief that it does, we tend to discount any experience which does not square with our preconception.

The human understanding when it has once adopted an opinion (either as being the received opinion or as being agreeable to itself) draws all things else to support and agree with it. And though there be a greater number and weight of instances to be found on the other side, yet these it either neglects and despises, or else by some distinction sets aside and rejects, in order that by this great and pernicious predetermination the authority of its former conclusions may remain inviolate.

Bacon's own example of this concerns those who argue for the power of prayer by pointing to pictures of sailors who prayed for a safe voyage and did indeed come home safely. Bacon says it was a good answer to ask: 'But where are they painted that were drowned after their [prayers]?' He concludes:

And such is the way of all superstition, whether in astrology, dreams, omens, divine judgements, or the like; wherein men, having a delight in such vanities, mark the events where they are fulfilled, but where they fail, though this happen much oftener, neglect and pass them by.

But with far more subtlety does this mischief insinuate itself into philosophy and the sciences; in which the first conclusion colours and brings into conformity with itself all that come after... (1620: 1, aphorism xlvi)

This is dead right. Popular belief in astrology survives because people mark the occasions when their horoscope was right (which is quite often since the astrological predictions are usually pretty vague), but neglect and pass over the occasions when it was not. Sometimes things are arranged to ensure that this will happen. When Uri Geller appears on television he sometimes tries to prove the mysterious power of thought by inviting the viewers to take out a broken watch and will it to start ticking again. But he only invites those whose watch started to telephone the studio! Thousands perform the experiment, twenty or thirty ring up, and we have twenty or thirty further illustrations of the truth of Geller's hypotheses! (Of course, Geller does risk the unlikely event that nobody rings up!)

Bacon is right about the problem: prior beliefs or preconceptions or prejudices can distort the message of the senses. Bacon proposes to solve the problem with his new method, which he calls the 'interpretation of nature'. Before we consider this, let us pause to note that in so far as Bacon thinks that error and uncertainty can be avoided by this new method, he also thinks error and uncertainty are our own fault. Error and uncertainty arise because we misuse our faculties, employ the wrong method, and indulge in premature speculation. So we have here an example of a conspiracy theory of error. We shall later see the rationalist philosopher Descartes proposing a very similar one.

How are error and uncertainty to be avoided? The first step, according to Bacon, is to empty the mind of all preconceptions or prejudices so that we can observe the world as it really is. He talks of purging the mind of prejudices to qualify it for dealing with the truth. He says that we are 'to become again as little children' who observe the world with an innocent eye undistorted by prejudice:

The understanding must be completely cleared and freed of [prejudice] so that access to the kingdom of man which is founded on the sciences, may resemble that to the Kingdom of Heaven, where no admission is conceded except to children. (1620: 1, aphorism lxviii)

After this, we are to avoid premature speculation:

The understanding must not...be allowed to jump and fly from particulars to [general conclusions]...The understanding must not therefore be supplied with wings, but rather hung with weights, to keep it from leaping and flying. Now this has never been done; when it is done, we may entertain better hopes of the sciences. (1620: 1, aphorism civ)

What are we to say of Bacon's idea of purging the mind of all preconceptions so that we can observe the world with the innocent eye of the child? It raises many questions. Can we in fact empty our heads of all preconceptions? Of course, we can try to do this and we may think we have succeeded: yet, we are rightly suspicious of the person who says that he or she takes a completely unprejudiced or unbiased view of some matter. What of those preconceived ideas which we are not aware of possessing? And should we try to empty our heads of pre-conceived ideas? May we not thereby avoid making mistaken perceptual judgements only at the price of making no jud-gements at all? Is it true, as Bacon supposes, that the little child does observe the world through an innocent eye? And finally, if our prior beliefs help us to resolve contradictions in our experience, as we have seen that they do, will we not be left with those contradictions if we abandon all prior beliefs? We shall pursue all of these questions.

Bacon himself pursues some of them, at least implicitly, when he gives further details of his new method. He first advocates collecting all the data about some problem, without any selection or interpretation in the light of preconceived ideas. But he soon realises that this is an unending task: if we are really to operate without preconceptions, then anything we observe might be deemed relevant to any question in which we are interested. Bacon then adopts the maxim 'Truth will more readily spring from error than from confusion'. We should not confuse ourselves by collecting masses of observations, most of which will prove to be irrelevant to our problem. Instead, we should formulate some tentative solutions to our problem, some hypotheses. These hypotheses are examples of the 'anticipation of nature' which Bacon previously condemned. But Bacon now advocates the really original feature of his new method: instead of seeking evidence in favour of our preconceptions, and ignoring evidence against them, we should adopt a critical policy. We should look for observations, and more important, seek to perform experiments, which will show our false hypotheses to be false. It is this critical method, and especially its emphasis upon experiment rather than casual observation, which made Bacon influential as a philosopher of science. Bacon thought that we could enumerate all the possible answers to any problem, eliminate the false ones one by one, and thereby arrive at the truth. This is a method which has come to be called 'eliminative induction':

> Now what the sciences stand in need of is a form of induction which shall analyse experience and take it to pieces, and by a due process of exclusion and rejection lead to an inevitable conclusion. (1620: Preface, 20)

There are many problems with Bacon's method of eliminative induction. Will we always be able to make observations, or devise experiments, which will show the falsity of any of our false hypotheses? And where we can, do we not rely uncritically on our senses to tell us what we have observed or the result of our experiment? What if we make an observational error which leads us to reject as false a hypothesis which is really true? Most important, can we ever actually enumerate all the possible answers to some question and hence be sure, when we have eliminated all but one of these, that the surviving hypothesis is the correct one? Bacon did not say anything about the first and last of these questions, and does not seem to have been aware of them. His answer to the second is very important. He says:

> For certain it is that the senses deceive; but then at the same time they supply the means of discovering their own errors; only the errors are [apparent], the means of discovery are to [be sought].
> The sense fails in two ways. Sometimes it gives no information, sometimes it gives false information. For first, there are very many things which escape the sense...And again when the sense does

apprehend a thing its apprehension is not much to be relied upon ... To meet these difficulties, I have sought on all sides diligently and faithfully to provide helps for the sense – substitutes to supply its failures, rectifications to correct its errors; and this I endeavour to accomplish not so much by instruments as by experiments. For the subtlety of experiments is far greater than that of the sense itself, even when assisted by exquisite instruments – such experiments, I mean, as are skilfully and artificially devised for the express purpose of determining the point in question. To the immediate and proper perception of the sense, therefore, I do not give much weight; but I contrive that the office of the sense shall be only to judge of the experiment, and that the experiment itself shall judge of the thing. (1620: Preface, 21–2)

An example will illustrate Bacon's point. Suppose people disagree about whether sunlight is essential for plant growth. Both parties to the dispute can support their point of view with casual observations, neither party can see what sunlight does or does not do for plants. A skilful artificial experiment will settle the question: get identical plants, in identical pots, with identical soil, and place one in the sunshine and the other in total darkness. Suppose the first plant thrives and the second dies. This simultaneously refutes the view that sunlight is not essential and establishes the view that it is. Of course, we must use our senses to determine what the outcome of the experiment is, and the possibility that we suffer an optical illusion or a hallucination in doing so remains. But this (ever present) possibility aside, the experiment has settled the question for us, in a way that no amount of casual observation could.

Sceptics will be unconvinced, and will point out sources of error quite apart from the reliance on the senses to determine the outcome of the experiment. Can Bacon be sure that if he performs the experiment on two further plants, its outcome will be the same? Can he be sure that something other than the presence and absence of sunlight does not explain the result – perhaps his plants were not quite 'identical' after all, and some factor other than the absence of sunlight led the second plant to die? This is the problem of enumerating and eliminating all possible hypotheses, in a slightly different dress. But we shall not pursue these further sceptical worries here.

Bacon's emphasis on the importance of controlled experiment, as opposed to casual observation, was his chief claim to
fame as a philosopher of science. He became the father of
'experimental philosophy' (the old name for experimental
science) and his views became the official views of the Royal
Society, the first and most important scientific society. (It is
worth noting that Uri Geller's experiment with the broken
watches is not a proper Baconian experiment: it is so devised
that it could only 'settle the question' in Geller's favour. For
more information on Bacon's importance as a pioneer philosopher of experimental science, see Urbach 1987.)

Bacon was quite optimistic about what might be achieved if
his new method of interpreting nature by means of controlled
experiment were adopted. He even thought that science might
be finished off in a few years, provided he could get a big
research grant from the king to employ assistants to make the
experiments. But he did not get his grant: the king dismissed
him from office instead. And instead of finishing off science,
Bacon himself was finished off by it. The story goes that he was
experimenting on stuffing chickens with snow to preserve them,
caught pneumonia on Hampstead Heath and died.

OBSERVATION IS THEORY-LADEN

So far we have considered several ancient sceptical arguments
against the senses as a source of certain knowledge. To end this
chapter I want to consider a very modern argument to the same
effect, which is, arguably, of greater importance than the
ancient ones.

Empiricists assume that we can learn from experience that
particular observation-statements are correct. For example, we
experience the table and thereby come to know that the
statement 'There is a table here' is true. But this overlooks the
gap which exists between the experiences we have when looking
at the table and the statement we formulate on the basis of those
experiences. We must formulate observation-statements, for
according to empiricism they are the ultimate premises from

which other statements are to be proved: experiences themselves are just happenings and cannot be the premises of any argument. But when we do formulate observation-statements, they transcend the experiences which prompt them. And what leads statements to transcend experience is the language in which the statements are formulated. For example, when we look in the direction of the table and declare 'There is a table here' we interpret certain sensory inputs as indicating the presence of a table. But if we did not previously know the meaning of the word 'table', or possess the concept of a table, then we could not formulate the observation-statement. A creature which did not possess the concept of a table could still see the table; but such a creature could not learn from this experience that there is a table here and could not formulate the observation report 'Here is a table'.

Philosophers have drawn a distinction between seeing and seeing-that (or more generally, between perceiving and perceiving-that). It is similar to the distinction between knowing and knowing-that. A cat may see the table, but if the cat does not possess the concept of a table then he cannot see that there is a table here. A person who does not possess the concept of a galvanometer (does not know what the word 'galvanometer' means) may see a galvanometer in a physics laboratory, but cannot see that there is a galvanometer there. Seeing-that is propositional and requires that the observer possesses the words or concepts needed to formulate the proposition in question. Seeing is not propositional and does not require the possession of any concept. What makes seeing-that possible is the prior understanding of language or concepts. It is language which enables us to see that (or more generally, perceive that) things are the case, and hence to formulate observation-statements. (The distinction between seeing and seeing-that is important, for it will later help us to avoid the pitfalls of linguistic or conceptual idealism': see Chapter 14, pp. 263–6).

Now, the gap between experiences and observation reports, a gap filled by language or concepts, is an important source of the fallibility of observation reports. We all see the table and do not hesitate to accept the observation statement 'There is a table'.

But what if someone were to fiddle around at the back of the 'table' and all of a sudden Beethoven's Fifth Symphony were to fill the room? Would we then be inclined to say that we were wrong, that the object was not a table after all but a rather swish and streamlined stereo? If we would say this, then in reporting 'There is a table' we were tacitly committed to the prediction that it would not emit Beethoven's Fifth. And because this prediction turned out to be mistaken, we were prepared to give up the observation report which committed us to it.

The point can be generalised. In attending to sensory stimuli and interpreting them in a certain way so as to formulate observation reports, we always employ words or concepts which commit us to certain predictions regarding our future experiences. Since any of these predictions might turn out to be mistaken, future experiences might always lead us to reject a past observation report. This is what we mean by saying that any observation report transcends the experience which prompts it and is therefore fallible.

How precisely does this transcendence come about? How can 'Here is a table' commit us to any prediction? In our particular example, the prediction actually arises not simply from the observation report but from a general principle also, as follows:

Observation report: Here is a table.
General principle: Tables, unlike stereos, do not play music.
Prediction: This object will not play music.

More generally, the structure of the predictive arguments is like this:

Observation report: A is an X.
General principle: X's do/do not do Y.
Prediction: A will/will not do Y.

Now the argument we have proposed says that since the predictions might always be mistaken, we might always be led to reject our observation report.

This suggests two ways in which the argument might be countered. First, notice that if the prediction does turn out to be wrong, we need not reject the observation report: we might instead reject the general principle. In our example, if the table emits Beethoven's Fifth, we might give up the general principle that tables do not play music and say instead that some tables are stereos. This is possible. But it would be absurd, I think, to recommend it as a general policy. And if it is not a general policy, then we might in any particular case reject the observation report instead – and our fallibilist conclusion stands.

The second way of countering the argument is simply to deny that in bringing the things we perceive under general concepts, we have any general principles employing those concepts which would commit us to any predictions. In our example one might simply deny that in reporting 'Here is a table' we possess any general principles about tables which might commit us to any prediction about how our 'table' will behave in the future. This response is implausible, for the point of bringing the things we experience under concepts is precisely that we will be able to anticipate how they will behave in the future. And this, in turn, is only possible if possession of a general concept goes hand in hand with possession of some general principles employing that concept.

So far I have said nothing about the nature of the general principles that we employ, and this is a matter which affects the cogency of both these replies to the original argument. There are two extreme views on the matter which have been defended by philosophers:

(A) The general principles are true by virtue of the meaning of the general concepts they contain: for example, knowing what the word 'table' means is knowing that tables do not play music, for this is part of the meaning of the word 'table'.

(B) The general principles are not true by virtue of the meaning of general concepts, but simply represent general beliefs, which might turn out to be true or might turn out to be false: for example, though we may believe that tables do not emit music, we might be prepared to admit that we were wrong.

If we accept the first view, then neither response to our original argument will work. If the table emits music, we cannot stick to our observation report that we have a table before us, only one that plays music, for it is part of the meaning of the word 'table' that a table does not play music. Moreover, once we understand the concept of a table, or know what the word 'table' means, we cannot claim that we have no expectations about tables or are committed to no predictions, for such predictions are built into the very meaning of the concepts we employ.

If we accept the second view, then matters are not so straightforward. The general principles are merely beliefs that we happen to possess. We might give them up if our expectations are disappointed, and we might not have had them in the first place. But to say that we must always give them up, and stick to our observation reports, is implausible. And to say that we never have any general belief when we employ some general concept is even more implausible.

In between the two extreme views (A) and (B) about the nature of the general principles, there is a compromise view:

(C) Some general principles are true by virtue of the meanings of the concepts they contain, and some are not, but merely represent beliefs that might turn out to be mistaken.

Which is the correct view to take? View (A) certainly seems to be correct and view (B) incorrect for dispositional words like 'brittle' or 'soluble' or 'poisonous'. 'Soluble' (more precisely, 'soluble in water') means 'will dissolve if placed in water'. Hence to describe something as soluble in water is to commit oneself to a prediction about how it will behave if placed in water. Similarly, if solubility in water is one of the 'defining conditions' of the term 'salt', then to describe something as a piece of salt is also to commit oneself to a prediction about how it will behave if placed in water. (Some terms carry with them, not predictions about the future behaviour of things which fall under the terms, but 'retrodictions' about the past behaviour or the causes of things which fall under them. 'This is a sedimentary rock' and 'This is a volcanic rock' entail different retrodictions about how the rock was formed, in virtue of the meanings of the terms 'sedimentary' and 'volcanic'.) The 'theory-laden' or 'dispositional' character of language is pretty pervasive. Whether it is all-pervasive, as view (A) requires, is a disputed question in the philosophy of language. We need not enter further into this dispute. For whichever of view (A) or view (C) we accept – view (B) having been refuted by the existence of dispositional words – the fallibility of observation reports will stand. (For more on this argument, see Musgrave 1983.)

CHAPTER 4

Empiricist psychology

We have seen how we employ our prior knowledge, or prior beliefs, to interpret our sense-experience. This is how we resolve contradictions in our experience, and declare some experiences veridical and some not. But where did this prior knowledge, or these prior beliefs, come from? If we say that they arose from experience, then we seem to be involved in an infinite regress since that experience will also have been interpreted in the light of beliefs acquired previously. Since none of us has lived forever, an infinite regress is impossible. It seems, then, that there are only two alternatives: either some beliefs are prior to all experience, or some experience is prior to all beliefs.

The second alternative is suggested by Bacon's theory that if we purge the mind of all preconceptions or prior beliefs we will be able to experience the world with the 'innocent eye' of a child. Does the child experience the world with an 'innocent eye', that is, with a mind empty of prior beliefs or preconceptions? Bacon seems to have thought so. Another empiricist philosopher, John Locke, certainly did. According to him the mind of the child is like an 'empty cabinet waiting to be supplied with the materials of knowledge'. And the 'materials of knowledge', according to Locke, are supplied through sense-experience.

We have already encountered the empiricist slogan 'Nothing is in the intellect which was not previously in the senses'. This slogan implies that before anything is 'in the senses', nothing can be 'in the intellect'. Hence the empiricists opposed the view that there are any innate or inborn or a priori ideas or beliefs, which would come before sense experience. Empiricists claimed

that the view that there are innate ideas or beliefs or knowledge
was adopted by their opponents, the rationalists. John Locke
was the most famous critic of this doctrine of innate ideas (in *An
Essay Concerning Human Understanding* 1, 1690).

We must be careful to distinguish philosophy from psychology
here. The philosophical question of which of our beliefs are
entitled to be called 'knowledge' is quite different from the
factual or psychological question of how our beliefs were
actually acquired. Empiricism as a philosophical theory is the
view that we can know only what our senses tell us and what we
can establish therefrom. This is quite consistent with our having
lots of beliefs which are not obtained from sense-experience
(and which are therefore not, for empiricists, entitled to be
called 'knowledge'). But the empiricists went further, and
claimed that as a matter of psychological fact all belief arises out
of experience. (Why, then, are not all beliefs entitled to be called
'knowledge'? That is the empiricist problem of error, and we
have seen how Bacon solved it.) It is this factual or psychological
thesis of empiricism which will concern us in this chapter.

The empiricist view that all belief arises from experience
seems to be obviously correct, and the rationalist view (or the
alleged rationalist view) that some belief precedes all experience
obviously incorrect. That matters may not be quite so straightforward may emerge if we compare our problem with a similar
one (Popper 1972: 346). Consider the well-known riddle:
'Which comes first, the hen (H) or the egg (O)?' We might
express our problem: 'Which comes first, the belief or hypothesis
(H) or the observation (O)?' The first riddle has a sort of
answer in evolutionary theory: hens are birds, birds evolved
from reptiles, reptiles from fishes, and fishes, given many more
evolutionary stages, from primitive unicellular organisms akin
to eggs. So if we accept the idea of evolution, we will say that
unicellular organisms (the eggs) came first. This is not a straight
answer, of course, because if the theory of evolution is to be
believed, there is no straight answer to the original question.

So the best answer evolutionary theory can give to 'Which
came first, the hen or the egg?' is 'A primitive sort of egg,
namely the unicellular organisms from which all others

evolved'. Perhaps the best answer we can give to 'Which came first, the hypothesis or the observation' is 'A primitive sort of hypothesis, namely...'. I shall be defending an answer like this, but we have ground to cover first.

THE BUCKET THEORY OF THE MIND

The empiricist theory of the acquisition of beliefs has been called the 'bucket theory of the mind' (by Popper 1972:61). The mind is a receptacle or bucket with holes in it, representing the senses, through which information about the outside world flows (see Figure 4). At first the bucket is empty. It is, as Locke said, an 'empty cabinet' or *tabula rasa* (an empty slate on which nature has yet to write anything). Then the senses begin to operate, and information flows into the mind. At first the information is pretty chaotic, but soon order imposes itself. Certain experiences are similar to one another and come to be associated together. Moreover, certain experiences are constantly conjoined with other experiences. We repeatedly see a fire and simultaneously feel the warmth which it gives us. The constant repetition of these two experiences instils in us a belief: fires make us warm. Having formed this belief, we come to expect to be warmed whenever we see the flames of the fire. Thus our beliefs help us find our way in the world, by enabling us to anticipate how things will behave.

Erroneous beliefs arise from the hasty or premature association of ideas. I may have had experience of a few red apples, and as a result jump to the conclusion that all apples are red. But this is too hasty, for some apples are green. This is the empiricist theory of error once again. The idea is that beliefs instilled in us by constantly repeated experiences will be correct, while beliefs acquired by jumping to conclusions will typically be mistaken. (The obvious problem here is: how much repeated experience will save us from error? We shall return to this problem.)

We can also exercise our imagination on the materials provided by experience. Having experienced horses and cows, we can imagine a creature like a horse except that it has a single

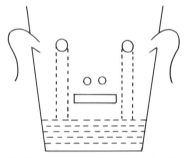

Figure 4. The bucket theory of the mind (after Popper 1972: 61)

horn in the middle of its forehead. Locke described imagination as forming a 'complex idea' out of the 'simple ideas' presented to the senses. We may even give the imagined creature a name ('unicorn'). And we may even form the erroneous belief that unicorns exist.

This picture of the acquisition of belief has two immediate consequences. The first is that the longer your bucket has been lying around, the more experience you will have had and the more beliefs you will have formed. The second is that if some of the holes in your bucket are stopped up (if you are born blind or deaf, for example), then whole areas of experience and hence belief will be unavailable to you. The blind person can know nothing of the colours of things, the deaf person nothing of the sounds they make. And if there are creatures with senses which we do not possess, then we can know nothing of what they experience with those senses.

This simple theory of belief-formation has been very influential. It has been elaborated by psychologists into theories of the association of ideas, conditioned reflexes and so on. (Psychology was once a branch of philosophy, and the empiricist philosophers were actually the founders of psychology.)

TRADITION AND THE IMPORTANCE OF LANGUAGE

Is the empiricist theory of belief-formation correct? The first point to note is that, as a matter of psychological fact, most of the beliefs which anyone possesses were not acquired from that person's experience but from other people. We acquire most of our beliefs by talking to other people, reading books and newspapers, listening to radios or watching television and so on. The most important source of knowledge (or rather, belief) is tradition, using the word in a rather broad sense to cover all cases of learning from other people.

This is an obvious point, and empiricists like Locke were not unaware of it. But Locke tended to play down tradition as a source of knowledge, for two reasons. First, he insisted that learning from other people is not an independent source of knowledge, but rather a special case of learning from experience: when I learn from other people I use my senses to hear what they say or see what they write. We will return to this point.

Locke's second point is that tradition is not a source of knowledge in the proper sense, but merely a source of unjustified belief or opinion. The information people give me in books or newspapers may always be mistaken. Even where it is not mistaken, I cannot be said to know something just because I heard it on the radio or read it in a newspaper, since I cannot justify it in my own experience. I may acquire beliefs or opinions from other people, but not knowledge:

I think we may as rationally hope to see with other men's eyes, as to know by other men's understandings...The floating of other men's opinions in our brains, makes us not one jot the more knowing, though they happen to be true. What in them was science, is in us but opiniatretry [mere opinion]. (1690: I, iii, 24)

This is a revolutionary point of view which bears decisively on the business of education. We popularly suppose that education is a process of acquiring knowledge. We claim to know that there is a lot of ice in Antarctica because our geography lecturer said so, or that sodium salts burn yellow because it says so in the chemistry text. But Locke says this is all wrong: lecturers and their textbooks impart beliefs rather than knowledge. To acquire genuine knowledge we must go to Antarctica and see for ourselves, or perform the experiment with sodium salts. Education does not impart knowledge of history, geography, chemistry, or whatever – it merely imparts knowledge of what is said or written by historians, geographers, chemists, or whoever. (It is partly in response to this kind of argument that science educators insist that their students perform experiments of their own and participate in field trips: the student must see for himself so that genuine knowledge can be obtained. Historians, alas, cannot make field trips into the past, and so history students never really know anything!)

According to Locke, then, all traditional sources of knowledge are to be set aside in favour of the one authoritative source, sense-experience. Now Locke is clearly right that some degree of uncertainty surrounds all of the beliefs that we acquire from tradition. Hence, if the only genuine knowledge is absolutely certain knowledge, we must confess that tradition is not a source of genuine knowledge. Yet the fact remains that most of our beliefs are acquired from tradition. And to play down tradition is also to play down our most important cultural heritage. If we were to set aside all the knowledge stored in libraries, and to believe only what we can personally verify with the senses, then we would not get far. If we try to start where Adam started, we are unlikely to get further than Adam got (Popper 1972: 122).

Tradition can remain a genuine source of knowledge if we do not require absolute certainty. That the chemistry text states that sodium salts burn yellow is a reason for me to believe it, though not an absolutely conclusive reason. And if a belief may be justified, and hence entitled to be called 'knowledge', by reasons that are less than absolutely conclusive reasons, then I can acquire knowledge from the chemistry text.

So whether we are willing to call any beliefs acquired from other people 'knowledge' depends upon how strictly we interpret the justification requirement. But quite apart from this, the knowledge (or belief, if you prefer) acquired from other people is often sufficient to make us question the evidence of our senses. The observer who sees a cat in the corner may come to suspect that he hallucinates if none of the other people present agree with him. The science student in the laboratory who fails to verify for himself what the science textbook says will be told to do the experiment again, only properly this time. So while we can agree with Locke that tradition is not a source of absolutely certain knowledge, we can point out against Locke that experience is not such a source either and that sometimes an appeal to tradition can show this. Locke played down tradition because it cannot yield certainty, thereby failing to see that tradition is an important source of the uncertainty which infects learning from sense-experience. If the senses reveal what tradition denies, the former may give way to the latter.

Locke's first point, recall, was that learning from other people is merely a special case of learning from experience, since we have to hear what they say or see what they write. Quite so. But we have here a very special sort of sense-experience. If we are to learn anything from such experiences, we must know something already, namely the language in which other people speak or write to us. If someone speaks or writes to me in Cantonese, I cannot learn anything from him. All I can learn from experience in this case is that a person made such-and-such noises or such-and-such marks on paper. But if I knew Cantonese, I would pay little heed to the particular noises or marks, and would 'see through them' so to speak, in order to grasp their meaning. Our desire to get at the meaning may lead us to overlook accidents of pronunciation and slips of the tongue, or accidents of hand-writing and slips of the pen. (This is why proof-readers should not attend too closely to the meaning of the text they are trying to check.) So in linguistic sense-experience (if we can call it that) the perceiver plays a very active role, using prior knowledge of the language to get at the meaning of what is said or written, rather than passively attending to the incoming stimuli (the noises or marks).

Not only is linguistic sense-experience peculiar, but the prior knowledge which makes it possible, knowledge of a language, is the most important knowledge that we possess. For it makes it possible for us to learn from other people, and opens up the whole of traditional knowledge to us. Without language, the only way for me to find out whether it will rain in London on 27 March 2004 is to go there and see for myself. With language, if I want to know I can telephone or write to a friend who happens to be there. Language does enable us to see with other people's eyes and know by other people's understandings. And this is what makes us the most successful creatures that there are.

Most children perform the amazing feat of acquiring this crucial knowledge by the age of two or three. Some do not and a famous case, that of Helen Keller, is an instructive one. Helen Keller became blind and deaf very shortly after birth. With the two most important 'holes in her bucket' stopped up, one would suppose that she would be condemned to a life of ignorance: surely at least two-fifths of human knowledge depends upon these two of our five senses? Yet Helen Keller became a very well-educated lady who wrote several books, including a most moving autobiography. The great event of her life occurred when she was eight, and was taught a language based upon touch. This put her in contact with other human beings for the first time, and according to Helen Keller, made her a human being herself. For she suggests that before she knew language, she had no real sense of herself as a human being. In her autobiography she attempts the impossible task of describing what a difference the acquisition of a language made to her. The passage I shall quote comes from a chapter entitled (significantly) 'Before the soul dawn':

Before my teacher came to me, I did not know that I am. I lived in a world that was a no-world. I cannot hope to describe adequately that unconscious, yet conscious time of nothingness. I did not know that I knew aught, or that I lived or acted or desired. I had neither will nor intellect. I was carried along to objects or acts by a certain blind natural impetus... I had a power of association... After repeatedly smelling rain and feeling the discomfort of wetness, I acted like those about me: I ran to shut the window. But that was not thought in any sense. It was the same kind of association that makes animals take shelter from the rain.

When I learned the meaning of 'I' and 'me' and found that I was something, I began to think. Then consciousness first existed for me. (Keller 1904: 141–3, 145)

The idea that consciousness requires a sense of self, and that this in turn depends upon the acquisition of a language, is an interesting speculation. The case of Helen Keller raises many such speculations. Another one arises when we consider the possibility that Helen Keller, having acquired a language, could also have acquired all the scientific knowledge that we possess about colour and sound. For she could have had 'read' to her scientific treatises about light and sound. Could she have understood such treatises? Could she have understood the word 'red' without ever having had a sensation of anything red? If we suppose, as many philosophers do, that the word 'red' stands for the sensation we get when we look at something red, then it would seem that a blind person can never understand the word 'red'. Yet humans can understand treatises about electro-magnetic fields despite the fact that, unlike some other creatures, we cannot sense the presence of those fields. So perhaps matters are not quite so straightforward. (We shall return to this question of the meaning of terms such as 'red': see p. 115).

We have discussed the peculiarity of linguistic sense-experience and the importance of learning a language. The peculiarity rests in the fact that what we learn depends very much upon our prior knowledge of the language and the ability which it gives us to select and interpret stimuli so as to grasp their meaning. The importance of learning a language rests in the fact that it makes the whole of traditional knowledge accessible to us. Now empiricists need not deny any of this. They may reply, however, that language is learned by a special kind of 'association of ideas' and that the experiences which knowledge of a language makes possible are peculiar and different from all others. I shall consider these points in turn. I shall be arguing that language is learned not by the association of ideas through repetition but by actively jumping to conclusions, and that this is typical of all learning. And I shall be arguing that ordinary sense-experience is not so different from linguistic sense-experience after all.

LANGUAGE LEARNING

The empiricist theory of belief-formation says that after repeatedly seeing fires and feeling their warmth, we come to associate the two, and form the belief that fires warm us. According to empiricists, it is basically the same with language learning. We repeatedly hear the word 'dog' in the presence of dogs and we come to associate the two together, and to expect to see a dog whenever we hear the word.

It may be objected that this theory applies, straightforwardly, only to the learning of the names of readily accessible objects, and that most words are not the names of such objects. There are names of unobservable things (like 'God' or 'light ray'). There are words which are not names at all (like 'quickly' or 'nice'). There are logical words (like 'or' or 'all' or 'not'). Somehow the empiricist has to elaborate his basic idea so that it can explain how such words are learned – for without them no sentence can be formed or understood.

It has also been objected that the incredible speed with which a complex thing like a natural language is learned makes the empiricist theory of language learning implausible. Most children, by the time they are three, are able to produce sentences which they have never heard at all, let alone heard repeatedly. Language learning is not simply the learning of the meaning of particular words, but more importantly the grasping of rules for the production of grammatical sentences. Could a rule be learned by repetition of associated stimuli, and if so, what kind of stimuli?

The rapidity of language learning and the complex nature of what is learned have suggested to Noam Chomsky that children are innately equipped with some kind of linguistic knowledge, which does not have to be learned and which can speed up and give structure to what does have to be learned. (In 1966 Chomsky wrote a book entitled, interestingly, *Cartesian Linguistics*: this is interesting because Descartes, from whose name the adjective 'Cartesian' is derived, was a prominent rationalist philosopher and a prominent defender of the rationalist view that some knowledge is 'innate'.) The problem with this view is to specify what kind of linguistic knowledge is innate. It cannot be knowledge of any particular natural language or its rules, whereby children born of English-speaking parents have some innate knowledge of English, children born of Chinese-speaking parents some innate knowledge of Chinese and so on. For the fact is that a Chinese infant raised in an English-speaking environment will master English just as well as his twin masters Chinese back home. And so, Chomsky conjectures, the innate knowledge must be of very general structural features of all natural languages. But the idea that all natural languages have some basic structural features in common ('linguistic universals' as they are called) is hotly disputed. It is also disputed whether the ability to acquire language is confined to human beings, in virtue of some specifically human innate knowledge. There have been widely publicised attempts to teach language to chimps.

Let us leave these interesting speculations of Chomsky's and look briefly at the way in which children learn language. The thing which has emerged from empirical studies of how children accomplish the amazing feat is that they are great generalisers; they have a great ability to jump to conclusions (often erroneous conclusions). They do not wait for frequent repetition to instil language into them. Thus, one investigator writes:

Children overgeneralize word meanings, using words they acquire early in place of words they have not yet acquired ... when a word first appears in a child's lexicon, it refers to a specific object but the child quickly extends the semantic domain of the word, using it to refer to many other things. Eventually the meaning of the word is narrowed down until it coincides with adult usage ... children most frequently base the semantic extension of a word on the shape of its first referent. (Moskowitz 1978: 92)

The sort of thing referred to here is really quite familiar. We have all heard the joke about the child who calls everybody 'Daddy' and embarrasses the vicar who has come to tea. One of my own daughters soon acquired the word 'birdie' which she applied to any non-human animal: a trip round London Zoo elicited cries of 'birdie' at the cage of every animal. (Wittgenstein once said: 'The limits of my language are the limits of my world.' My daughter's world, at that stage of her career, contained Mummies, Daddies and Birdies.) Moskowitz cites the child whose first word was 'moon' which was successively applied to cake, round marks on the windows and, in books, the letter 'o', and so on. Another child's first word was 'fly' which was then applied to specks of dirt, dust, small insects, the child's toe, crumbs and a toad! Not only is this kind of thing familiar to anyone who has watched a child master language, it is also pretty sensible behaviour on the part of the child. If you wish to communicate, but do not have many words at your disposal, then why not make the ones that you have work overtime? An important philosopher of language called Humpty Dumpty also thought this sensible, and said:

When I make a word do a lot of work like that I always pay it extra. Ah, you should see 'em come round me of a Saturday night, for to get their wages, you know. (Carroll 1865/71: 270)

Even more interesting is the mastery of grammatical rules. The rule for forming plurals in English is to add the sound 's' or 'z' to the singular, though there are many irregular plurals ('feet' not 'foots', 'men' not 'mans'). Children acquire singulars, and sometimes an irregular plural which they use interchangeably with the singular. Then they somehow grasp the rule. And straightway they apply it universally to all the words they know: they say 'foots' and 'mans'; and if they knew an irregular plural before, they apply the rule to that, too, and doubly pluralise it into 'mens' or 'feets'. It is similar with the rule for forming past tenses, add 'ed' to the present, again with many irregular cases ('came' not 'comed', 'went' not 'goed'). A child first acquires present tenses and perhaps a few irregular past tenses used interchangeably. Then the rule is mastered and is applied universally: they say 'comed' and 'goed', and even get carried away into 'camed' and 'wented' in the case of previously acquired irregulars. Their grasp of rules leads them to make numerous grammatical mistakes. And at this early stage they are quite impervious to correction of their mistakes, and will persist in them no matter how often they are corrected. Little children soon become little men and women of principle: their attitude is 'I have my principles, don't bother me with the facts'. It takes years for a child to correct all of these rule-based mistakes and to master all the exceptions to the rules.

None of this explains how the child acquires its first words or its first grammatical rules; it merely describes what they do with them once they have got them. Obviously experiences such as hearing a word in the presence of the thing it names play a role in the learning of that word. But then the child generalises, overgeneralises, imposes order where it does not exist and, as a result, makes mistakes. If the child can jump to conclusions in this way after having acquired a word, it is plausible to suppose that the child does the same thing in acquiring the word in the first place. And if this is correct, then frequent repetition of associated stimuli may not be necessary to enable a generalising animal to associate them.

Language learning is a very specialised and still very mysterious thing. But perhaps the sort of thing that goes on when children acquire language is actually typical of all learning from experience, both by humans and by other animals. This we shall pursue in the next section.

THE ROLE OF REPETITION

An important part of the empiricist theory of the acquisition of beliefs is that they are instilled into us by the frequent repetitions of associated stimuli. Is this theory of learning by repetition correct? There are lots of quite familiar situations which suggest that both animals and humans can acquire beliefs without repetition. The child who burns himself on the electric fire is unlikely to repeat the experiment. Instead, the child will henceforth avoid touching the fire, showing that in some sense or other he has formed a belief ('Touching the fire will always hurt me') on the basis of only one trial. Similarly, a puppy had a lighted cigarette pushed under his nose, did not like it, and ran away sneezing. Thereafter, the appearance of a cigarette or anything vaguely resembling a cigarette elicited the same response (Popper 1962: 44). Creatures learn very rapidly from painful or unpleasant experiences: they jump to conclusions on the basis of single experiences of this kind. And of course, what is painful or unpleasant depends upon the observer.

In a similar way, the notion of repeated experiences or of similar experiences is a little naive. What is to count as a repetition depends upon the point of view of the observer (Popper 1959: 421). Which of the drawings in Figure 5

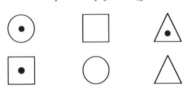

Figure 5. Similarities?

are similar to one another? If we focus on the shapes we will give one answer, if we focus on the presence or absence of the central spot we will give another. One experience is similar to another, or a repetition of another, only from a certain point of view. But this means that something like a point of view must precede the recognition of similarities in experience. What one observer regards as similar experiences repeated may be regarded by another observer, with a different point of view, as quite dissimilar experiences.

This is not to deny that there is something like learning from repetition. But the typical case here is that of learning to do something automatically or without thinking which one previously had to do deliberately (Popper 1962: 43). The pianist who repeats a difficult passage does so in order to be able to play it automatically. And in unnatural circumstances something like a belief may be instilled in a creature by repetition. The classic case here is that of the conditioned reflex: Pavlov repeatedly rang a bell before feeding a dog, and finally the dog would salivate in the expectation of being fed at the mere sound of the bell. Yet, as the animal psychologist David Katz says, this is by no means necessary and applies only to artificial associations. Speaking of the anti-smoking puppy, Katz writes:

According to Pavlov many…repetitions are usually needed to establish a conditioned reflex; yet under the natural conditions of a real situation a single experience was sufficient to set up something very like one. (Katz 1937: 104)

The idea that beliefs are formed very often by jumping to conclusions has, of course, been recognised by certain empiricists. Bacon was the first to recognise it and deplore it, as we have seen. Another empiricist, David Hume, admitted that we often form general beliefs on the basis of single experiences, but explained this by saying that previous repetitions have instilled in us the habit of forming beliefs from experience. We only jump to conclusions after a great deal of repetitious experience has instilled conclusions in us. But as John Watkins has said (1968: 277, Note 1), on this view grandparents should be reckless generalisers compared with their cagey grandchildren. The reverse seems to be the case.

For a long time psychologists based their learning theories on the basic empiricist idea of learning by repetition. One psychologist has claimed that learning by repetition (which he calls 'induction') is a myth:

Induction is a myth... our normal tendency is to leap to conclusions after a single observation... Several experimental situations, from classical conditioning to concept formation, have been suggested as primitive models of the inductive process... they all seem to be yielding similar results. If we examine the simplest conditioning models, we find that learning is or can be instantaneous, that the basic association typically appears full-blown after a single exposure. Evidence to this effect comes from operant conditioning... aversive conditioning... punishment... and work on causality... Rather than passively registering each succeeding instance in inductive increments of belief, the picture is emerging of an organism who actively hypothesizes and integrates in accordance with his hypotheses. Increment theory is not moribund, but the more psychology looks for a pure inductive process, the more it finds an organism who jumps to conclusions. Furthermore, it can be shown in many of the above cases that, once the organism has adopted a hypothesis, he can be almost impervious to numerous disconfirming instances. (Singer 1971: 1011)

The last sentence here is of particular significance for us: it confirms what Bacon complained of centuries ago, the propensity to set aside experiential evidence which tells against preconceived ideas.

So the general picture of belief-formation which emerges is as follows. The observer is not passive, waiting for experiences to enter the 'bucket' and for beliefs to be formed by repetition. Instead, the observer is active. Certain stimuli are selected and attention is paid to them; certain experiences are recognised or classified as similar to one another, depending on the point of view of the observer; and the observer is constantly jumping to conclusions on the basis of experiences which are important to that observer. What we learn from experience depends always upon two things, the stimuli which impinge upon our sensory systems and the prior contents of the 'bucket' (in the form of interests, points of view, or previous expectations).

Now the philosophical importance of this is that, since what we learn from experience is not merely a function of the incoming stimuli, what we learn can always be mistaken. This is obvious in the case of jumping to some general conclusion on the basis of one or two experiences. It is less obvious, but is also true, simply of learning from experience that some particular observation statement is correct. Here, too, we jump to conclusions, as the argument about theory-ladenness of the last chapter showed.

INNATE IDEAS OR INBORN KNOW-HOW?

We have argued that what the perceiver learns from experience always depends upon two things, the incoming stimuli and the prior contents of that perceiver's 'bucket' in the light of which it selects, interprets and responds to stimuli. It might be objected, however, that while all this may be true of the mature perceiver whose 'bucket' already contains concepts, beliefs and expectations, it cannot hold for all perception. If there is nothing in the 'bucket' to start with, then there is nothing with which the perceiver can select and interpret incoming stimuli. The first perceptions must, therefore, be passive receptions of incoming stimuli, without selection or interpretation. At birth our 'buckets' are empty and we do therefore, as Bacon said, see the world with an 'innocent eye'.

This brings us to the question of innate or inborn ideas or knowledge. It brings us to the analogue of the hen-egg problem: which comes first, an observation (O) or an expectation or hypothesis (H)? And as I said before, I shall answer that what comes first is a primitive kind of expectation or hypothesis.

Research on animal behaviour and animal perception is of considerable interest here. It shows that animals come into the world equipped with inborn or innate or instinctive responses to

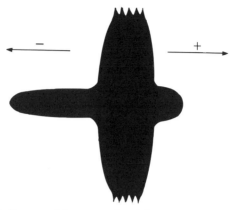

Figure 6. Perceptual interpretation (after Tinbergen 1953: 216)

certain specific stimuli. Animals are 'tuned', so to speak, to select certain stimuli as being important to them, to interpret them in a particular way, and to respond accordingly. (Though we must not, of course, assume that this 'selection' and 'interpretation' is a conscious process.) There are countless illustrations of this, but some of the nicest are to be found in Tinbergen's book *The Herring Gull's World* (1953).

Newly hatched herring gull chicks must obtain food from their parents by pecking at the parent's beak: only if the chick pecks will it be fed, so that blind chicks are simply left to starve. Tinbergen shows that what elicits this innate response is the red spot on the end of the parent's beak. Present a chick with a cardboard beak containing the spot, and it will peck; present a chick with a cardboard beak without the spot and it will not. The spot is crucial: a very rough beak-model with a dark spot (which does not have to be red) will elicit the response, while a very accurate beak-model without a spot will not. The response is quite instinctive and does not have to be learned.

Again, newly hatched chicks are capable of an escape-response to dangerous stimuli: they run to hide under anything handy and 'freeze'. Tinbergen shows that this response is elicited if you move a cardboard shape like the one in Figure 6 over the chicks in the direction of the plus sign. The response is not elicited if the shape moves in the opposite direction. It is also quite instinctive and does not have to be learned from the parents: chicks hatched in an incubator display it from the start. We say of the situation that the shape moved to the right looks like a hawk, which is a predator, while the shape moved to the left looks like a swan, which is not a predator. The one looks like something dangerous, the other does not. But we must not suppose that the chicks think along these lines: for all we know, they do not think at all, but respond purely instinctively. But right from the start, certain stimuli are selected (unconsciously) and interpreted (unconsciously) in quite specific ways.

There is a further perceptual phenomenon called imprinting which is especially interesting. A charming example of it is described by Konrad Lorenz in his book *King Solomon's Ring* (1952). Newly hatched geese have the instinctive ability to follow their parents around and to respond to their calls. But how do they 'know' who their parents are? They learn this from experience, but in a very special way: the 'parent' is actually the first middle-sized moving thing that they see (Lorenz 1952: 62). Normally this first middle-sized moving thing will actually be the parent, and hence this bit of instinctive knowledge is an obvious advantage to the chicks. But Lorenz tells the story of how he hatched some goose eggs in an incubator, so that he was the first moving object that the newly hatched babies saw. Straightway they adopted him as their parent, and try as he might he could not stop them gathering at his feet and following him around! He even had to learn to make goose-calls so as to keep his new family out of trouble. The babies were 'imprinted' upon him as the parent, and took little notice of the real parent when Lorenz brought her to them. Further research showed that you could imprint baby geese upon pretty well any object of the right size, provided that it moved: one lot of baby geese even adopted a large balloon pulled on a piece of string. It also turned out that specific 'imprinting' must take place at specific times in the life of animals, and that the response dies away if the appropriate stimulus is not presented at the right time. Baby geese will adopt nothing as a 'parent' if nothing of the right size moves in their vicinity in the first few days of their life.

Now the baby geese learn from experience who is their

parent, and do not know this instinctively or innately. But this
is a very special learning from experience, which requires only
a single experience, because what the babies do seem to 'know
innately' is that the first moving thing of an appropriate size is
their parent. Armed with this bit of instinctive knowledge, only
one experience is required and it elicits a whole repertoire of
very specific behavioural responses. (It is even conjectured that
the ability to direct sexual behaviour at a member of the
opposite sex is partly due to imprinting, so that animals reared
in artificial isolation from members of the opposite sex will
become homosexual and will prefer members of their own sex
even when the opposite sex becomes available. But this is a
much more controversial business; see Sluckin 1964: 121.)

Now the instinctive perceptual abilities we have been
speaking about have obvious survival value for the animals
which possess them (this is a point to which I shall be returning).
But they can also lead to error. Normally there is not a student
of animal behaviour around presenting baby herring gulls with
cardboard beaks, cardboard hawks and so forth. But when
there is, the instinctive responses to various stimuli become
erroneous or inappropriate. And because the responses are
quite automatic, it is quite easy to 'fool' the creatures which
possess them. (The automatic nature of these responses is also a
warning against anthropomorphism: the parent herring gull is
not callously indifferent to the blind and hungry chick, but is
simply unable to feed it because it does not elicit food in the
right way.)

One of Lorenz's nicest stories concerns water-shrews (Lorenz
1952: 126–9). These fierce little creatures have an excellent
sense of smell, but poor eyesight. Yet they tear around quickly,
avoiding obstacles, and getting from their nests on land to the
water very quickly. How do they do it? Lorenz placed some
shrews in a box on a wooden platform surrounded by water.
They emerged slowly, went this way and that, and finally came
to the water by a very circuitous route as if by chance. They
jumped in, swam around for a while, jumped out at precisely
the point where they had jumped in, and returned to the box by
precisely the circuitous route they had originally taken!

Thereafter they always followed this route, running along it very quickly. A path-habit is formed out of one experience, because the shrews actually lay a scent trail which they then follow again. Very gradually the 'corners' of the trail are smoothed out, and it becomes closer and closer to a straight line. Lorenz placed a stone on the path: the shrews scuttled along and bumped into it, backed up and bumped into it again, and finally went around it or jumped over it. When he removed the stone, the shrews still went around or jumped over the place where the stone had been as if it were still there. Only gradually was this complication in their habit removed and the original direct route restored. (Foraging ants or termites also lay scent trails, and when they return along them laden with good food, others set out along them, too, reinforcing the scent for as long as the food-supply lasts.) Recently, some even more remarkable discoveries have been made. It seems that some of these instinctive responses, some of these specific ways of selecting and interpreting stimuli, are built into the sense-organs themselves. It is possible to detect, by using sensitive electrodes, when particular cells or groups of cells in the eyes of animals are sending messages to the brains of those animals. It turns out that the visual systems of animals are 'tuned' to respond to very specific types of visual stimuli.

Frogs eat flies. But a frog surrounded by immobile but otherwise perfectly appetising flies (appetising for a frog, that is), starves to death. The reason is that immobile flies are not seen as food at all. Certain cells in the frog's eyes only send a message to the frog's brain when a fly (or something small which moves jerkily like a fly) enters the visual field, and only if these cells send a message will the frog try to catch and eat the fly. The frog's eye is so structured that certain things are seen as food and other things are not. Here are the conclusions of those who discovered this:

What are the consequences of this work? Fundamentally, it shows that the eye speaks to the brain in a language *already highly organized and interpreted* ... every point is seen in definite contexts. The character of these contexts, generally built in, is the physiological [innate knowledge] ... the language in which they are best described is the language

of complex abstractions from the visual image. We have been tempted,
for example, to call the convexity detectors 'bug perceivers'. Such a
fiber responds best when a dark object, smaller than a receptive field,
enters that field, stops and moves about intermittently thereafter. The
response is not affected if the lighting changes, or if the background is
moving, and is not there if only the background, moving or still, is in
the field. Could one better describe a system for detecting an accessible
bug? (Lettvin *et al.* 1959: 230–55)

Similar things have been discovered concerning the visual
systems of cats. And it seems that monkeys have eyes which are
specially designed to see monkey hands. Here is a newspaper
report of some research carried out in America:

Establishing the trigger features of cells in the visual pathway involves
the delicate feat of placing a micro-electrode within a single cell. This
is done without pain to the animal. In their monkey experiment, the
Americans produced their first weak response from the detector cell
when they placed before the animal's eyes an outline of a crown.
Encouraged, they fiddled with the crown outline, elongating it until
they had a shape rather like a human hand. The cell fired more
vigorously.

  They tried it with the shape of a human hand and the stuttering
impulses from the cell showed that they were close to discovering its
purpose. Finally they presented the monkey with the shape of a
monkey hand. 'The cell went crazy... electric discharges flowing from
it at the rate of 1,000 a second.' The experiment proved that the job of
that one cell in the monkey brain was to recognise the monkey hand.
(*Otago Daily Times*, 26 February 1972: 18)

Now so far as I know, very specific responses like those of the
frog or the monkey have not been established for the human
eye. There is some evidence, however, that the human eye is
specially programmed to see horizontal lines (as are the cat's
eyes). Such lines would normally represent the edges of surfaces,
things over which a kitten or a crawling baby might fall.

  Countless philosophers have regarded seeing as a simple
business, the place where the theory of knowledge must begin.
Countless books start by imagining a perceiver confronted with
an orange (sometimes it is a tomato), and ask what the perceiver
sees, or 'really sees', and what he can infer from it. But we can
see (in a different sense) that seeing is not a simple business at

all, from a scientific or biological point of view. What is seen and how it is 'interpreted' depends very much upon the creature doing the seeing. As Norwood Hanson put it (1969: 61): 'There is more to seeing than meets the eye'. The human eye responds to only a part of the whole spectrum of electro-magnetic radiation (the so-called 'visible portion' of the spectrum), while other creatures' eyes are different (bees, for example, respond to ultraviolet light). But the differences are far more specific than this: as we have seen, different creatures are programmed to select certain stimuli and to respond to them in quite specific ways, and some of this programming is even built into the very structure of the sense-organs. It seems that there is no wholly passive perceiving and that no creature (including humans) ever sees the world with a wholly 'innocent' eye. So if we are forced to answer our 'hen-egg'question ('Which comes first, the hypothesis H or the observation O?') the best answer seems to be that what comes first is a primitive sort of hypothesis, a primitive and inborn mechanism for 'selecting' and 'interpreting' perceptual stimuli (Popper 1972: 344).

How does all this bear upon the empiricist theory that there is nothing in the intellect that was not previously in the senses? John Locke is famous for his defence of this view, and his attack upon 'innate ideas'. According to Locke, all belief and knowledge is formed out of 'ideas' and all ideas are the product of sense-experience (counting our ability to introspect our thoughts and feelings as a sort of 'sixth sense'). It follows immediately that before the senses have operated there are no 'ideas' and hence no belief or knowledge. Locke argues at length and with some ingenuity against the opposite opinion in Book 1 of his *Essay Concerning Human Understanding*.

Has the kind of research we have just considered established the existence of 'innate ideas'? Well, certainly not in Locke's sense. For example, we have been careful not to attribute conscious 'ideas' or conscious thought to the animals which display innate responses to selected stimuli. But for Locke the notion that an idea might be unconscious, that a creature may have an 'idea' and yet not be aware that it has it, is nonsense.

Locke was, in fact, well aware of animal instinct. Indeed, he was asked, with reference to his attack on 'innate ideas', about birds who know how to construct their nests and what materials to use, without having learned this from experience. He gave the question a pretty dusty response: 'I did not write my book to explain the actions of beasts' (1690: 1, 205, Note 2). Yet, elsewhere Locke admitted the existence of innate propensities or dispositions in human beings, such as the propensity to avoid painful stimuli and seek pleasurable ones. Now this innate disposition enables humans to pay special attention to certain stimuli and to respond to them in particular ways. It means, in other words, that the human perceiver plays an active role, rather than passively receiving incoming 'data'. Locke was unaware of the detailed discoveries about the innate perceptual abilities of animals – we can hardly blame him for that, since they have been discovered only recently. Perhaps, if confronted with them, he would have denied that human perception was of the same kind.

Such a denial may seem plausible. Human infants are not born with the detailed apparatus of inborn responses which herring gull chicks have. Compared with baby herring gulls, human babies are pretty helpless creatures. Also compared with baby herring gulls, human babies are pretty clever creatures who learn most of what they come to know and do not need to know it innately. Herring gulls do not learn much in life, and therefore most of their behaviour has to be instinctive. However, human babies are not entirely devoid of innate responses to quite specific stimuli. The new-born baby knows how to suck, that is, is tuned to respond in a quite specific way to certain quite specific tactile stimuli. Similarly, new-born babies know innately how to grip things, that is, they respond in a quite specific way to a different kind of tactile stimulus. The human eye may be innately 'tuned' to perceive the world in quite specific ways, as the monkey-eye does. And if Chomsky is right, humans may have some sort of inborn knowledge of the general structure of language. More important than any of these things (with the possible exception of the last, if it exists) is an innate propensity to seek regularity in experience, which leads infants to generalise or 'jump to conclusions'.

There are certainly no 'innate ideas' in Locke's sense, no products of sense-experience before the senses start to operate. Is there any inborn knowledge? Can the sort of thing we have been discussing really count as the possession of knowledge prior to any sense-experience?

We have seen that all of the instinctive responses we have considered may be erroneous or inappropriate in certain situations. Since a piece of knowledge has to be true, the most we could say is that there are innate beliefs here rather than innate knowledge. Thus, we might attribute to newly hatched herring gulls the innate or instinctive belief that anything hawk-shaped moving overhead is dangerous. Yet, even this seems odd. It commits us to ascribing to creatures beliefs which are not merely unconscious, but which could well be beliefs of which the creature can never become conscious. It commits us to ascribing unconscious ideas or concepts to these creatures, for one cannot believe that *P* (either consciously or unconsciously) without possessing (consciously or unconsciously) the concepts which *P* contains. But do baby herring gulls possess the concepts of 'hawk-shaped' things or 'dangerous' things? Perhaps there is a minimal sense of 'possessing the concept of *X*' in which they do, a minimal sense in which one possesses the concept of *X* if one can sort out the *X*s from the non-*X*s. But we are in danger here of saying that a machine for sorting out small apples from big ones possesses the concepts 'small' and 'big'.

A distinction we drew earlier may help here, the distinction between knowledge-that (and belief-that) and knowledge-how. What cannot be denied, I think, is that animals and humans possess instinctive or innate know-how. The baby herring gull knows instinctively how to respond to a hawk-shaped object moving overhead, and so on for all the other examples. Even those who think that knowledge or belief that something is the case requires the knower or believer to possess appropriate concepts, and those who think that animals cannot be said to possess concepts, can still accept this way of describing the situation. (I myself think it does make sense to attribute beliefs, and concepts, to animals, but I shall not argue the point here.)

The possession of innate know-how means that the senses are

never passive and unselective recorders of data. And this in turn means that what is learned from sense-experience may always be mistaken, if, for example, we are in a situation where our innate know-how lets us down. It is this which justifies us in concluding that what comes first is not observation but a primitive form of expectation or hypothesis.

We saw earlier how the possession of languages enables us to formulate statements reporting our experience, but that these statements always transcend the experience they 'report' and are corrigible in the light of future experience. This is a point emphasised by Popper (1972: 24–5). He also emphasises a further point: that language, in enabling us to formulate our beliefs and inspect them, also enables us to criticise them consciously. He makes the point by saying that the only difference between the amoeba and Einstein is the latter's ability to criticise the conclusions to which he has jumped (which depends upon his possession of language). Lorenz's baby geese illustrate the point well: they were placed in a situation where their innate know-how led them to 'jump to the wrong conclusion' (that Lorenz was their mother). If Lorenz had been less of an animal-lover, this mistake would probably have been fatal. Einstein, not to mention lesser mortals, also jumps to many mistaken conclusions. But he can formulate them, try to criticise them, and eliminate the mistaken ones without himself being eliminated. Where mistakes are built into the behavioural repertoire of a creature, they are likely to be fatal. Where they can be formulated in language, and behaviour based upon them held in abeyance, they need not be. The possession of language makes a new kind of mistake possible, as we have seen. But it also makes a new kind of learning from mistakes possible.

CHAPTER 5

Idea-ism, appearance and reality

The last chapter about empiricist psychology was really a long digression from our main theme. For questions about how the senses actually operate and how beliefs are actually formed are questions of psychology and/or physiology, factual questions rather than philosophical ones. However, these factual questions have repercussions for philosophical views, and so our digression had a point. The fact that the perceiver plays an active role in perception and in the acquisition of beliefs explains why the senses are not an infallible source of knowledge about the world and why beliefs erected upon the evidence of the senses are not thereby entitled to be called 'knowledge'.

A NEW EMPIRICISM — IDEA-ISM

I now want to return to more philosophical matters, and to consider a new answer to the sceptical attack on the senses. This new answer is very widespread: the essence of it is already to be found in Greek philosophy. It was elaborated by the great trio of British empiricist philosophers, Locke the Englishman, Berkeley the Irishman, and Hume the Scotsman. Locke called it the 'new way of ideas'. It has persisted right down to the twentieth century, where it came to be called the 'theory of sense-data'. I shall call it 'idea-ism'. The term is unfamiliar and is not to be confused with the term 'idealism' which is well known in philosophy. Idea-ism and idealism are not the same doctrine, though they are related to one another. To state the difference baldly, idea-ism is an epistemological doctrine and idealism an ontological or metaphysical doctrine. I shall be saying more about this difference.

When a philosophical view is as widely accepted as idea-ism is, and when it persists for as long as idea-ism has persisted, we must expect it to be very plausible and to have some powerful arguments in its favour. This is the case with idea-ism. Yet, once idea-ism is accepted, it leads to some very strange problems and to some even stranger solutions to those problems. Idea-ism is proposed by philosophers who want to rely upon the senses, yet it leads to such strange conclusions that one is inclined to say that philosophers who accept it have taken leave of their senses. This is how an early critic of the doctrine, Thomas Reid, saw the situation. Reid is an unjustly neglected philosopher who founded a school of 'common-sense philosophy'. He said of idea-ism:

The theory of ideas, like the Trojan horse, had a specious appearance both of innocence and beauty; but if those philosophers had known that it carried in its belly death and destruction to all science and common sense, they would not have broken down their walls to give it admittance. (1764: 87)

I shall end by agreeing with Reid. But before then my strategy will be to explain the doctrine and the arguments for it as best I can, and to look at the problems to which it leads and the queer views produced in response to those problems. Only after this will I return to the beginning to see whether any alternative to idea-ism is possible.

What is the doctrine of idea-ism? If we return briefly to the sceptical attack on the senses, we will recall that Sextus Empiricus distinguished appearance and reality, and emphasised that he did not doubt that the senses tell us how things appear to be. He wrote:

And when we question whether the underlying object is such as it appears, we grant the fact that it appears, and our doubt does not concern the appearance itself but the account given of that appearance. (1933–49: I, 19–20)

Here lies the clue which leads to an answer to the sceptic. For Sextus is not an out-and-out sceptic regarding the senses. He grants that the senses give us certainty about how things appear to be though not about how they really are. The senses are an infallible source of immediate knowledge, not about the outside world and the objects in the outside world, but about the appearances presented to us by the outside world. So-called perceptual errors arise because we go beyond the immediate information provided by the senses. So-called contradictions in sense-experience, of which the sceptic makes much, arise from the same source. If we confine ourselves to reporting how things appear to be, then no error or contradiction can arise. Consider again the example of the coin viewed from above and from the side. If as a result of viewing the coin in these two ways, we issue observation-statements like:

The coin is round
The coin is elliptical

then our reports contradict each other and one must be mistaken. But if we confine ourselves to reporting:

Now the coin appears to be round
Now the coin appears to be elliptical

then our reports do not contradict each other, both of them are true, and both of them are immediately known for certain to be true.

Similarly, everything that we said earlier about how prior beliefs or expectations (or even innate perceptual responses) influence what we learn from experience (or how we respond to stimuli) can be accepted. But it will be insisted that all of these influences only affect the way we interpret stimuli (or respond to them). It will be insisted that none of this casts any doubt upon the immediate information which the senses provide. It may be difficult in some cases to separate the immediate data from the interpretations or inferences based upon that immediate data. But in principle this can always be done.

According to this view, then, the senses never lie and the immediate information they give us is never mistaken. Errors only arise in the interpretations that we place upon the immediate data. Humble observation-statements like 'The coin is round' are actually interpretations of, or inferences from, the immediate data. Such interpretations or inferences might always be mistaken, but the immediate data are not. And this applies even in the extreme cases presented by the sceptic, such as dreams or hallucinations. If I dream that I am on a mountain-top and, mistaking my dream for reality, actually believe that I am on a mountain-top, then I am mistaken. But I am quite right to say that it now appears to me (in my dream) that I am on a mountain-top. If the hallucinating drunk reports that there are pink rats in the room, he is mistaken. But if he reports that it appears to him that there are pink rats, then he is quite right.

So a chief line of argument in favour of idea-ism is that it is the only way to avoid the sceptical attack on the senses as a source of certain knowledge. We begin with naive or direct realism regarding sense-experience, the view that the senses give us direct and infallible information about external objects. Sceptics attack this position in all kinds of ways. Empiricists repulse these attacks by abandoning perceptual realism and claiming that the senses give us direct and infallible information about the 'appearances' or 'ideas'. Their argument is:

(1) The senses give us certain knowledge either about external objects or about ideas or appearances.
(2) The senses do not give us certain knowledge about external objects.
     Therefore, the senses give us certain knowledge about ideas or appearances.

This argument is valid: if we accept its premises as true, we must also accept its conclusion as true. Moreover, the sceptical arguments we have considered do seem to show that premise (2) is correct. Premise (1) is the cornerstone of empiricism – it says that the senses give us certainty about something. If we accept (1) also, then the idea-ist conclusion is inescapable.

REIFYING THE DATA

But we have not yet arrived at the doctrine of idea-ism. The further step we have to take is to *reify* 'the appearances', to turn them into the things of which I am immediately aware in sense-experience. This is a subtle step but an important one. We might mark it verbally as follows. Instead of saying:

Now the coin appears to be elliptical

idea-ist philosophers say, more clumsily but apparently equivalently:

I am now immediately aware of an appearance of an elliptical coin

or:

I am now having or receiving an appearance of an elliptical coin.

Now the ideas of the doctrine of idea-ism, or the sense-data of the doctrine of sense-data, are reified appearances of this kind. Instead of saying:

Now the coin appears to be elliptical

idea-ists say such things as:

I am now having or experiencing a visual idea or visual sense-datum of an elliptical coin.

This further step, the reification of appearances or ideas or sense-data, is actually quite crucial. It is needed if we are to say that the immediate objects of perception, what we are immediately aware of in perception, are not external objects but rather appearances or ideas or sense-data produced in our minds by external objects. If I say 'Now the coin appears to be elliptical', I still claim to be perceiving the coin or to be aware of the coin. If I say 'I am now experiencing or am aware of a visual idea or visual sense-datum of an elliptical coin', then I no longer claim to be perceiving the coin or to be aware of the coin. These two formulations are not, therefore, merely different ways of saying the same thing, though many philosophers write as if they were. Are there good reasons to reify appearances or ideas or sense-data, as the second formulations do?

There do seem to be good reasons to reify appearances or ideas or sense-data. When I view a coin from the side, I certainly see or am aware of something, and what I see or am aware of is elliptical in shape. But the coin is not elliptical in shape, and therefore what I see or am aware of is not the coin. When I look at a stick half-immersed in water, I certainly see or am aware of something bent. But the stick is not bent, and therefore what I see or am aware of is not the stick. When the hallucinator sees pink rats, he certainly sees or is aware of something (for we say, after all, that he is 'seeing things'). But there are no pink rats, and therefore what he sees or is aware of is not pink rats. In all these cases what the perceiver actually sees or is immediately aware of are appearances or ideas or sense-data. And the same goes for cases of so-called 'veridical perception'. When I view the coin from above, or the stick out of water, or some real brown rats, the immediate object of perception is also an appearance or idea or sense-datum. Veridical and non-veridical perception do not differ in their immediate objects. Rather, they differ in whether the appearances or ideas or sense-data resemble reality: in veridical perceptions they do, in non-veridical perceptions they do not.

The arguments implicit in the foregoing are as follows:

(1) When I view a round coin from the side I see something elliptical.
(2) The round coin is not elliptical.
Therefore, when I view a round coin from the side I do not see the coin.

(1) When I view a straight oar half-immersed in water, I see something bent.
(2) The straight oar is not bent.
Therefore, when I view a straight oar half-immersed in water, I do not see the oar.

(1) When I hallucinate pink rats, I see pink rats.

(2) There are no pink rats.
Therefore, when I hallucinate pink rats I do not see pink rats.

(I am well aware that this last argument is very peculiar indeed – I shall return to the matter.)

These arguments, and others like them, trade on the cases, endemic in the sceptical literature, in which appearance and reality do not match up (so-called 'non-veridical perceptions'). Some philosophers have been tempted to respond that in them the circumstances of perception are somehow unusual or abnormal, and that when usual or normal circumstances prevail and we have veridical perceptions we become immediately acquainted not with 'ideas', but with external objects. These philosophers try to resist the view that in both non-veridical and veridical perception the immediate object of perception is the same – an idea or sense-datum.

But this is implausible: view a coin from the side (which is surely the usual way we view coins), and then slowly tilt the coin until it is vertical to the line of sight. Are we aware of a series of sense-data steadily becoming less elliptical and more circular in shape, and then suddenly aware of a circular external object? Surely it is more plausible to assume that we are always immediately aware of sense-data or 'ideas', only one of which (the one we receive when the coin is held vertical to the line of sight) resembles the coin in shape. Once we have reified ideas or sense-data into the things of which we are immediately aware in some cases of perception, it is natural to do the same thing for all cases of perception. And there are other arguments which tend to the same conclusion.

THE CAUSAL THEORY OF PERCEPTION AND THE TIME-LAPSE ARGUMENT

Another argument, or cluster of arguments, in favour of idea-ism is based upon scientific analysis of how the process of perception actually occurs. Such arguments have been as influential in the twentieth century as they were in the seventeenth, so we will consider some modern versions of them.

Science teaches us that perception involves some more or less complicated causal interaction between the object perceived and the perceiver. For example, in order for us to see a table, light must be reflected from the surface of the table, enter the eye, stimulate the retina, then the optic nerve, then the visual cortex of the brain, where (all being well) they cause a visual experience of a table. Similar stories can be told for the other senses. This is the causal theory of perception.

Notice that it is couched in thoroughly realist terms. It tells us, for example, that in order to see a table a certain causal interaction must take place between the table and the perceiver. Scientific analysis of how perception occurs says nothing to convince us of the idea-ist thesis that the objects of perception (things seen, heard, smelled, tasted, or touched) are not external objects but rather ideas or sense-data. Science merely teaches us that perception is a more or less indirect process: the perceiver is separated from the object perceived in space and time, and is linked to it by a more or less elaborate causal process, rather than being in direct 'contact' with it.

This last point gives us the key to a new philosophical argument for idea-ism. Suppose we accept direct realism, the view that perception must have its immediate objects, that it must be a direct or immediate process. Then the causal theory of perception teaches us that we are not directly or immediately aware of external objects, that they cannot be the immediate objects of perception. And we will have to posit ideas or sense-data as the assumed immediate objects of perception. The argument goes, then, like this:

(1) The senses give us direct or immediate information either about external objects or about ideas or sense-data.
(2) The senses do not give us direct or immediate information about external objects.

Therefore, the senses give us direct or immediate information about ideas or sense-data.

The argument is valid: accept its premises and you must also accept its conclusion. The second premise seems to have been established by scientific analysis of the process of perception. The first premise is another cornerstone of empiricism – that the senses give us direct or immediate information about something. Accept it, too, and the idea-ist conclusion is inescapable.

The argument has a slightly paradoxical flavour to it, which is well captured in a famous passage from Bertrand Russell, another prominent defender (at times) of the theory of sense-data. Russell writes:

Physics assures us that the occurrences which we call 'perceiving objects' are at the end of a long causal chain which starts from the objects, and are not likely to resemble the objects, except, at best, in certain very abstract ways... The observer, when he seems to himself to be observing a stone, is really, if physics is to be believed, observing the effects of the stone upon himself. – Naive realism leads to physics, and physics, if true, shows that naive realism is false. Therefore naive realism, if true, is false; therefore it is false. (1940: 13)

Russell writes relatively recently. But the argument we are now considering is actually a very old one. Perhaps its first clear statement is by the rationalist philosopher Descartes, who as a rationalist was anxious to expose the naiveties of his empiricist opponents. But it was also used in one form or another by empiricists like Locke, Berkeley and Hume, who adopted idea-ism as a way out of the dilemma.

A special case of this general argument has become famous and is worth stating separately because it puts the point especially sharply. I refer to the so-called 'time-lapse argument', invented by Bertrand Russell but popularised by C. E. M. Joad. This is how Joad formulates the argument:

Let us suppose that I am looking at a star, Sirius say, on a dark night. If physics is to be believed, light waves which started to travel from Sirius many years ago reach...the earth, impinge upon my retinae and cause me to say that I am seeing Sirius. Now the Sirius about which they convey information to me is the Sirius which existed at the time when they started. This Sirius may, however, no longer exist; it may have disappeared in the interim. To say that one can see what no longer exists is absurd. It follows that, whatever it is that I am seeing, it is not Sirius. What, in fact, I do see is a yellow patch of a particular size, shape and intensity. I infer that this yellow patch had an origin...several years ago and many million miles away. But this inference may be mistaken...What, then, if the physicist and physiologist are right, we in fact know [in perception] are certain events taking place in our own brains. The outside world is not itself known [in perception]; its existence is merely an inference...If we accept the teachings of physics and physiology, what we know in perception are not the movements of matter, but certain events in ourselves connected with these movements; not objects external to ourselves, but the effect of the impact of light-rays and other forms of energy proceeding from those objects upon our bodies. (1943: 113–16)

Here Joad takes an extreme case, that of seeing a star many light years away from us. But the argument can be generalised to cover all cases of visual perception, and indeed to all perceptions of whatever sense. Let us see how this can be done.

First of all, we should correct a slip which Joad makes. At a crucial step in his argument he writes: 'To say that one can see what no longer exists is absurd.' But his argument does not really rest upon the assumption that Sirius no longer exists, that it has in fact exploded since the light was emitted from it. If it did, we could simply point out that the assumption is false (or at any rate, that Joad has no reason to suppose it true). What Joad's argument really assumes is that Sirius *may* have exploded since the light was emitted from it. And this assumption is certainly correct: it is certainly logically possible that Sirius has exploded in the interval between the emission of the light and its reception by the eye of the perceiver. So we can strengthen his argument by reformulating the crucial step as follows: 'To say that one can see what may no longer exist is absurd.'

Now the Sirius case is extreme because it takes a long time for the light from Sirius to reach the earth. If T is the time of emission of the light, and $T+t$ the time of its reception by the eye, then in the Sirius case t is several years (since Sirius is several light years away from the earth). But the size of the interval t is not important from a philosophical point of view. If I look at a nearby table, then light is reflected from the table at T and enters my eye at $T+t$, where t is now an incredibly small but finite time. I must admit the logical possibility that the table has ceased to exist between T and $T+t$ (God might just have zapped it out of existence). If it is absurd to say that I can see (at $T+t$) what may no longer exist (at $T+t$), then it is absurd to say that I can see a table. What I see must be the effect of the table upon me, a table-like sense-datum which does exist at $T+t$. Similarly for all cases of visual perception.

The argument will also go through straightforwardly for hearing and smelling things. To hear something, sound waves must be emitted from it, enter the ear, and cause an auditory sensation. To smell something, molecules must be emitted from it, enter the nose, and cause an olfactory sensation. In both cases the causal process takes time, and we must admit that the heard or smelt thing may have ceased to exist during that time. Since it is absurd to say that I can hear or smell something which may no longer exist, it is absurd to say that we hear or smell things. Nobody ever hears or smells a rat, rather we hear rat-noises and smell rat-smells, auditory and olfactory sense-data produced by rats. (If the reader is starting to smell a rat in all this, let the reader be patient a little longer.)

The argument can also be pushed through, though not so straightforwardly, for tasting and even touching things. Here we do seem to be 'in direct contact' with the things. But physiology teaches us that it takes a very small but finite time for stimulations of nerves in the fingertips or the tongue to be transmitted to the brain where they cause tactile and gustatory sensations. The touched or tasted thing may just have ceased to exist during that time. It is absurd to say that I can touch or taste something which may no longer exist, so it is absurd to say that we touch or taste things. Nobody ever touched a table or tasted an orange, rather we touch tactile sense-data and taste gustatory sense-data. (By now the reader ought to be smelling a rat.) So the time-lapse argument can be generalised to all cases of perception (though when we do generalise it, it looks less plausible). If we accept the general argument, then once again we are driven to the idea-ist conclusion that the immediate objects of perception are always ideas or sense-data.

So much for the various arguments in favour of idea-ism. What of the doctrine itself? The first thing to be said is that it is far removed from the common-sense view of the matter. The common-sense view is that when I look at a table what I see or am aware of is the table. The common-sense view is the realist view. (It is less obvious that the common-sense view is direct or naive realism.) The proverbial man-in-the-street, asked to tell what he sees, never says things like 'I immediately experience a visual idea or sense-datum of a table, from which I infer that there is a table in front of me'. Ideas or sense-data are not part of common-sense; rather, they are posited by philosophers anxious to secure the infallibility of the empirical basis.

This is not an argument against idea-ism. Common-sense views have often turned out to be wrong, and perhaps the common-sense realist view of perception is wrong. (Certainly the sceptics and scientists show that naive or direct realism is wrong). But it is a good principle of method in philosophy not to give up a common-sense view unless there are good reasons or arguments to do so. So we will have to return to the arguments we have considered, and see whether their idea-ist conclusion can be evaded. For the moment, however, let us look rather at the consequences of accepting idea-ism.

Idea-ism is the view that what we are immediately aware of in perception are appearances or ideas or sense-data. Sometimes (it is supposed) these ideas are produced in our minds by external objects and resemble those objects. This is veridical perception. Sometimes ideas are produced by external objects but do not resemble them (illusions). Sometimes ideas are not produced by external objects at all (dreams and hallucinations). In the second and third cases we have non-veridical perception.

One happy consequence of this view for those who wish to defeat the sceptic is that it enables us to obtain certainty from sense-experience, that it preserves the infallibility of the em-pirical basis for knowledge. Older empiricists adopted direct or naive realism: 'We directly perceive external objects as they really are.' For older empiricists, therefore, the senses gave us immediate knowledge of the truth of observation-statements about external objects and their properties. But sceptical and scientific arguments show that naive direct realism is incorrect. So empiricists replace it with idea-ism: 'We directly experience ideas or sense-data as they really are.' Now the senses give us immediate knowledge not about external objects, but about ideas or sense-data in our own minds. The old sceptical arguments are quite powerless against this theory.

Before asking whether the sceptic has any new argument against idea-ism, let me illustrate my earlier contention that idea-ism has seemed to many to be an eminently plausible view. It is worth noting that the great trio Locke, Berkeley and Hume do not so much argue for the position as assume it as an axiom. All of them begin their works by stating idea-ism as if it were self-evident. Locke writes:

Since the mind, in all its thoughts and reasonings, hath no other immediate object but its own ideas, which it alone does or can contemplate, it is evident that our knowledge is only conversant about them. (1690: IV, i, 1)

Is it really evident that we cannot contemplate tables or trees or stars, but only ideas of tables or trees or stars? Well, Berkeley thinks it is, too:

It is evident to any one who takes a survey of the objects of human knowledge, that they are either ideas actually imprinted on the senses, or else such as are perceived by attending to the passions and operations of the mind, or lastly ideas formed by help of memory or imagination, either, compounding, dividing, or barely representing those originally perceived in the aforesaid ways. (*Principles*, Part I, 1; 1949, 41)

Hume agrees, though he changes the terminology: the original sensory ideas he calls 'impressions', reserving the term 'idea' for copies or images of these which persist in the mind. He writes:

All the perceptions of the human mind resolve themselves into ... IMPRESSIONS and IDEAS. The difference betwixt these consists in the degree of force and liveliness with which they strike upon the mind ... Those perceptions which enter with most force and violence, we may name *impressions*; and under this name I comprehend all our sensations, passions and emotions, as they make their first appearance in the soul. By *ideas* I mean the faint images of these in thinking and reasoning. (*Treatise*, I, i, 1; 1888: 1)

I also said earlier that idea-ism persisted right up to the twentieth century. Here, in justification of that claim, are a few more passages in which philosophers and philosopher-scientists take idea-ism for granted, though they all express it rather differently. A. J. Ayer produces it immediately as a response to the sceptic's infinite regress argument:

A way of escaping the infinite regress ... would be to rely on the notion of incorrigible propositions. The regress would terminate when one arrived at a proposition which was, as it were, self-guaranteeing. The candidates for this role would be propositions which ... recorded the subject's immediate experiences, propositions which described what he felt, or how things appeared to him, or what he seemed to remember. (1969: 119)

Ayer is one of the twentieth century's most prominent defenders of idea-ism (the theory of sense-data). Scientists, too, think idea-ism obvious. Arthur Eddington writes:

The only subject presented to me for study is the content of my consciousness. According to the usual description, this is a heterogenous collection of sensations, emotions, conceptions, memories, etc. (1939: 195)

Nobel Prize winner Eugene Wigner thinks that there are two kinds of reality:

... there are two kinds of reality or existence: the existence of my consciousness and the reality or existence of everything else. This latter reality is not absolute but only relative ... excepting immediate sensations and more generally, the content of my consciousness, everything is a construct ... but some constructs are closer, some farther, from the direct sensations. (1967: 189)

One might expect scientists to think that they can study things like stars or rocks or atoms or the human brain. But scientists-turned-philosophers seem to know better. Eddington says that the only subject I can study is the 'content of my consciousness'. Wigner goes even further: stars, rocks, atoms and human brains are 'constructs' (whatever that means) out of 'immediate sensations', and their existence is 'only relative' (whatever that means) to that of the sensations. Actually, Wigner has turned idea-ism into idealism. Berkeley did the same thing before him, and when we discuss Berkeley's philosophy we shall see what is meant by saying that physical objects are 'constructs out of sensations'.

THE SCEPTIC FIGHTS BACK — APPEARANCE AND REALITY AGAIN

We have seen that a chief motive or argument for idea-ism is anti-sceptical: the empirical basis for knowledge must be rescued from sceptical attack and made infallible. How might the sceptic respond to this? She might try to show that the new empirical basis for knowledge is not absolutely secure or infallible after all. Or she might concede that it is (as Sextus Empiricus did) but deny that it could be an adequate foundation for knowledge. The second objection is far more important than the first. As we will see, it leads us to pose the old problem of appearance and reality in a new, sharper and more radical form.

But let us begin by discussing the first objection briefly. Earlier we made the finicky-sounding but important point that the basis for knowledge must consist of statements rather than, say, experiences, since only a statement can justify another statement. Idea-ism makes the empirical basis consist of statements about the ideas or sense-data that perceivers experience. They will be statements like 'Now I am aware of a visual idea of a bent stick', 'Now I experience a table-like sense-datum', 'Now I am aware of an olfactory idea (smell) like that of bad eggs' and so forth. The locutions are curious. It is also interesting that when we try to describe our (supposed) ideas or sense-data, we have to do so in terms which are parasitic upon ordinary talk about physical objects ('table-like sense-datum', 'smell like that of rotten eggs' and so on). Ordinary language contains very few special words for sensations, like the words 'itch' and 'tickle' (which shows again that the theory of ideas or sense-data is a philosophical rather than a common-sense theory).

Our question is whether reports like those above are infallible or whether they could turn out to be mistaken. Here we exclude the case where a person tells lies about his ideas, declaring falsely that he is having a table-like sense-datum when it is actually a chair-like sense-datum of which he is aware. We also exclude the case where a person issues a false report because of a slip-of-the-tongue, saying 'table-like sense-datum' when he meant to say 'chair-like sense-datum'. These cases are uninteresting, for lies and slips-of-the-tongue can occur regarding any statement about what is going on in our minds (or heads if you prefer), and they do not really impugn the claim that our knowledge of these goings-on is incorrigible. To exclude these uninteresting cases, let us suppose we have a perfectly sincere reporter who is not trying to deceive us, and a reporter with a complete command of the language who makes no slips-of-the-tongue or other verbal mistakes. Could such a reporter be wrong about the ideas or sense-data he is experiencing?

Sceptics have produced some pretty far-fetched arguments designed to show that he could. Consider the following series of sense-data reports: 'Now I am having an olfactory sense-datum of rotten eggs. Now I am having a visual sense-datum of a rotten apple. I see that my first report was wrong: the olfactory sense-datum was not of rotten eggs but rather of a rotten apple.' If this series is possible, then it shows that sense-data reports are corrigible in the light of future sense-data reports (in much the same way as we earlier saw that observation-statements are corrigible in the light of future observations). If we believe that sense-data come in families (to use the jargon), so that smelling rotten eggs will be succeeded by seeing them, too, if we look, then we must admit that my current sense-data reports are corrigible in the light of future experience. The only way to avoid this is to insist that my current sense-data reports imply nothing whatever about what future sense-data I shall or shall not receive (which is tantamount to ridding ourselves of the belief that sense-data come in 'families'). If the new empirical basis is to be really secure, then it must be really narrow.

Two other sceptical arguments against the infallibility of sense-data reports are even more far-fetched. The first points

out that there is presumably a small time-lag between experiencing the sense-datum and formulating the report about it.
Hence I rely upon my memory in formulating the report and
since memory is fallible, so is any sense-datum report. It has
been suggested that we can get over this objection by transforming the sense-datum report into a report on my present
memory-images: we do not say 'Now I am having a table-like
sense-datum' but rather 'Now I am having a memory-image of
having had a table-like sense-datum a little while ago'. But if
there is also a time-lag between the occurrence of the 'memory-
image' and the formulation of a report about it, then an infinite
regress threatens.

This far-fetched argument does serve to draw attention to a
problem, or cluster of problems, to which idea-ist philosophers
pay some attention: the problem of memory. The problem is
epistemological: can I be sure on the basis of my present ideas
or sense-data that I have previously had ideas or sense-data?
And a related problem is: how can I distinguish those of my
current ideas or sense-data which are produced by perceiving as
opposed to remembering or imagining?

The last sceptical objection seizes upon the fact that all sense-
data reports contain the word 'I': we all report our own ideas
or sense-data. But this is to assume that there is a continuing
subject of all my experiences, a single thing which has all of the
experiences which I call my own. Now this, the sceptic might
object, is a wild hypothesis not justified by the existence of the
experiences or sense-data themselves. It has been suggested that
we can get over this objection by transforming sense-data
reports into something like 'Now there occurs a table-like sense-
datum' and 'Now there occurs a chair-like sense-datum', in
which it is not assumed that a single continuing subject is aware
of both sense-data.

This far-fetched argument serves to draw attention to another
problem to which idea-ist philosophers pay some attention: the
problem of personal identity. Again, the problem is epistemological: can I be sure, on the basis of my present ideas or
sense-data, that I exist as the continuing subject of all my ideas
or sense-data? This problem is linked to the problem of memory,

because many idea-ists have assumed that memory is the key to personal identity: what makes a past experience mine rather than yours is my present ability to remember it. The problems of memory and personal identity are not problems which arise only for idea-ist philosophers. But they do arise in particular and rather acute forms for idea-ist philosophers. I do not propose to discuss them further.

So much for the rather bizarre way in which some sceptics have challenged the infallibility of sense-data reports as a basis for knowledge. The more important sceptical response was to challenge, not the security of the new empirical basis, but its adequacy. It is obvious that the security of the empirical basis has been bought at a very heavy price. For the empirical basis has become much narrower than before: naive realism gave us immediate knowledge of the external world; idea-ism gives us immediate knowledge only of the (sensory) contents of our own minds. Now anything we say about the external world has become mediate or derived knowledge (or belief). Narrowing the basis for knowledge may have secured it from sceptical attack, but only at the price of making it more difficult to establish any other knowledge on that narrow foundation.

As we have seen, Sextus Empiricus himself conceded that the senses gave us infallible information about the appearances. He obviously thought that empiricism could not survive the admission that the senses do not yield certainty about how things really are. The Greek philosophers seemed to have agreed with him. Some tried to rescue empiricism by saying that on occasions the senses do tell us with certainty how things really are. This was Aristotle's view. Others abandoned empiricism because the senses told us only about 'the appearances', and opted for a rationalist view. This was the response of Plato. But now we have a new form of empiricism which accepts that the senses tell us only about 'the appearances'. Locke was right to call it the new 'way of ideas'.

Can we establish on the basis of our ideas or sense-data any statement about what reality is like? This is the old problem of appearance and reality again. But within idea-ism it assumes a sharper form. We can pose it in three stages by asking three questions in ascending order of seriousness (or you may think, ridiculousness) :

(1) Can I be sure on the basis of ideas or sense-data what the real colour (shape, size, texture, temperature, taste, smell...) of a thing is? Which idea or sense-datum of the colour (shape, size...) resembles the thing's real colour (shape, size...)?

This is the question which we already considered. Sceptics like Sextus Empiricus said that we could never be sure which 'appearance' resembled reality. I shall say no more about this first question, for there are more radical questions that we must ask. To see this, notice that our first question takes two things for granted or makes two presuppositions: it presupposes that there are things or external objects and it presupposes that they have real colours (shapes, sizes...). Questioning these two presuppositions, in reverse order, leads to our second and third problems.

(2) Can I be sure on the basis of ideas or sense-data that things possess real colours (shapes, sizes, textures, temperatures, tastes, smells...)? Perhaps some of the apparent properties of things are not possessed by those things at all, but exist only as ideas or sense-data produced by those things. If colour is such a property, if things are not themselves coloured but merely produce colour-sensations in the minds of perceivers, then the question 'What is the real colour of a thing?' ceases to apply and sceptical worries about which colour-sensation resembles reality evaporate. This second question is more fundamental than the first: before we can sensibly ask which apparent P is the real P (for any property P), we must first establish that things or external objects possess a real P. But there is a more fundamental question yet. For our second question continues to take for granted or presuppose that there are things or external objects which have some real properties of their own.

(3) Can I be sure on the basis of ideas or sense-data that there are external objects at all? Perhaps none of the apparent

properties of things really belong to things because there are no things, but only ideas or sense-data of things. We take for granted the fundamental hypothesis of an external world, containing things or objects which cause our ideas. Can I establish on the basis of ideas or sense-data that this fundamental hypothesis is true? This third question is more fundamental than the second: before we can sensibly ask which apparent properties really belong to external objects, we must first establish that there are external objects. So we have here arrived at the most fundamental facet or sub-problem of appearance and reality. It has a special name: the problem of the external world.

Idealism (with an 'l') is the metaphysical or ontological view that only ideas or sense-data (and perhaps the minds which have them) exist. The problem of the external world is whether we can prevent idea-ism from turning into idealism, whether we can establish on the basis of ideas that something other than ideas exists. There is an even more extreme way to put the problem. Each person's ideas or sense-data seem to be private to that person: my experiences may be similar to yours but my experiences are mine and yours are yours, and we cannot literally be said to have the same experience. Solipsism is the lunatic version of idealism which says that only my ideas or sense-data (and perhaps my mind) exist. (Solipsism sidesteps another problem facing idea-ists, the problem of establishing on the basis of ideas present to my mind that other minds exist.) The most extreme version of our problem asks whether we can prevent idea-ism from turning into solipsism, whether I can establish on the basis of my ideas that other minds with ideas exist and that external objects exist also.

The second and third of our questions lead us into strange territory indeed. To say that objects may not have colours or may not exist at all seems bizarre. Idealism is a peculiar philosophy and solipsism a lunatic one. The solipsist view that the world is my dream has the megalomaniac consequence that I am responsible for Beethoven's music or Rembrandt's paintings (Popper 1972: 41). If anyone actually claimed to be a solipsist, we should straightway lock him in a lunatic asylum. So why take such views and the problem which prompts them seriously?

This is to overlook the fact that our questions are epistemological questions. No philosopher takes solipsism seriously to the extent of thinking it true. Both Hume and Berkeley were accused of being solipsists, but this is a mistake. Actually, Bertrand Russell tells (1948: 196) of receiving a letter from Mrs Ladd-Franklin in which she professed to being a solipsist and sought Russell's help in convincing other people. But if she had really been a solipsist, what was she doing writing to Russell or trying to convince other people? The problem of solipsism is not whether solipsism is true (all agree that it is not) but rather whether we can prove (on the basis of ideas or sense-data) that solipsism is false. Many philosophers have taken this problem seriously. Many philosophers have adopted what Rudolf Carnap called 'methodological solipsism' and have begun from the solipsistic position where they are immediately acquainted only with their own ideas or sense-data. But the task was always to get beyond this starting-point and to establish the existence of other minds, external objects and so forth. This is the programme which we find stated more or less explicitly in Locke, Berkeley, Hume, Mill, Russell and Carnap himself. Solipsism is obviously crazy but 'methodological solipsism' is not.

So our questions are epistemological questions, and in particular epistemological questions which arise out of the doctrine of idea-ism. Yet, we must not overlook the tremendous anti-sceptical virtues, if virtues they be, of idealist metaphysical views of one kind or another. Indeed, the chief attraction of idealist metaphysics is its potential for defusing scepticism. Let me try to explain this.

Idea-ists propose to defeat the sceptic by confining immediate knowledge to the 'appearances' or 'ideas' or 'sense-data'. But the sceptic's immediate response is that this leaves the problem of appearance and reality untouched, indeed, that it heightens the problem. Confining ourselves to talk of (different) apparent colours of things may remove the contradictions in colour-experiences, but we still do not know which apparent colour is the real colour. But now suppose we opt for the idealist view that things have no 'real colour'. Straightway the sceptical question evaporates: there is no 'real colour' for the sceptic to raise difficulties about. If we extend this ploy to all of the apparent properties of things, and say that the things do not have real Ps for any of the properties P that we experience, then the entire problem of appearance and reality in its original form (question (1) of page 103, above) evaporates. Having gone this far, and declared that things have none of their apparent properties, we might as well take the further step of doing away with the things themselves. On the idealist view that only minds and their ideas exist, the rest of the problem of appearance and reality (questions (2) and (3) of page 103, above) also evaporates. The sceptic now has only the problem of other minds to fall back upon. But if we opt for solipsism, scepticism cannot get any grip upon us at all.

Now as I already emphasised, no sane philosopher travels all the way down the idealist road and opts for solipsism. Most philosophers stop well short of solipsist lunacy. But many idea-ist philosophers have travelled some of the way down the idealist road. And the prospect of thereby pulling the rug from under the sceptic's feet is the single most important reason why they have done so. I shall be illustrating this contention.

CHAPTER 6

Primary and secondary qualities

I now want to consider an important answer to the second part
of the problem of appearance and reality, the question of which
apparent properties of things are real properties of things. The
answer is the doctrine of primary and secondary qualities. It is
associated with John Locke, the first member of our trio of great
British empiricist philosophers. According to this doctrine, the
apparent properties of things fall into two groups. There are the
primary qualities and the secondary qualities. There is some
dispute as to which properties to place in which group, but a
standard classification is this:

> Primary qualities: shape, size, weight, being in motion or at
> rest, being one in number or several.
> Secondary qualities: colour, taste, smell, sound, texture, heat
> or cold.

Now I said earlier, and it is true, that the doctrine of primary
and secondary qualities was defended by John Locke. But
Locke did not invent the doctrine, he took it over from scientists
whose work he knew and admired. These scientists did not
defend the doctrine on epistemological grounds but rather on
scientific or metaphysical ones. And it is interesting that the
view Locke actually defended was different from, and I think an
improvement upon, the view of some of his scientific precursors.
The crucial difference concerns the subjectivity of the secondary
qualities. A careful reading of Locke reveals that he denied this
part of the doctrine, though for various special reasons this does
not always emerge clearly from what he says.

To clarify all this, I will first look briefly at the history of the doctrine, then at how Locke took over and modified it. Finally I will ask whether a consistent idea-ist can really defend any version of the theory of primary and secondary qualities.

The doctrine of primary and secondary qualities (though not this name) actually has its origin in the speculative metaphysics of the ancient atomists Democritus and Lucretius. They thought that the real world consists of atoms and the void: the atoms are unchanging and indivisible ('atom' means 'uncuttable'), and all apparent changes in the world are to be explained as rearrangements of various kinds of atoms in the void (empty space). Now the Greek atomists realised that if we try to explain the observed properties of collections of atoms, there are two ways we can proceed. We explain why blood is red by saying that most of the smaller collections of atoms which compose the blood (namely the red blood corpuscles) are red. But this is a relatively shallow explanation, for it leads immediately to the question of why the red blood corpuscles are red, a question of the same kind as the one with which we started. Clearly it will not do to say that red blood corpuscles are red because the atoms which compose them are red, or that lemons taste bitter because 'lemon atoms' are bitter and so on. A deeper explanation will reduce the observable properties of atoms or collections of atoms to other properties which atoms or collections of atoms possess. For example, Democritus had the nice hypothesis that lemons are bitter, not because the lemon atoms are bitter, but because they have jagged shapes which do not fit nicely into the 'pores' in the collections of atoms which form our tongues. Other things taste sweet, on the other hand, because their atoms have nicely rounded shapes and roll smoothly over the tongue and fit nicely into its 'pores'. And we should not pooh-pooh this speculation, for it is still with us: the idea that the tastes and smells of substances are to be explained in terms of their molecular structure is still actively being pursued.

So already in Greek atomism the idea developed of explaining some of the observable properties of things in terms of other properties possessed by atoms or collections of atoms. There is a conundrum involved here. On the one hand, explaining the bitterness of lemons by imputing bitterness to the lemon atoms seems to get us nowhere. On the other hand, how can things which are not themselves bitter produce sensations of bitterness by virtue of their shape?

Atomism has had a long history, and down the centuries the list of primary properties (properties possessed by the atoms themselves) has changed and become more abstract or further removed from experience. Democritus explained why some substances are more difficult to break into pieces than others (cohesion) in terms of the atoms of cohesive substances having lots of little hooks on them which bind them all together. Newton objected that this was not true to Democritan principle, since it leads immediately to the question of how the hooks on the atoms cohere with the atoms. Newton explained cohesion by attributing attractive forces to the atoms of cohesive substances (1730: 388). Attractive forces are stranger than hooks. Some of the properties attributed to atoms or to sub-atomic particles today are stranger still (including the property of 'strangeness').

The idea that certain of the apparent properties of things are subjective (exist only in the minds of perceivers) was first stated sharply by Galileo. In his little book *The Assayer* (published in 1623), Galileo writes:

Now I say that whenever I conceive any material or corporeal substance, I immediately feel the need to think of it as *bounded*, and as having this or that *shape*; as being *large or small* in relation to other things, and in some *specific place* at any given time; as being *in motion or at rest*; as *touching or not touching* some other body; as being *one in number, or few, or many*. From these conditions I cannot separate such a substance by any stretch of my imagination. But that it must be white or red, bitter or sweet, noisy or silent, and of sweet or foul odour, my mind does not feel compelled to bring in as necessary accompaniments. Without the senses as our guides, reason or imagination unaided would probably never arrive at qualities like these. Hence I think that tastes, odours, colours and so on...reside only in the consciousness. Hence if the living creature were removed, all these qualities would be wiped away and annihilated.

To excite in us tastes, odours, and sounds I believe that nothing is required in external bodies except shapes, numbers and slow or rapid movements. I think that if ears, tongues and noses were removed, shapes and numbers and motion would remain, but not odours or tastes or sounds. (Galileo 1957: 274, 276–7)

An interesting point about this passage is that Galileo does not arrive at his view from sense-experience. On the contrary, he asks what properties reason compels us to ascribe to bodies and says that without the senses as our (misleading) guides reason would never attribute tastes, odours, colour and so on to external objects. The primary properties are those which reason dictates, the secondary properties those which sense-experience (mistakenly) suggests. Galileo here speaks as a rationalist rather than an empiricist. And when he speaks of 'reason' he means mathematical and particularly geometrical reasoning. He actually arrives at his position from a metaphysical assumption to the effect that the real world has a geometrical structure and can therefore be comprehended by geometrical methods. As he puts it, the 'Book of Nature' which we read in experience is written in the 'language of mathematics':

Philosophy is written in this grand book, the universe, which stands continually open to our gaze. But this book cannot be understood unless one first learns to comprehend the language and read the letters in which it is composed. It is written in the language of mathematics, and its characters are triangles, circles, and other geometric figures without which it is humanly impossible to understand a single word of it; without these, one wanders about in a dark labyrinth. (Galileo 1957: 237–8)

Galileo's 'mathematical metaphysic' has been very popular among philosophers and scientists: the rationalist philosopher Descartes and the physicist Einstein are two others who accepted it. Its adherents do not deny that we must use our senses to get knowledge about the world, to read the 'Book of Nature'. Unaided reason will never be able to tell us how many chairs there are in a room, or whether the table there is round or square. But before we can read the 'Book of Nature' we must know the mathematical language in which it is written. Unaided sense-experience will lead us to 'wander about in a dark labyrinth' and to ascribe to the world features which exist only in our minds. It is reason (the mathematical metaphysics), rather than sense-experience, which leads Galileo and others to the idea that the 'secondary qualities' are subjective. And it is no accident that all of Galileo's 'primary qualities' (shape, size, number, motion...) can be described in mathematical terms.

Galileo's view that the secondary qualities are subjective runs counter to common sense. It means that common-sense judgements like 'My tie is red' or 'Sugar is sweet' are strictly speaking mistaken: my tie is not red or any other colour, nor is sugar sweet or bitter. Adherents of the doctrine do not, however, reject such judgements out of hand. Instead, they reinterpret them. They say that what 'My tie is red' means is something like 'My tie will appear red to, or cause an idea of redness to arise in the mind of, a normal human observer under normal lighting'. And what 'Sugar is sweet' means is something like 'Sugar will appear sweet, or cause an idea of sweetness to arise in the mind of, a normal human observer who tastes it.' The alternative view, which is closer to common sense, is that 'My tie is red' means what it says, and that it is because the tie is really red that it will look red to normal human observers under normal lighting. The difference here is a subtle one: the common-sense view is that 'My tie is red' might entail a statement about how it will look to 'normal observers'; the philosophical view is that this entailment exhausts the meaning of 'My tie is red'.

Some famous riddles are relevant here. 'If a tree falls in a deserted forest, does it make a noise?' Those who think that noises are secondary qualities which exist only as 'auditory experiences' in the minds of perceivers will say that it does not. 'Do things have colours in the dark or when nobody is looking at them?' Those who think that colours are secondary qualities which exist only as 'colour sensations' in the minds of perceivers will say that they do not. The common-sense view is that the falling tree does make a noise but there is nobody in the deserted forest to hear it, and that things have colours in the dark or when nobody is looking at them but nobody is experiencing their colours.

The distinction between primary and secondary qualities, first hinted at by the Greek atomists and stated explicitly by Galileo and Descartes, was also accepted by Locke's contemporaries Isaac Newton and Robert Boyle. Boyle wrote a book, *On the Origin of Forms and Qualities*, full of speculations about how various perceived qualities are produced in our minds by the interaction of atoms or 'corpuscles' with our sense-organs. Now Locke knew and admired Newton and Boyle, and simply borrowed the distinction from them. It was not Locke's idea-ist theory of knowledge which led him to the distinction, but his admiration for the scientific and metaphysical views of Newton and Boyle. (Indeed, we shall see that if Locke had stuck firmly to his idea-ist theory of knowledge, he could have hardly accepted the distinction at all.)

LOCKE'S THEORY

Locke did not merely take over the doctrine from the scientists, he modified it so that it did not involve the subjectivity of the secondary qualities. He was not always consistent in this. The following passage, for example, is very reminiscent of Galileo's view:

> The particular bulk, figure and motion of the parts of fire or snow are really in them, whether anyone's senses perceives them or no; and therefore they may be called real qualities, because they really exist in those bodies. But light, heat, whiteness, or coldness, are no more really in them than sickness or pain is in manna. Take away the sensation of them; let not the eyes see light or colours, nor the ears hear sounds; let the palate not taste, nor the nose smell, and all colours, tastes, odours, and sounds ... vanish and cease. (1690: II, iii, 17)

Now, as I say, this is very reminiscent of Galileo: secondary qualities exist only in the minds of perceivers, and disappear when those perceivers disappear. This was what many of Locke's readers, including his immediate successor Berkeley, took him to be saying.

But a careful reading reveals a different Lockean view. The

passage I have just cited, when its missing portions are restored, ends as follows:

> ...all colours, tastes, odours, and sounds, *as they are such particular ideas*, vanish and cease, and are reduced to their causes, i.e. bulk, figure, and motion of parts.

Now what this says is that 'ideas' of colours, tastes, odours and sounds (that is, colour-sensations, taste-sensations...) vanish when perceivers vanish. And this is trivial: where there are no perceivers there are no perceptions. But the causes of 'ideas' or sensations do not vanish when perceivers vanish. And these causes Locke thinks can be analysed in terms of the 'bulk, figure, and motion' of the particles of which things are composed. Elsewhere Locke distinguishes ideas of secondary qualities (such as colour-sensations) from secondary qualities (such as colours), and describes the secondary qualities as powers which objects have to produce ideas or sensations. The secondary qualities

> are nothing in the objects themselves but powers to produce various sensations in us by their primary qualities, i.e. by bulk, figure, texture, and motion of their insensible parts... (1690: II, viii, 10)

Thus, for example, to say that a stone is red is to say that:

> It has, indeed, such a configuration of particles, both night and day, as are apt, by the rays of light rebounding from some parts of that hard stone, to produce in us the idea of redness... (1690: II, viii, 19)

Now if redness is a power in things to produce particular sensations in human observers (given appropriate circumstances), then a thing can have this power whether or not it is exercising it. A red stone is red in the dark, and it is red when no one is looking at it. We can even imagine a second *Day of the Triffids* in which all human beings are rendered, not blind (as in John Wyndham, 1951), but colour-blind: red things will remain red but no more will there be 'ideas of redness' in the minds of humans.

The difference between primary and secondary qualities, on this second Lockean view, is not that the former are real or objective and the latter unreal or subjective. The difference is

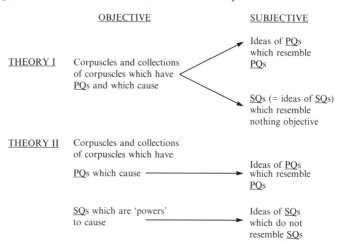

Figure 7. Galileo and Locke on secondary qualities

that ideas of primary qualities resemble primary qualities (apparent shape and real shape are both shapes), while ideas of secondary qualities do not resemble secondary qualities (apparent colours or colour-sensations are nothing like the properties of surfaces which produce them). A further difference is that secondary qualities are to be explained as properties of collections of corpuscles and in terms of the (primary) properties of the corpuscles which make them up. (So there is a sense in which corpuscles and their primary properties are more real or more fundamental than collections of corpuscles and their secondary qualities.)

We can depict these two theories of primary and secondary qualities (PQs and SQs) in a diagram as shown in Figure 7 (the terminology is Locke's). Notice that on the first theory, secondary qualities are identified with ideas of secondary qualities (e.g. colours with colour-sensations). This is what justifies adherents of this theory in saying that if perceivers and their ideas or sensations disappear, so do the secondary qualities.

I think that it is the second theory which Locke really wants to maintain. It must be admitted that this is not always clear from his writings, so that those who (like Berkeley) attribute the first theory to him can find support for their interpretation.

Some of the reasons for Locke's unclarity are peculiar to his system, such as his failure always to distinguish 'ideas of secondary qualities' (e.g. colour-sensations) from secondary qualities (e.g. colours). But one of the reasons for Locke's unclarity is of more general interest.

Locke, together with other idea-ists, subscribed to a superficially plausible theory of the meaning or reference of words. According to this theory, the meaning of a word is the 'idea' for which it stands. If we apply this theory to the words we use for the secondary qualities, some interesting results follow. The word 'red' for example, will refer to our 'idea of redness', to a particular colour-sensation. It cannot refer to a 'power' to cause this particular sensation, because we have no 'idea' of such a power (we cannot see, touch, smell, taste, or hear such 'powers'). On this theory of language, talk of 'powers', 'insensible particles', 'forces', and such things, is meaningless: there is no 'idea' for which such words might stand. Locke did not notice this consequence of his theory of meaning; other idea-ist philosophers who subscribed to the theory were more consistent. Locke did notice, however, that if the word 'red' stands for a particular colour-sensation, and if a blind person never has had that sensation, then a blind person cannot use the word 'red' meaningfully and cannot understand what others mean when they use the word – given the subjectivist theory of meaning to which Locke subscribed.

If we apply this subjectivist theory of meaning to the names of secondary qualities, then it immediately follows that the secondary qualities are subjective. If 'red' stands for a secondary quality, and 'red' stands for an 'idea', then obviously the secondary quality is an idea. A drop of blood is not red, for there are no 'ideas' or sensations in a drop of blood for which the word 'red' might stand. Of course, the same will go for names of primary qualities. A drop of blood is not round either, for there are no 'ideas of roundness' ('roundness-sensations') in a drop of blood for which the word 'round' might stand. The subjectivist theory of meaning is absurd: it means that all our apparent talk about objects and their properties is actually talk about our 'ideas'. Locke's acceptance of this theory made mischief in his writings: it is, I think, what is ultimately responsible for this failure always to distinguish ideas of things from the things. But Locke did not consistently adhere to the theory, and so was able to defend a theory of secondary qualities according to which they are not subjective.

ARE SECONDARY QUALITIES SUBJECTIVE?

Which theory of the secondary qualities should we accept? Locke's theory (from now on I will refer to 'THEORY II' of Figure 7 as 'Locke's theory') is certainly closer to common sense than Galileo's theory (from now on I will refer to 'THEORY I' of Figure 7 as 'Galileo's theory'). For it is part of common sense that things have colours when nobody is looking at them, and this is accepted by Locke, but not by Galileo. Yet a common-sense opinion might always be wrong. And in fact it remains a controversial matter in philosophy which of these two theories is correct.

Yet, Locke's theory is closer, it can be argued, to science as well as to common sense. For scientists try to analyse the 'powers' in things which enable them to cause certain sensations in (human) observers. Scientists try to say, for example, precisely what the redness of a surface consists in: a surface is red, roughly speaking, if it absorbs all radiation in the visible spectrum other than that in the red region. (Here the references to the 'visible spectrum' and the 'red region' of it can be replaced by specifications of bands of wavelengths.) This scientific account also makes the redness of a surface a 'power' or disposition of that surface, but one which makes no reference to observers and their ideas or sensations. And it makes the redness of a surface a perfectly objective property of that surface, which it possesses even if no light is falling upon it or even if no observer is around to respond to any light which is falling upon and reflected from the surface.

Although Locke's account of redness is closer to the scientist's account than Galileo's, it must be admitted that there is a certain tension between them. For investigations of the mechanisms of colour vision and of the redness of surfaces have revealed that the connection between a surface's being red and its causing sensations of redness is far less close than Locke supposed (or than many modern philosophers suppose). Red surfaces do not always cause sensations of redness, and sensations of redness are not always caused by red surfaces. Here the scientists merely reinforce the sceptical points made long ago by Sextus Empiricus: the fact that a surface looks red on a particular occasion by no means guarantees that it is red. The great variability of colour-sensations means that Locke's account of redness should be replaced by the scientist's account.

Similar points hold in other cases where we have scientific analyses of secondary qualities. For Locke the word 'hot' refers to a power in an object to cause a particular kind of tactile sensation (heat-sensations). Science replaces this with an elaborate theory of heat, including ways of measuring the temperatures of things. Once again it turns out that the senses are often unreliable guides to the temperatures of things, a fact already noted by Sextus Empiricus when he said that to a cold hand lukewarm water appears hot.

Some of the secondary qualities continue to resist scientific analysis. While we have scientific accounts of the colours and temperatures of things, their tastes and smells turn out to be more difficult. So far as I know, scientists do not yet know what it is about a substance that makes it taste sweet to (human) observers. If this is so, then regarding sweetness we cannot pass beyond a Lockean account: it is that (unknown) power of a substance to cause a particular kind of taste-sensation in (human) observers. Where a secondary quality can only be specified by reference to (human) observers, to that extent it might be said to be 'subjective'. To what extent is a secondary quality 'subjective' if it can only be specified by reference to (human) observers? Only to the extent that it becomes a relational property between objects and human beings. It is not 'subjective' in the sense that it exists only 'in the mind', or would cease to exist if perceivers ceased to exist.

So far I have argued that Locke's theory of the secondary qualities is closer to common sense and to science than Galileo's theory. However, returning to more philosophical matters, we must also realise that Locke's theory is closer to scepticism. We pay an epistemological price for any theory, like Locke's which makes the secondary qualities objective. The price is simple: the senses cease to be infallible guides to the secondary qualities of things. From the fact that a thing looks red or feels hot, it does not follow that it is red or hot. Sceptical questions still can get a grip: which apparent colour is the real colour? Can you be sure, just because a thing appears to have property *P*, that it really does have property *P*?

Such sceptical questions get no grip on any theory which, like Galileo's, makes the secondary qualities subjective. Here the secondary qualities are only 'appearances' or 'ideas' or sensations. There is no 'real colour' for the sceptic to ask about. If we have infallible knowledge of our own ideas, then we have infallible knowledge of the secondary qualities. There is nothing else to be mistaken about.

The theory that the secondary qualities are subjective is the first step on the road from idea-ism to idealism: that colours, tastes and smells exist only 'in the mind' is an idealistic thesis. If our first priority is to defeat the sceptic regarding (our knowledge of) secondary qualities, then idealism regarding them will seem attractive. The battle-lines are becoming clear: on the one side, common sense, science and scepticism; on the other side, dogmatism regarding the senses and idealism.

BERKELEY'S CRITIQUE OF LOCKE

Locke, despite his professed idea-ism, did not himself take the first step down the road from idea-ism to idealism. But was this consistent? Can one be a consistent idea-ist and maintain Locke's theory of the secondary qualities or, for that matter, of the primary qualities? George Berkeley argued that one cannot. He took Locke to be defending the old theory of the subjectivity of the secondary qualities, the theory that colours and smells are nothing but various ideas in the minds of observers. And he claimed that any argument to the effect that the secondary qualities are subjective will show equally well that the primary qualities are subjective also. For example, if the variability of perceived colour implies the subjectivity of colours, then the variability of perceived shapes or sizes will imply the subjectivity of these qualities also. The so-called primary qualities are in exactly the same boat as the secondary qualities.

Berkeley was clearly right here. But there are two ways we can jump: we can say (as Berkeley did) that all the properties are subjective, or we can say (as Locke, properly understood, did) that all are objective. Berkeley's misunderstanding of Locke regarding the subjectivity of the secondary qualities was a quite natural misunderstanding. Locke borrowed the distinction from scientists like Newton and Boyle. If Locke had stuck consistently to his idea-ist theory of knowledge, then all of the scientific speculations of Newton or Boyle would have become very problematic. We cannot sense the atoms or corpuscles of which material objects are said to be composed. To talk of configurations of particles reflecting rays of light and thereby having a 'power' to produce an 'idea of redness' is to talk of things of which we have no ideas. It is, in fact, to talk nonsense according to Berkeley, for it is to use words where we have no corresponding 'idea'. Locke is dimly aware of the difficulty. Despite his great admiration of Newton and Boyle, he says that 'natural philosophy is not capable of being made into a science' (1690: IV, xii, 10). What this means is that we cannot know anything for certain about physical objects and the way in which our ideas or sensations are produced. Berkeley agreed and concluded: 'So much the worse for natural philosophy.'

Could colours be subjective and shapes objective? Only if we can imagine something which has a definite shape but no colour. But Berkeley argued that we cannot imagine or form an idea of a thing which has shape but no colour: shape is simply the boundary of colour. Hence to talk of colourless shapes is to talk nonsense, to use words to which no idea can correspond. Colour and shape are inseparable, and if one is subjective then so is the other. This inseparability argument is less convincing. A blind person can, on Berkeley's own principles, acquire (through the sense of touch) ideas of shapes, and yet have no ideas of colour. A blind person can, it would seem, form an idea of a colourless square or circle.

Berkeley's most important argument was directed against Locke's view that the ideas of primary qualities resemble the primary qualities while the ideas of secondary qualities do not resemble the secondary qualities. Berkeley points out that we can only say that A resembles B if it is possible for us to be aware of both A and B so as to be able to compare them. If I say, rightly or wrongly, that a picture A resembles the object B it is a picture of, then I can, in principle anyway, compare A with B to check whether my statement is correct. But on Locke's own view, all we are ever aware of are ideas, and we can never get hold of the qualities themselves, to check whether our ideas resemble them. Locke's view is therefore one which, on Locke's own premises, we could never have any evidence for. The sceptic will be delighted with it. As for Berkeley, he says that the only thing that can be said to resemble an idea is another idea.

So Berkeley argued that, given Locke's idea-ist epistemology, all the apparent properties of objects, primary and secondary, are subjective, exist only as ideas in the minds of perceivers. Objects have no colours or smells – and they have no shapes or sizes either! The thought becomes irresistible that perhaps the objects themselves do not exist at all. And this was precisely Berkeley's view, as we will see in the next chapter.

CHAPTER 7

Berkeley: idea-ism becomes idealism

George Berkeley (1685–1753) is the Irishman of our famous trio of British empiricists. Educated at Trinity College in Dublin, he published his major philosophical works before he was thirty: *Essay Towards a New Theory of Vision* in 1709, *Principles of Human Knowledge* in 1710 and *Three Dialogues between Hylas and Philonous* in 1713. He then became involved in an abortive scheme to set up a college in the American colonies, and lived from 1728 until 1731 on Rhode Island. (It is said that the University of California *at Berkeley*, founded much later, is named after him.) Finally, in 1734 he was made Anglican Bishop of Cloyne, in Ireland, where he lived until his death.

Berkeley is famous for having denied the existence of matter, an opinion so absurd that one might suppose that only someone who has taken leave of his senses might defend it. Yet Berkeley thought that it was the only opinion which could preserve the evidence of the senses. Our first task is to explain this riddle.

HOW TO TURN APPEARANCE INTO REALITY

Can one be a consistent idea-ist and defend a theory of primary and secondary qualities such as Locke's? As we have seen, Berkeley argued that one could not. More generally, Berkeley saw that the idea-ist theory of knowledge is plagued by the problem of appearance and reality. And he found a novel way to solve (or perhaps better, dissolve) this problem: turn the 'appearances' into reality. Sceptical worries about appearance and reality presuppose that 'appearances' or 'ideas' or 'sense-

data' are one thing and reality or the real world or external
objects another. The problem then is to justify beliefs about the
latter on the basis of our immediate knowledge of the former.
Berkeley thinks that this problem is insoluble. But we can
dissolve the problem if we deny its presupposition, and maintain
instead that appearance and reality are one. The way to defeat
the sceptic is to pass from the idea-ist theory of knowledge to an
idealist metaphysic. Berkeley called his idealist metaphysic
'immaterialism', because of its denial that matter or material
objects exist. Most of Berkeley's readers think that immaterialism is an absurd philosophy. Berkeley claimed that it was
the only philosophy which could avoid an even greater
absurdity, namely scepticism. As he saw it, the choice lay
between materialism and scepticism or immaterialism and
certainty.

Here a terminological point is necessary. I just used the term
'materialism' for the view (the opposite of Berkeley's immaterialism) that material objects exist in the world independently of the minds of perceivers. In philosophy materialism
is more often taken to be the much stronger view that only
material objects exist in the world (so that, for example, the
'minds of perceivers' are just a special sort of material object,
namely, brains). In the rest of this chapter I shall use the term
'materialism' for the weaker view that material objects exist,
not for the strong view that only material objects exist.

Berkeley was quite clear about wishing to defeat scepticism,
so I shall quote him:

Colour, figure, motion, extension, and the like, considered only as so
many sensations in the mind, are perfectly known...But if they are
looked on as...images, referred to things...existing without the mind,
then we are involved all in scepticism. We see only the appearances,
and not the real qualities of things...So that, for aught we know, all we
see, hear, and feel, may be only phantom and vain chimera, and not
at all agree with the real things...All this scepticism follows, from our
supposing a difference between things and ideas, and that the former
have a subsistence without the mind, or unperceived. It were easy
to...shew how the arguments urged by sceptics in all ages, depend
on the supposition of external objects. (*Principles*, Part i, 87;
78–9)

Upon the common principles of philosophers, we are not assured of the existence of things from their being perceived. And we are taught to distinguish their real nature from that which falls under our senses. Hence arise scepticism and paradoxes. It is not enough that we see and feel, that we taste and smell, a thing. Its true nature ... is still concealed. For ... we have made it inaccessible to all our faculties. Sense is fallacious, reason defective. We spend our lives doubting those things which other men evidently know, and believing those things which they laugh at and despise. (*Three Dialogues*, Preface: 167)

Berkeley's solution to the problem of scepticism is, once again, to give up the distinction between 'real things' and ideas, to turn the ideas into the real things – the solution, in a word, is idealism.

We have seen how Berkeley established, against Locke, that given the idea-ist epistemology, the theory that our ideas are caused by external objects which have certain real properties of their own cannot be established as true and cannot even have any empirical evidence in its favour. But might it not be true even so? Berkeley thinks not, and produces two further arguments.

The first argument rests upon the principle that all causes are active, and on the assertion (which Berkeley borrows from the materialists themselves) that material objects are inactive. It follows, says Berkeley, that a material object cannot cause anything, and *a fortiori* that it cannot cause ideas. This is a weak argument, because the materialist (he who believes that material objects cause ideas or sensations) might dispute either of its premises. He might simply deny that all causes are 'active' (whatever this means), or he might accept this and simply assert that material objects are 'active' (whatever this means) in that they do cause ideas.

Berkeley's second argument is that the hypothesis of materialism cannot be true because it is meaningless. For a word to have meaning, it must stand for an idea. The word or phrase 'material object' does not stand for any idea, since (by assumption) we do not experience material objects (only ideas). Hence the materialist (who believes that ideas are caused by material objects) talks nonsense. This is also a weak argument, since the theory of meaning upon which it rests is highly dubious. Indeed, Berkeley himself was to modify this theory, when he came to consider (as he did) the question of what caused our ideas.

But we have yet to consider Berkeley's most important argument against materialism and in favour of idealism. It goes as follows:

Wood, stones, fire, water, flesh, iron and the like things which I name and talk about, are things that I know. And I should not have known them unless I perceived them by my senses; and things perceived by the senses are immediately perceived; and things immediately perceived are ideas; and ideas cannot exist without [i.e. outside] the mind; their existence therefore consists in being perceived; when therefore they are actually perceived, there can be no doubt of their existence. Away with all that scepticism, all those ridiculous philosophical doubts. (*Third Dialogue*: 230)

Fundamentally the same argument is stated again at the very end of Berkeley's *Three Dialogues* when Philonous (Berkeley's spokesman) says:

I do not pretend to be a setter-up of *new notions*. My endeavours tend only to unite and place in a clearer light that truth, WHICH WAS BEFORE SHARED BETWEEN THE VULGAR AND THE PHILOSOPHERS: the former being of the opinion, that *those things they immediately perceive are the real things*; and the latter, that *the things immediately perceived, are ideas which exist only in the mind*. Which two notions put together, do in effect constitute the substance of what I advance. (*Third Dialogue*: 262)

Hylas (the other character) replies that for a long time it seemed that scepticism was being advanced, but in the end the conclusion is directly opposed to scepticism. Philonous says:

Just so, the same principles which at first view lead to scepticism, pursued to a certain point, bring back men to common sense. (*Third Dialogue*: 263)

This argument plays such an important role in Berkeley's philosophy that we might christen it 'Berkeley's masterargument.' The crucial steps in the argument can be set out as follows:

(1) Common sense: We perceive such things as trees or stones.
(2) Idea-ism: We perceive only ideas and collections of ideas.
(3) Ideas and collections of ideas cannot exist unperceived.
Therefore, such things as trees or stones are ideas or collections of ideas which do not exist unperceived.

Now the argument is, I think, a perfectly valid one. If we accept all of its premises, then we must accept its conclusion also. Contrariwise, if we wish to reject Berkeley's idealist conclusion, then we must reject at least one of Berkeley's premises. What are the possibilities here?

There is little to be said for giving up (3), though some philosophers have actually done so. ('There is no opinion so absurd or incredible that it has not been maintained by some philosopher or other', as Descartes once said.) These philosophers talk of unsensed sense-data (or unsensed sensa, as they prefer to call them), which really exist although no perceiver is perceiving them. But this is a desperate thesis advocated by philosophers already convinced that tables and chairs consist of sense-data, and anxious to accommodate the common-sense view that tables and chairs continue to exist when nobody is perceiving them. (Berkeley faces the same problem, but solves it differently, as we will see.) There is, of course, the quite respectable view that there are unconscious ideas, ideas which exist in some mind but which that mind is unaware of, and which are therefore 'unperceived' in some sense or other. Neither Locke nor Berkeley accepted that there could be unconscious ideas. But Berkeley could easily reformulate his 'master-argument' to accommodate them: instead of saying, in (3), that ideas cannot exist unperceived, he could say that they cannot exist outside the mind (and similarly in the conclusion). Unconscious ideas would, however, require Berkeley to amend the nice slogan with which he summed up his philosophy: that where ideas are concerned, to be is to be perceived ('esse est percipi'). This would have to become to be is to be perceived or to be perceivable. Unsensed sensa are also perceivable, one supposes, but they differ from unconscious ideas in that they are not supposed to exist in minds, but to float around somewhere else waiting for minds to 'latch onto them'.

If we accept Berkeley's third premise, but wish to avoid his conclusion, then only two options remain. One has already been chosen by Locke, who gives up the common-sense view that we perceive wood, stones, and such things, denies the 'vulgar opinion' that the things we perceive are the real things. This, Berkeley complains, is the royal road to scepticism: if we do not perceive real things, then we cannot know anything about them either.

The only remaining alternative is to reject the second premise, idea-ism, which both Locke and Berkeley take for granted. This would be to revert to a realist theory of perception whereby the things perceived are external objects rather than ideas. Whether such a theory is viable, given all that sceptics and scientists say about perception, is a question that we will postpone a little longer. What should be said here, though, is that although Berkeley never really considered this possibility, had he done so he would no doubt have considered it merely as an alternative road to scepticism. Idea-ism makes the empirical basis of knowledge (statements reporting the ideas we experience) secure: to renounce idea-ism is to deprive us, therefore, even of a secure empirical basis. But more of this later.

IMMATERIALISM

So far we have focused on the negative part of Berkeley's philosophy, his attempt to demolish any theory which, like Locke's, postulates external or material objects existing independently of perceivers and causing their perceptions. Now we must turn to the more positive part of his theory. One way to characterise this is as Berkeley's attempt to avoid solipsism. Berkeley's idealism says that ideas are the real things and that trees or stones are collections of ideas which do not exist unperceived. But the only ideas of which Berkeley is immediately aware are his own ideas. So how can he prevent his idealism from turning into solipsism? How can he establish, for example, on the basis of his own ideas, that other people exist who have ideas also? Another way to characterise the positive part of Berkeley's philosophy is as an attempt to answer many of the rather obvious objections to the view that external or material objects do not exist. What is remarkable is that Berkeley himself raised most of these objections and answered them; in this respect Berkeley was his own best critic. However, it is often rather difficult to understand Berkeley's answers, because we have to try to express them in ordinary language, and ordinary language is thoroughly infected with views which Berkeley rejects. (This fact, which will become apparent as we proceed, tells against Berkeley's claim that he rescues common sense from the ravages of philosophical scepticism. That Berkeley's view is far from commonsensical emerges when we try to explain it in ordinary language.)

Dr Johnson was once asked what he thought of Berkeley's immaterialism. 'I refute it thus,' he declared, kicking a stone along the path and, we may suppose, hurting his toe. Berkeley once called upon his friend Jonathan Swift and knocked politely on the door. Swift refused to open it, declaring that if the door was merely a collection of (Berkeley's) ideas, he ought to be able to walk right through it or wish it away. These stories illustrate a very basic objection to Berkeley: that he denies the existence of things such as stones or doors, or affirms that stones or doors are not real.

Berkeley simply denies that this is the case. All he denies is that stones or doors exist as material objects external to minds. Stones and doors exist, or are real things, but they consist of particular collections of ideas in people's minds. A stone, for example, is a particular collection of visual ideas, tactile ideas, auditory ideas and so forth. The real stone is the thing that people can see, touch, even kick; and it consists of the ideas people have when they see, touch, or kick it. Berkeley adds, and this is important, that it is not up to me which ideas I shall have. More precisely, he distinguishes ideas of sensation or perception from ideas of imagination or memory, and says that while it is up to me what I shall imagine or remember, it is not up to me what I shall sense or perceive. The world is not my dream. Thus I cannot kick a stone without experiencing a particular tactile sensation, and I cannot kick it hard without hurting my toe (experiencing a painful sensation). Similarly, I cannot walk through a door or wish it away: I must open the door, or somebody must open it for me.

But why, it may now be objected, do we say that the stone or the door is a collection of ideas? Why do we not rest content with particular and distinct ideas (the visual idea of the stone, the tactile idea of the stone and so forth)? Why, if there is no single external object causing all these ideas, do we lump them together into a collection or bundle?

Berkeley's answer to this question is, in a word, experience. It is a matter of fact, which we learn from experience, that certain ideas are always associated with other ideas. We receive a visual impression of an apple. We learn from experience that if we reach out we will receive a certain tactile impression, that if we sniff we will receive a certain olfactory impression, that if we bite the apple we will receive a certain gustatory impression and so on. Berkeley calls these regularities in our experience laws of nature. As Berkeley formulates them, they do not look much like the laws of nature of the scientists. Instead, they are reports of regular associations of ideas: something like 'Apple visions are regularly associated with apple touches, apple smells, apple tastes'. And it is because of these laws of nature, which we learn from experience, that we come to lump ideas together into groups, and coin the term 'apple' to refer not to any particular sensation, but to the entire group of them. Furthermore, the laws of nature are what enable us to anticipate our future experiences: having seen the apple (received a particular sort of visual idea), we confidently expect it to taste like an apple if we bite into it. If it tasted like a banana, that would be a miracle (a violation of the laws of nature).

The theory that objects, or 'sensible things' to use the term that Berkeley prefers, are collections of ideas does have some strange consequences. The common-sense materialist view is that two people can see the same thing. But two people cannot have the same visual idea (though they might have similar ones), and one person's visual ideas are very different from his tactile ideas. Is Berkeley not committed, therefore, to denying that two people can see the same things or that one person can both see and touch the same thing?

Berkeley does deny these common-sense assertions if they are taken to imply the existence of things independent of perceptions, to which our senses give us access. Berkeley insists, however, that this implication is not part of the common-sense understanding of these assertions. According to Berkeley, '*A* and *B* see the same tree' means something like '*A* has a visual idea of a tree, and *B* has a quite distinct visual idea of a tree, and both *A*'s and *B*'s visual ideas are part of the one collection of ideas which form the sensible thing we call the tree'. And according to Berkeley, '*A* both sees and touches the tree' means something like '*A* has a visual idea of a tree, and *A* also has a quite different tactile idea of a tree, and both *A*'s visual idea and his tactile idea are part of the one collection of ideas which form the sensible thing we call the tree'. Now I doubt that this is what we do ordinarily mean by such statements: I think we mean that two people can literally see the same tree, or that one person can literally see and touch the same tree. And if this is so, it casts real doubt on Berkeley's claim that this theory is consistent with our common-sense views. Be this as it may, Berkeley can, after a fashion, allow that these common-sense views are correct: they are correct if interpreted (*re*interpreted?) in the ways indicated.

Implicit in all of this is Berkeley's answer to another common objection: that his theory obliterates the distinction between illusion and reality, between dreams and reality, between hallucination and reality, between our imaginings and reality. In each case, Berkeley's answer is basically the same. In the *Dialogues* Hylas asks:

But according to your notions, what difference is there between real things, and chimeras formed by the imagination, or the visions of a dream, since they are all equally in the mind?

Philonous, Berkeley's spokesman, answers:

The ideas formed by the imagination are faint and indistinct; they have, besides, an entire dependence on the will. But the ideas perceived by sense, that is, real things, are more vivid and clear, and ... have not a like dependence on the will...And though [dreams, hallucinations, or imaginings] should happen to be ever so lively and natural, yet by their not being connected, and of a piece with the preceding and subsequent transactions of our lives, they might easily be distinguished from realities. In short, by whatever method you distinguish *things* from *chimeras* on your own scheme, the same, it is evident, will hold on mine. For it must be, I presume, by some perceived difference, and I am not for depriving you of any one thing that you perceive. (*Third Dialogue*: 235)

Berkeley's basic answer is that contained in the last two sentences of this passage: that he can use whatever his opponents use to distinguish illusions, hallucinations, dreams and imaginings from reality. Perhaps it is the 'faint and indistinct' nature of our imaginings. Perhaps it is their 'dependence on the will'. Most important of all, since it is applicable where the first two criteria fail, is the fact that 'chimerical ideas' do not fit the regular course of nature as revealed in sensory experience. Macbeth has a visual idea of a bloodstained dagger, but knows that it is a hallucination because he cannot touch the dagger also. (But the sceptic might ask what defends the primacy of touch here.)

Of course, Berkeley cannot go on to give the same account of illusions and such things as the materialist gives. Berkeley cannot say, of our stock example of the oar which looks bent in water, that the oar is really straight, meaning that the real, independently existing material object is straight – for according to Berkeley there is no real, independently existing material object. According to Berkeley, when we say that the oar is not really bent, all we mean is that it will not look bent out of the water or that it will not feel bent if we run our hand along it. Hylas asks: 'How can a man be mistaken in thinking...an oar with one end in the water crooked?' Philonous answers:

He is not mistaken with regard to the ideas he actually perceives; but in the inferences he makes from his present perceptions. Thus in case of the oar, what he immediately perceives by sight is certainly crooked; and so far he is in the right. But if he thence conclude, that upon taking the oar out of the water he shall perceive the same crookedness; or that it would affect his touch, as crooked things are wont to do; in that he is mistaken. (*Third Dialogue*: 238)

Thus the visual idea of the bent oar in water is just as much a part of the collection of ideas which make up the oar as any other idea, and is just as real as any other idea in this collection. It is simply that, as an illusory idea, it does not fit in with other ideas in the collection, as evidenced by the mistaken inferences we might make. (You may be wondering why, according to Berkeley, collections of ideas occasionally have such 'stray' members. Can he give the same explanation as the materialist scientists give? This is a very good question, to which we shall return.)

In discussing the objections we have considered so far, we have talked (it is hard to avoid doing so) of such doings as kicking stones, walking through doors, reaching out to touch apples. We have talked, in other words, of moving our body in various ways. But, it may be objected, Berkeley cannot talk this way without contradicting himself, for to do so is to talk of one rather special external or material object, namely our body. Can Berkeley really maintain that the body, like other real or sensible things, is just a collection of ideas?

The answer is that Berkeley can, and does, maintain exactly this: that the body is a collection of ideas, though a rather special one for each of us. It is special first, because we know about it, in part, through a special 'sixth sense' which provides us with bodily sensations. Each of us knows, through bodily sensations, whether or not his eyes are open or whether he is standing or sitting. To know whether your eyes are open, or whether you are standing or sitting, I have to look at you – but it is not the same for myself. The second reason why the body is special is that it accompanies me everywhere and at all times. A basic regularity in our experience (so basic that we hardly are aware of it) is that whenever I am having visual sensations they are accompanied by those particular bodily sensations I call 'having my eyes open'. Other such regularities are that the bodily sensations of 'having my eyes open' and 'putting my hand in front of my face' are regularly accompanied by the visual sensation of a hand, or that the bodily sensations of 'having my eyes open' and 'looking down' are regularly accompanied by a visual sensation of a pair of feet. 'My body' is just the name each of us gives to this special collection of ideas which includes the bodily sensations as well as visual ideas of my hands or feet, olfactory ideas of how I smell, and so forth. The third reason why this collection of ideas which I call 'my body' is special is that it is under my control: each of us can determine which particular ideas it will contain (to some extent, at any rate). When I decide to open or close my eyes, I determine that certain bodily sensations will belong to the collection of ideas I call 'my body'. And more than this: if I open my eyes it is not generally up to me which visual ideas I shall experience; but if I open my eyes and place my hand in front of my face, it does seem that I bring it about that I have a certain visual idea, namely, the vision of my hand. It is my (partial) control over it, that is, over the 'ideas' it contains, that distinguishes the collection of ideas I shall call 'my body' from the collection of ideas I call 'that apple'. And this leads Berkeley to qualify his previous view that ideas of sensation (as opposed, say, to ideas of imagination) are not under our control: some ideas of sensation, those which belong to the collection 'my body', are under my control.

Now, returning to the objection of the paragraph before last, when Berkeley talks of kicking a stone, he does not tacitly presuppose the existence of at least one external or material object, namely, his body. 'I kick the stone' is to be analysed, according to Berkeley, as a statement about a particular sequence of ideas: something like 'Bodily sensations of moving my leg in a particular way, accompanied by visual sensations of a leg approaching a stone, are succeeded by (painful) tactile sensations in the foot of touching the stone, which are in turn succeeded by visual sensations of the stone moving away from the big toe'. And similarly for other statements about moving our body in various ways.

GOD AND OTHER MINDS

So far we have taken it for granted (it is hard to avoid doing so) that as well as Berkeley and his ideas, there are lots of people who also have ideas. We have taken it for granted, in other words, that Berkeley-solipsism (only Berkeley and his ideas exist) is false, that Musgrave-solipsism (only Musgrave and his ideas exist) is also false and so on. But, it can be objected, how can Berkeley prove on the basis of his own ideas that other people (other minds) also exist and have ideas? This is the problem of other minds.

Berkeley points out, first of all, that this is just as much a problem for materialists as for his immaterialist view. This is true and important: it means that one cannot object against Berkeley that his theory faces a problem which the rival theory does not.

Berkeley then proceeds to solve the problem in two stages. The first stage shows the hypothesis of other minds to be a reasonable hypothesis, while the second stage proves it (or so Berkeley claims). The first stage proceeds as follows. Each of us learns from experience that we have a body, in the sense we have just explained. Each of us also learns from experience that there are other human bodies around just like ours, possessing sense-organs like ours and so on. Moreover, we learn from experience that these other bodies behave like ours behaves: they avoid bumping into closed doors, thrusting hands into open fires, and they talk to us about their experiences in a way which suggests that they have ideas like ours, learn from experience the way we do, and regulate their behaviour accordingly. All this makes it plausible to assume that these other bodies are associated with experiencing minds, as ours is. We shall see in a little while how Berkeley thinks he can turn this into a proof of other minds.

The next objection leads us to the most important part of Berkeley's theory. We have seen that Berkeley distinguishes ideas of imagination or memory which are under our control or caused by us, from ideas of perception which we cannot (generally) control and which are not caused by us. Berkeley claims that perceptual ideas must have some cause. He claims, moreover, that what causes them must be a mind or spirit, since only spirits are 'active'. Now experience shows that the spirit which causes my perceptions must be extremely powerful: it has no trouble giving me (and other minds, if such there be) all kinds of different perceptions in different circumstances. Moreover, this spirit must be extremely wise: my perceptions may be of many different kinds, but numerous regularities (laws of nature) hold for them, showing that they could only be caused by a spirit which knows (or perhaps institutes) all of the laws of nature. Finally, the fact that my experience is governed by law shows that the spirit which causes my experience is benevolent towards me (and towards other people, if such there be); the spirit does not confuse me by causing me to have an idea of a table before I blink and an idea of an elephant after I blink (nor does the spirit seem to confuse other minds either). In short, the spiritual cause of our perceptual experience is all-powerful, all-wise and all-loving. The cause of our perceptions is, in a word, God.

Berkeley regards this as a proof of the existence of God. For a sceptic, however, it leaves much to be desired, since virtually every step might be challenged. How does Berkeley know that my perceptions must be caused? Why does he assume that they have only one cause? Why cannot I cause them myself, unknowingly, which would, presumably, be a solipsist's view? How does Berkeley know that what causes perceptions must be active and that only spirits are active? Perhaps external material objects cause them, as the materialist supposes. Finally, my experience only seems to be governed by law to a limited, though important, extent. Reflection on our experience might entitle us to conclude that the cause of it is pretty powerful, quite smart, and by and large benevolent, but the move to the all-powerful, all-knowing and perfectly benevolent God of Christianity seems unwarranted. (It is worth remembering that, as a Bishop of the Anglican Church, it is the God of Christianity that Berkeley seeks to establish.)

The sceptic will point out, quite rightly in my view, that one cannot really prove the existence of anything other than ideas on the basis of ideas alone. This holds as much for the God of Berkeley's immaterialism as for the external objects of the materialist. What we can do is regard Berkeley's God and the materialist's external objects as two very basic hypotheses introduced to explain our experience. Bertrand Russell once wrote:

Berkeley retains the merit of having shown that the existence of matter is capable of being denied without absurdity... (1912: 13)

There is some truth in this. It is worth realising that materialism, the metaphysical view which we tend unthinkingly to accept, is not the only metaphysic capable of explaining our experience. The question is: which is the best explanation, the materialist's or Berkeley's?

Before turning to this question, let us see how having established the existence of God, Berkeley puts Him to work. We can now prove the existence of other minds. For God would deceive Berkeley if he so ordered his experience as to make the postulation of other minds reasonable (in the way that we have seen) and yet not create other minds to go along with the other bodies which Berkeley experiences. God is no deceiver, so Berkeley knows for sure that other minds exist.

Once again, a sceptic might drive a coach and horses through this 'proof'. God is no deceiver when He makes oars appear bent in water: any mistakes we make in this case are our erroneous inferences from the sense-data. So why should not the hypothesis of other minds be our larger-scale erroneous inference from the data also? It would, of course, verge on solipsistic megalomania for Berkeley to suppose that he and God were the only two spirits. But whether he can prove that this is not the case is another matter.

The most famous, or infamous, task of Berkeley's God is that of keeping the universe ticking over while nobody is experiencing it. We might object to Berkeley that if the table in his study is a collection of ideas, and if ideas do not exist unperceived, then the table ceases to exist when Berkeley's study is deserted. To which Berkeley replies:

The table I write on, I say, exists, that is, I see it and feel it; and if I were out of my study I should say it existed, meaning thereby that if I was in my study I might perceive it, or that some other spirit actually does perceive it... (*Principles*, Part 1, 3; 42)

Now there are actually two different answers here. The first is 'that some other spirit [God] actually does perceive' Berkeley's table whenever his study is bereft of human observers. This is the theory of God as the omnipresent perceiver, keeping everything in existence, that is, continually having ideas belonging to the collections of ideas which make up every 'sensible thing'. It is this theory which Ronald Knox made fun of in a famous limerick:

> There was a young man who said, 'God
> Must think it exceedingly odd
> If He finds that this tree
> Continues to be
> When there's no one about in the Quad.'

> *Reply*
> Dear Sir:
> Your astonishment's odd
> *I* am always about in the Quad
> And that's why the tree
> Will continue to be
> Since observed by
> Yours faithfully,
> God.

According to this first theory, the world is not Berkeley's dream, but it is, in a sense, God's dream. Berkeley's favourite biblical text is reputed to have been 'In God we live, and move, and have our being' – for Berkeley this was almost literally true.

Yet, there are peculiar problems in supposing that God perceives Berkeley's table when neither Berkeley nor anyone else is looking at it. Does God perceive as humans do, using sense-organs? Are perceptual ideas passively received or registered by God, as they are by human perceivers? Is God subject to perceptual pains and pleasures, as human perceivers are? Berkeley, as a good Christian, would presumably wish to answer all these questions in the negative.

Because of these difficulties, Berkeley's real position on the continued existence of the table is a more subtle one. Berkeley states this second view when he says that to say that his table exists when he is out of his study means 'if I was in my study I might perceive it'. According to this view, God does not perceive the table, rather He fixes things up so that if Berkeley or anyone else were in Berkeley's study (that is, having ideas of the inside walls of Berkeley's study) then that person would also perceive Berkeley's table. God does not perceive things, rather He causes humans to perceive things in a regular fashion. A sensible thing is not a collection of all the ideas in the minds of humans and God, rather it is a collection of ideas which humans actually have and would have (possible ideas, if you like) if they were in the appropriate circumstances. This second theory brings Berkeley close to a view which later came to be called 'phenomenalism'.

Does 'Object O continues to exist when nobody is observing it' mean 'Object O would be perceived if anyone were in the appropriate circumstances'? This is what Berkeley and the phenomenalists maintain. Now the first statement certainly entails the second: if the first statement is true, then the second statement will be true also. Moreover, the only way to verify the first statement is to place oneself in appropriate circumstances and look. Or to put it another way, since we cannot experience an unexperienced object, whatever experience would falsify the first statement would also falsify the second. So far as experience goes, the two statements are equivalent. If we adopt a theory of meaning to the effect that statements which are equivalent so far as experience goes are equivalent *full-stop* (a verifiability theory of meaning), then our two statements will mean the same. Contrariwise, if we wish to deny that the first statement means the same as the second (as opposed to entailing it), then we must reject the verifiability theory of meaning.

God obviously plays a crucial role in Berkeley's metaphysical system. Yet, the introduction of God has often been regarded as the really weak link in the system. Some have even objected that in introducing God as the cause of our perceptions, Berkeley contradicts himself. He objected to the materialist hypothesis that it was meaningless because we have no idea corresponding to the word 'material object'. But we never perceive God either, so the word 'God' is also meaningless. The objection runs deeper than this: we never perceive our own mind or spirit, so these words also are meaningless, as is talk of minds or spirits other than our own.

Berkeley raises this objection against himself and answers it by modifying the theory of meaning according to which every meaningful word must stand for an idea. A word is also meaningful, he says, if it stands not for an idea but for a notion. He claims that each of us has a clear notion of his own mind, that is, of an active thing which perceives, remembers, imagines, hopes and fears, and so on. He claims that by analogy we can form the notion of other finite minds like ours, and by extrapolating away the weaknesses of finite minds, we can form the notion of an infinite mind or spirit (the notion of God).

This modification of the theory of meaning means that Berkeley can no longer accuse materialism of being meaningless: why can we not form a notion of matter or of material objects? Berkeley claims that any such notion, though not meaningless, will be contradictory, since it postulates an inactive cause of ideas and all causes are (by virtue of the meaning of the term 'cause') active causes. Talk of inactive causes is as contradictory as talk of married bachelors. This is an argument whose weakness we have already pointed out. The upshot seems to be, once again, that there are two consistent theories about the cause of our experience, materialism and Berkeley's theory.

The idea that God causes our perceptions lands Berkeley squarely in the problem of evil: the bad things that happen in the world of sensible things are caused to happen by God, yet God is supposed to be benevolent or opposed to evil, and He is also supposed to be omnipotent or able to prevent it. Berkeley replies, quite rightly, that this is a problem not peculiar to his system, but one which arises for anyone who postulates an omnipotent and benevolent deity. He then avails himself of the standard Christian solution to it: that God gave humans free will, and that the evils in the world result from the exercise of human freedom. This connects with a rather esoteric point mentioned earlier, whether or not each of us causes the ideas of our own bodily movements. Suppose a murderer freely decides to stab his victim: does the murderer also cause the sequence of ideas, including movements of his arm, which constitute the stabbing? If he does, then not all ideas of sensation are caused by God. If he does not, then it seems that the murderer's decision forces God to bring about the sequence of ideas involved in his actually doing the deed. It is not too clear which view Berkeley wants to maintain. What is clear is that Berkeley is quite correct to say that the problem is not confined to his system. The materialist who postulates an omnipotent and benevolent deity has the problem of explaining why God does not at the last moment turn the murderer's dagger into a feather-duster. Berkeley has the problem of explaining why God does not at the last moment fail to bring about the sequence of ideas which constitutes the stabbing.

The introduction of God brought Berkeley trouble in another, purely internal, respect. Berkeley wanted his God to be the God of orthodox Christianity. But is Berkeley's metaphysic consistent with orthodox Christian belief? For example, does not the story of the creation in the Book of Genesis state that material objects were created first and human perceivers rather late in the piece? Berkeley took some pains to show that his theory was consistent with Christian orthodoxy (suitably reinterpreted). For example, what was created early on in the piece was not matter but various 'possibilities of perception'. Berkeley's endeavours in this regard are as convincing (or unconvincing) as his attempts to reconcile his theory with common-sense views.

Berkeley also argues that it is materialism, rather than his own theory, which is a real threat to Christianity. To begin with, the idea that God created the material world which then causes our ideas is impious: since an omnipotent God could create our ideas directly, why credit Him with a redundant and wasteful creation? More important, once we postulate a material world independent of our minds, will we not be tempted to make it independent of God's mind also? Why suppose that it was created by God at all, when we can suppose that it has always existed? For Berkeley, materialism is a royal road to atheism, and only his own immaterialism could save us from it.

IMMATERIALISM, PHENOMENALISM AND SCIENCE

Given the problems with Berkeley's proof of the existence of God, and the difficulties which surround the role of God in Berkeley's metaphysics, we might wonder what happens if we simply remove God from the picture. The result is phenomenalism proper, a theory which has been remarkably popular among philosophers. John Stuart Mill accepted it at one point, and summarised it in the slogan that matter is 'the permanent possibility of sensation': actual and possible sensations or ideas comprise the universe, and it is not asserted that they are caused either by material objects or by God. In the twentieth century phenomenalism became extremely popular and was formulated not as a metaphysical thesis about the world but as a thesis about alternative ways of talking about the world. The claim was that there is ordinary physical object language and there is phenomenalist language, that the two are inter-translatable, and that it is therefore a matter of linguistic convenience which we adopt. Mountains of paper accumulated concerning the possibility of 'translating' humdrum statements like 'Berkeley's desk is in Berkeley's study' into statements about actual and possible sense-data. We have already seen the kind of thing involved here, and I shall say no more about it now except that most philosophers came to agree that phenomenalist 'translations' could not literally be provided. Pouring idealist metaphysics into linguistic bottles did not improve its quality: the new wine was just terribly cloudy, for straightforward questions like 'Do material objects exist?' were met with obfuscating answers like 'It is not a matter of what exists, but of how we prefer to talk'.

It might be supposed that by removing God from Berkeley's picture, the phenomenalists improved upon Berkeley. But it can be shown that in one respect this is not the case, and that God, as well as being a weak link in Berkeley's scheme, was also one of its strengths. Materialism, Berkeley's immaterialism, and phenomenalism are three metaphysical theories. As such, none of them can be refuted by experience: whatever we experience will be consistent with each of these theories. How are we to evaluate theories like this so as to choose rationally between them? One thing we can do is look at the philosophical arguments in favour of the various theories, and see how good these arguments are. Another thing we can do is see how well the different theories solve problems which are common to them all. Let us consider just one such common problem and see how well the various theories solve it. The problem I have in mind is that of explaining the apparent continued existence of objects when they are not being perceived, which manifests itself in our experience in countless ways: I look at the table and have certain visual experiences, I briefly close my eyes, and when I open them again I have very similar visual experiences of a table. Our three theories deal with the problem thus:

Materialism: The table is an independently existing material object which causes perceptions. The reason why we continue to perceive the table is that it is still there to be perceived.

Berkeley's immaterialism: Our perceptions are caused by a wise and benevolent God who would not wish to confuse us by first giving us table-perceptions and then, after we have blinked, gorilla-perceptions. The order and regularity in our experience (the laws of nature) are a manifestation of God's goodness.

Phenomenalism: There is no explanation of the order and regularity in experience: it is just a brute fact, and a rather fortunate one.

We can see that the phenomenalist pays a price for removing God from Berkeley's metaphysic: he ceases to be able to explain something which Berkeley can explain. In this respect, then, phenomenalism (Berkeley's immaterialism minus God) is a worse theory than Berkeley's. However, materialism also explains the apparent continued existence of objects. And this line of argument can be developed further to show that Berkeley's theory gives a worse explanation of the regularities in our experience than does the materialist theory.

To develop this point, we must first consider what becomes of physical science if we accept Berkeley's philosophy. Physical scientists propose all kinds of theories about material objects, about how they are structured and how they behave. If immaterialism is true, then all of these theories are false since the 'matter' which they postulate does not exist. It would seem that Berkeley is committed to putting a stop to the physical sciences!

In fact, Berkeley did not wish to put a stop to physical science – but he did wish to put physical science in its place. No longer could the physical scientists aim to tell us truths about the world: the truth about the world was contained in immaterialist metaphysics. What then could the scientists aim to do? To answer this question, Berkeley developed a new philosophy of science, which has come to be called 'instrumentalism'. (Most philosophers think that Berkeley did not invent instrumentalism, and that it actually has a very long history going back far beyond Berkeley. I think that this is a mistake, but it would take us too far afield for me to argue the point here; see Musgrave 1977a and 1991b for details.)

Berkeley's instrumentalism distinguishes two kinds of scientific statements. The first kind we have encountered already: they are statements of regularities in our experience, what Berkeley calls 'laws of nature'. Berkeley has nothing against these: suitably translated into statements about the orderly succession of ideas, they can be true; and they are useful in enabling us to anticipate our future experiences. (Where such statements are true, they are true only on God's sufferance, so to speak: God could always work a miracle and violate any of His laws of nature.) The second kind of scientific statements are the theories which physical scientists propose to explain the laws of nature, by describing a reality which lies behind the appearances. Berkeley calls them 'mathematical hypotheses' and insists that literally construed they are all false: there is no reality behind the appearances except God. However, Berkeley concedes that 'mathematical hypotheses' might also be useful, as a way of summarising and classifying laws of nature. Geometrical optics deals with light rays, how they behave, and how they are affected by various physical objects. Taken literally, it is a fairy-tale: there are no light rays and no physical objects to affect them. But its mathematical hypotheses yield lots of laws of nature about how things cast shadows, how they look in mirrors, how oars look bent in water, and so forth. They are useful devices for summarising these laws.

But physical science, the heir to common-sense materialism, does not seek merely to summarise known 'laws of nature' – it also predicts new laws. Suppose that geometrical opticians inspect their theory and see that if the theory is true then a certain arrangement of lenses will make objects appear larger or closer than they really are. (I do not vouch for the historical accuracy of this tale: it is the principle which concerns me, and the story is only meant to illustrate a principle.) The success of such a prediction is the best kind of evidence for the truth of the theory in question. But would Berkeley make predictions of this kind? It is hard to see how he could. Berkeley can certainly predict that known regularities in our experience will continue (God willing). But Berkeley can hardly predict that God will choose to make objects look bigger when viewed through a telescope. God could perfectly well choose to make them look smaller, to disappear altogether, to turn into ducks, or whatever else we care to imagine. Of course, when it turns out that telescopes enlarge objects, Berkeley can accommodate the fact – but he could not predict it. (Or at least, he could not predict it without postulating that God causes ideas so as to make it seem that the 'mathematical hypotheses' dreamt up by the scientists are true – which would be a pretty cruel deception on His part!)

If the successful prediction of new laws of nature is a virtue, then we must conclude that physical science has virtues which Berkeley's immaterialism does not possess. And since physical science is a development of common-sense materialism, this virtue also devolves upon common-sense materialism. (For more information and details on this, see Musgrave 1988.)

We have seen that Berkeley's philosophy has a negative part and a positive part. In the negative part Berkeley demolishes the attempt to establish materialism on idea-ist foundations. He shows, to put it crudely, that if all we can know are our own ideas and what can be proved therefrom, then we cannot know anything of external material objects or their properties. In the positive part of his philosophy Berkeley claims that on the basis of ideas we can establish the existence of God who causes our ideas and of other minds who receive ideas from God. The negative part of Berkeley's philosophy is much more successful than the positive part. But if we accept the former and reject the latter, we are left with the view that all we can know on the basis of ideas are ideas, and each of us his own ideas. We are left, in other words, with the view that the only reasonable position (the only position we can know for sure to be true) is solipsism. This was the rather gloomy conclusion drawn by the third of our trio of British empiricists, David Hume. But Hume found a new way out of the problem, a new way to avoid solipsism – and this was to reject reason. This will be the topic of the next chapter.

CHAPTER 8

Hume: idea-ism becomes irrationalism

David Hume (1711–76) is the Scotsman of our famous trio of British empiricists. His most important writings on the theory of knowledge are Book I of his *Treatise of Human Nature* (1739) and his *Enquiry Concerning Human Understanding* (1748). The relationship between these two books has been much discussed by Hume scholars. Hume was disappointed that his *Treatise* 'fell dead-born from the press without reaching such distinction as even to excite a murmur among the zealots' (Mossner 1954: 612). So he rewrote it, streamlined it, omitted some of its more difficult sections and tempered some of its more radical doctrines. The result was the *Enquiry*. But the *Enquiry* was a tempered version of an already tempered work; in 1737, while preparing the *Treatise*, Hume wrote to his friend Henry Home:

I am at present castrating my work, that is, cutting off its noble parts, that is, endeavouring it shall give as little offence as possible. (Klibansky and Mossner 1954: 3)

What was likely to give offence were Hume's sceptical views about religion, which were not published until after his death (in his *Dialogues Concerning Natural Religion*, 1779).

HUME'S IRRATIONALISM

Like Locke and Berkeley before him, Hume took for granted the doctrine of idea-ism, the doctrine that we are immediately acquainted only with our own ideas. Hume's terminology was different: Lockean 'simple ideas' he called 'impressions', reserving the term 'idea' for remembered impressions, 'the faint images of these in thinking and reasoning'. (Hume scholars discuss how, if at all, we can sort impressions from ideas: how can you tell that you are seeing an elephant as opposed to imagining or remembering one?)

What can we know (prove to be true) on the basis of impressions or ideas? Locke thought we could know of the existence of external objects and of some of their properties. Berkeley had criticised this view, claiming instead that we could know of the existence of other minds and of God as the cause of our ideas. Hume objected to both of them. We cannot prove that external objects exist, that God exists, that other minds exist, even that our own mind exists. The only reasonable position (the only position we can prove) is solipsism – reason leads to total scepticism about anything other than my own impressions and ideas.

Was Hume a solipsist and a sceptic? Many of his early readers thought so – but I think that they missed the really original feature of his position, which was irrationalism. Hume thinks that since reason leads to solipsism and scepticism, we must reject reason. For we cannot actually be solipsists or sceptics. In our philosophical moments we convince ourselves that belief in anything beyond our own impressions and ideas is rationally unfounded. But we cannot persist in this conclusion for more than a moment: human nature or custom or instinct takes over, and we find ourselves believing once again in all sorts of things which philosophy declares unreasonable. Scepticism and solipsism are the most reasonable views – but human nature compels us to be unreasonable. At the end of Book 1 of his *Treatise* Hume sums all this up in a famous passage:

The intense view of these manifold contradictions and imperfections in human reason has so wrought upon me, and heated my brain that I am ready to reject all belief and reasoning, and can look upon no opinion even as more probable or likely than another...

Most fortunately it happens, that since reason is incapable of dispelling these clouds, nature herself suffices to that purpose, and cures me of this philosophical melancholy and delirium...I dine, I play a game of backgammon, I converse, and am merry with my friends; and when after three or four hours amusement, I wou'd return to these speculations, they appear so cold, and strain'd, and ridiculous, that I cannot find in my heart to enter into them any further.

Here, then I find myself absolutely and necessarily determined to live, and talk, and act like other people in the common affairs of life...I may, nay I must yield to the current of nature, in submitting to my senses and understanding; and in this blind submission I shew most perfectly my sceptical disposition and principles. (*Treatise*, I, iv, 7; 268–9)

Hume's position is rather subtle. On the one hand he asks what we all believe and why we all believe it and cannot help believing it. On the other hand he asks whether these natural or instinctive beliefs can be rationally justified. His answer to this second evaluative question is invariably a negative one. So the upshot is that we cannot help having unreasonable beliefs. The Greeks thought man was by nature a rational animal – Hume thought man was by nature an irrational animal.

So much for Hume's general position, as I interpret it. Others interpret it differently. They do not see Hume as a sceptic in philosophy and an irrationalist in life. Instead they see him as a defender of the reasonableness of our 'natural' or 'customary' or 'instinctive' beliefs, and as a critic of the impossibly high standards of reasonableness demanded by the sceptic. I do not think this rather cosy view of Hume is supported by the texts (especially not by the *Treatise*). But I shall not argue the exegetical point here. The question of whether the cosy view just mentioned is defensible (whether or not we attribute it to Hume) will be taken up later, in Chapter 15.

HUME AND EXTERNAL OBJECTS

As an example of Hume's general position, let us see how he deals with the problem of the external world. (His discussion occurs in the *Treatise*, I, iv, 2, entitled 'Of scepticism with regard to the senses'.) He begins, characteristically, by insisting that we all do believe in an external world populated with 'bodies' which have a 'distinct and continued' existence (they exist outside the mind and continue to exist unperceived). Even sceptics believe this:

Thus the sceptic still continues to reason and believe, even tho' he asserts, that he cannot defend his reason by reason; and by the same rule, he must assent to the existence of body, tho' he cannot pretend by any arguments of philosophy to maintain its veracity. Nature has not left this to his choice, and has doubtless esteemed it an affair of too great importance to be trusted to our uncertain reasonings and speculations. We may well ask, *What causes induce us to believe in the existence of body?* but 'tis in vain to ask, *Whether there be body or not?* That is a point, which we must take for granted in all our reasonings. (p. 187)

Well, what causes do induce us to believe in the existence of bodies? We are not induced to have this belief by any rational argument. We do not perceive bodies outside the mind, but only impressions and ideas inside it. Nor can we argue from premises about what we do perceive to conclusions about what we do not perceive:

This sentiment, then, as it is entirely unreasonable, must proceed from some other faculty than the understanding. (p. 193)

The faculty it proceeds from (or is caused by) is the imagination. There is a 'constancy and coherence' in our experience: we have a visual impression of a table, blink our eyes, and have another visual impression of a table; we are warmed by the fire, nod off and wake up to be warmed by it again. Our imagination induces us to fill in the gaps in our experience, by imagining that tables or fires are external objects distinct from our experiences and continuing to exist unexperienced. (This answer, which is sensible enough, is incompatible with the official idea-ist theory of what 'the imagination' can accomplish – but I let this pass.)

Is this natural belief or 'sentiment' of ours a reasonable belief? Hume thinks not. He asks exactly what kind of thing it is that we believe has a 'distinct and continued' existence. The 'vulgar' think they are the things we experience, the 'philosophers' think they are not the things we experience. Neither belief is reasonable:

Accordingly, we find, that all the conclusions which the vulgar form on this head, are directly contrary to those, which are confirm'd by philosophy. For philosophy informs us, that every thing, that appears to the mind, is nothing but a perception, and is interrupted and dependent on the mind; whereas the vulgar confound perceptions and objects, and attribute a distinct and continu'd existence to the very things they feel and see. This sentiment…is entirely unreasonable… (p. 193)

Do 'the philosophers' (that is, Locke) do any better? They distinguish objects from ideas and say that objects have a distinct and continued existence and actually cause the ideas. Hume objects:

But as no beings are ever present to the mind but perceptions; it follows that we may observe a relation of cause and effect between different perceptions, but can never observe it between perceptions and objects. 'Tis impossible, therefore, that from the existence or any of the qualities of the former, we can ever form any conclusion concerning the existence of the latter, or ever satisfy our reason in this particular. (p. 212)

Hume adds that we could have no scrap of evidence for the view that any of our perceptions, or properties of them, resemble objects, or properties of them, since we never perceive the objects.

So the upshot is this. We cannot help believing in objects. But this is either to believe (with the vulgar) in unperceived perceptions or to believe (with the philosophers) in things for which we could have no scrap of evidence as to their existence, their properties, their causing our perceptions. Either belief is quite irrational. Hume embraces irrationalism, concluding his discussion as follows:

What then can we look for from this confusion of groundless and extraordinary opinions but error and falsehood? And how can we justify to ourselves any belief we repose in them?

This sceptical doubt…is a malady, which can never be radically cur'd but must return upon us every moment, however we may chace it away, and sometimes may seem entirely free from it. 'Tis impossible upon any system to defend either our understanding or our senses; and we but expose them farther when we endeavour to justify them… Carelessness and inattention alone afford us any remedy. For this reason I rely entirely upon them; and take it for granted, whatever may be the reader's opinion at the present moment, that an hour hence he will be persuaded that there is both an internal and an external world... (p. 218)

Hume's discussion of the problem of the external world is important. His arguments against the 'vulgar' and the 'philosophical' opinion both depend crucially upon idea-ism: 'every thing that appears to the mind, is nothing but a perception' (p. 193) or 'no beings are ever present to the mind but perceptions' (p. 212). We can regard Hume as having established the following conditional proposition: if idea-ism is correct, then belief in external objects is unreasonable. Hume himself, of course, accepted the antecedent of this conditional and therefore its consequent also. But one might accept the conditional, deny its consequent, and therefore deny its antecedent also. This would be to regard Hume's argument from idea-ism to irrationalism as a *reductio ad absurdum* of idea-ism. We shall take up this possibility in Chapter 15.

But first we have some unfinished business with Hume. Hume thought that what went for the belief in external objects also went for any other belief which transcended experience (impressions and ideas). In all such cases the sceptic is right and the only remedy is 'carelessness and inattention'. We are not going to consider Hume's detailed arguments regarding belief in other minds, one's own mind, God, or anything else. Instead we are going to consider perhaps his chief claim to philosophical fame, his sceptical critique of inductive reasoning. For this is the second major sceptical objection to the empiricist theory of knowledge.

The first major sceptical objection concerned the security of the empiricist's basis for knowledge. This gave rise to the problem of perception, the retreat into idea-ism, and the problem of appearance and reality. The second major sceptical objection concerns, not the security of the empirical basis, but its adequacy. Hume's own discussion of it is couched in the terminology of 'impressions' and 'ideas', a terminology invented to try to deal with the first objection. It is also intricately bound up with Hume's views on causality. But it is important to see that Hume's objection is independent both of his idea-ism and of his views on causality. This is how I propose to present this second objection, though it means departing from the letter (though not from the spirit) of Hume's own presentation. So let us set aside the sceptical critique of the reliability of the senses and return to the naive realist view that the senses give us certainty about external objects. We can know for certain, let us assume, that observation-statements such as 'That table is brown' or 'This fire is hot' or 'It is raining' are true.

HUME'S INDUCTIVE SCEPTICISM

Hume realised that all of us go beyond the evidence of the senses, and form beliefs (or have expectations or make predictions) about things we have not experienced, beliefs in the light of which we regulate our behaviour. We all do this every day of our lives, in countless ways, naturally and without thinking. Our hands are dirty, and to clean them we put them in water rather than in the fire. Why? Because we expect that the water will clean them, while the fire would hurt them. Offered a sandwich on a plate, we reach for the sandwich rather than the plate. Why? Because we believe that the sandwich will be nourishing while the plate would not. We take the stairs to get down to the ground, rather than jumping out of the window. Why? Because we predict that taking the stairs will leave us in one piece, while jumping out of the window would not.

But are these beliefs of ours (and the actions based upon them) reasonable beliefs? Can they be justified? Empiricists think that beliefs must be justified on the basis of experience. Asked how he knows that, say, putting your hand in the fire will hurt it, the empiricist answers 'From experience'. But to appeal to past experience to justify beliefs or expectations about the future is to engage in inductive reasoning. We think the bread we are about to eat will nourish us because bread nourished us when we ate it in the past. We can set out the tacit reasoning we use as follows:

Bread nourished me on Monday.
Bread nourished me on Tuesday.

Bread nourished me on Wednesday.
Bread nourished me on Thursday.
Bread nourished me on Friday.
Bread nourished me on Saturday.
Therefore, bread will nourish me tomorrow (Sunday).

Let this simple, somewhat artificial, and rather pedantic example be our stock example of inductive reasoning in what follows.

Hume thought that as a matter of psychological fact we cannot help reasoning inductively. He even thought that the 'we' here included animals: cats and dogs are inveterate inductive reasoners, too (*Treatise*, 1, iii, 16). Nor did he dispute (at least not in this context) that the premises of such arguments could be known for certain to be true from past experience. His objection is that inductive arguments are logically invalid: the truth of the premises does not guarantee the truth of the conclusion, it is possible for the conclusion to be false even though all the premises are true, the conclusion does not follow from the premises. In our little example, the fact that bread nourished me from Monday to Saturday does not guarantee that the bread I eat on Sunday will not poison me. (Contrast our invalid inductive argument with this valid deductive one: 'Bread always nourishes, therefore bread will nourish me tomorrow (Sunday).' Here, if the premise is true, the conclusion must be true also. Contrariwise, if Sunday's bread poisons me, the premise that bread always nourishes is false.) Hume insisted that because inductive arguments are invalid, the appeal to past experience cannot prove or justify or give a reason for beliefs about the future. But a belief is only reasonable if we can prove or justify or give a reason for it. Hence no belief about the future is reasonable. A reasonable person will be a total sceptic about the future (or about unexperienced cases).

But although such scepticism is the only reasonable position, it is not a position we can actually adopt. Human (and animal) nature being what it is, we cannot help reasoning inductively. Repeatedly nourished by bread, we cannot help believing that the next piece of bread we eat will nourish us also. Repeatedly burned by fires, we cannot help expecting the next one to burn us if we go too close. Reason might lead us into scepticism – but human nature leads us out. Hume's solution (if it is a solution) is once again to embrace irrationalism. We can set out Hume's argument as follows:

(1) We do and must reason inductively.
(2) Inductive reasoning is invalid.
(3) To reason invalidly is unreasonable.
Therefore, we are and must be unreasonable.

The problem of induction can be formulated as follows: can Hume's irrationalist conclusion be avoided? (Popper 1962: Chapter 1, 1972: Chapter 1). This is not the only way to formulate the problem, nor is it the usual way it is formulated; but it is the best way to formulate it. Common formulations like 'Can induction be justified?' or even 'How can induction be justified?' beg the question against some of the possible responses to Hume.

Many philosophers have struggled with this problem. One of them wrote of its importance as follows:

It is important to discover whether there is any answer to Hume... If not, there is no *intellectual* difference between sanity and insanity. The lunatic who believes that he is a poached egg is to be condemned solely on the ground that he is in a minority, or rather – since we must not assume democracy – on the ground that the government does not agree with him. This is a desperate point of view, and it must be hoped that there is some way of escaping from it. (Russell 1946: 646)

Before we look at any attempts to answer Hume, a few preliminary points need to be made. The first is that so far we have considered only one type of inductive argument, though it was the type considered by Hume himself. That type of inductive argument came later to be called 'singular predictive inference', because its conclusion is a singular prediction. A second type of inductive argument moves from premises reporting past experience to a general conclusion. A simple standard example might be:

Bread nourished me on Monday.
Bread nourished me on Tuesday.
Bread nourished me on Wednesday.
Bread nourished me on Thursday.
Bread nourished me on Friday.
Bread nourished me on Saturday.
Therefore, bread always nourishes.

Such inductive arguments are called, for obvious reasons, 'inductive generalisations'. Hume's strictures apply to them, too: if singular predictive inference is invalid, so is inductive generalisation, only more so (if it makes sense to speak of degrees of validity and invalidity). By 'inductive argument' we shall mean an argument of one of these two types.

This is a more restrictive definition than has become customary. Some define an inductive argument as any argument which is not deductively valid; this is to include deductive fallacies among the inductive arguments. Others define an inductive argument as any argument which is not deductively valid but whose premises provide a reason for believing the conclusion. This is not helpful until we are given an account of how one statement can provide a reason for believing another which does not follow from it. Some attempt to give such accounts, as we will see. Others write as though it were obvious when one statement is a (non-conclusive) reason for believing another – which it is not. The terminology here is especially confusing because some valid deductive arguments are called 'inductions'. There is 'demonstrative induction', exemplified by:

Emeralds are all the same colour.
This emerald is green.
Therefore, all emeralds are green.

There is Bacon's 'eliminative induction', exemplified in its simplest form by:

Either the butler did the dirty deed or the footman did the
    dirty deed.

The butler did not do the dirty deed.
Therefore, the footman did the dirty deed.

Finally, there is 'mathematical induction', which in its simplest form goes like this:

O has the property P,
Whenever n has the property P so does $n+1$.
Therefore, all natural numbers have the property P.

This is a valid deduction in arithmetic, once we add as a 'missing premise' the axiom (or axiom-schema) of mathematical induction, telling you that if the two premises are true then so is the conclusion. Having mentioned all these terminological complications, let us set them aside in favour of the simple idea that an inductive inference is either a singular predictive inference or an inductive generalisation.

Our problem is, can Hume's irrationalist conclusion be avoided? If we look at the argument Hume gave for that conclusion, stated on page 153, above, it is possible to give a taxonomy of possible solutions. For Hume's argument is a valid one. Hence, if we are to reject the conclusion, we must reject (at least) one of the premises. Since Hume's argument has three premises, this immediately gives us three options:

Deny premise (1) and say instead that we do not, or need not, reason inductively. This is the deductivist solution of Karl Popper and his followers.

Deny premise (2) and say instead that inductive reasoning is valid. This is, historically, by far the most popular solution. It is not, of course, the absurd view that inductive arguments as we have presented them so far are valid. Rather it is the view that so far we have not presented inductive arguments properly, and that when we do they will turn out to be valid. Now there are two ways to turn an argument which is invalid as presented into a valid argument: one can strengthen the stated premises so that the conclusion follows from them; or one can weaken the stated conclusion so that it follows from the premises. Both ways of 'validating' inductive arguments have been tried.

Deny premise (3) and say instead that it is not unreasonable to reason invalidly. This is the nondeductivist solution of Wittgenstein and Strawson and their followers.

In the next chapter we will consider these various solutions, beginning with those in the second category.

CHAPTER 9

Countering Hume on induction

Hume thought inductive arguments were invalid. But perhaps he misconstrued them, perhaps he omitted an assumption which all such arguments implicitly contain. If we make this assumption explicit, and include it among the premises of our inductions, then those inductions will be seen to be valid after all. This assumption is the general 'principle of induction'. What is the principle of induction? Some of the simplest attempts to formulate it are: 'The future resembles the past', 'Unobserved cases resemble observed cases' or 'Nature is uniform'. Other formulations are more complicated, for a reason we will see in due course.

It must be admitted, to begin with, that if we add 'The future resembles the past' (or something equally strong) to the premises of our two simple examples of inductive reasoning, then those inductive arguments become perfectly valid *de*-ductive arguments:

The future resembles the past.
Bread nourished me from Monday until Saturday.
Therefore, bread will nourish me tomorrow.

(And similarly for the corresponding inductive generalisation.) But, Hume would object, it is only reasonable to employ an inductive principle in our reasonings if we know that principle to be true (or can justify our belief in it). And this we cannot do.

We cannot justify our belief in the principle of induction by any argument from experience. For this would be to argue as follows (by analogy with our simple example):

> The future resembled the past on Monday.
> The future resembled the past on Tuesday.
> The future resembled the past on Wednesday.
> The future resembled the past on Thursday.
> The future resembled the past on Friday.
> The future resembled the past on Saturday.
> Therefore, the future (always) resembles the past.

But this is an invalid inductive argument again. If we try to validate this second argument by appealing to a second inductive principle, then we are clearly going to be involved in an infinite regress.

Nor can we justify our belief in the principle of induction by any argument which is *not* based on experience. For what would such an argument be like? The only way to show that something is true without relying upon the teachings of experience (or upon any additional assumption of any kind) is to argue by *reductio ad absurdum*: show that something must be true because its negation leads to a contradiction. But we cannot argue that the principle of induction must be true because its negation leads to a contradiction. No contradiction results from the supposition that the future will *not* resemble the past. Hence no argument which is not based upon experience (no *reductio* argument) can justify our belief in the principle of induction.

It follows, said Hume, that belief in the principle of induction is quite unreasonable:

> ... the supposition, that the future resembles the past, is not founded on arguments of any kind, but is deriv'd entirely from habit. (*Treatise*, I, iii, 12; 134)

And so his old conclusion stands: we are in the habit of arguing inductively but cannot show that it is reasonable to argue this way.

There is a possible way out of this argument. At one point Hume assumes that the only things knowable independently of experience are statements whose negation involves a contradition. This might be denied. It might be claimed that we can show the inductive principle true by an argument which is not based upon experience and yet which is not a *reductio ad absurdum* argument. Immanuel Kant was to make such a claim. Bertrand Russell said at one point that the only way to save inductive reasoning is to endorse Kant's claim. (Elsewhere Russell flirted with the idea that, despite Hume and despite appearances, the principle of induction could be proved by *reductio* after all.)

This is a desperate way out. It is utterly mysterious how we could know independently of experience that nature is uniform or that the future resembles the past or any such principle. Moreover, the view abandons empiricism in a quite fundamental way, by saying that any argument from experience, if it is to be valid, requires a principle among its premises which is not learned from experience. On this view, any knowledge which transcends the immediate evidence of the senses requires this important piece of non-empirical knowledge. This is not a small concession on the part of the empiricist, it is an admission that empiricism is fundamentally flawed. Yet Russell, who is generally sympathetic to empiricism, was once driven to this desperate measure by the desire to answer Hume (Russell 1946: 647).

Does not Hume himself abandon empiricism when he concedes that we can prove some truths independently of experience? For did not the empiricist claim that all knowledge is derived from experience? Some empiricists did claim this. But on reflection even the most hard-headed empiricist would concede that the truth of statements like 'All bachelors are unmarried' follows from the meanings of the words they contain, so that the negations of such statements involve contradictions – for to suppose that not all bachelors are unmarried is to suppose that someone is both married and unmarried. (Hard-headed empiricists would insist that we learn the meanings of words from experience. But even they would say that having learned the meaning of the word 'bachelor', we do not need to check whether all bachelors are unmarried, as we would with more interesting claims like 'All bachelors are unhappy'.) So the empiricist concession on such truths (which Hume called 'relations of ideas') is not much of a concession. They are all uninteresting truths, verbal trivialities, which tell us nothing about the world, only about the way we use words.

The hard core of the empiricist position concerned the interesting truths about the world (which Hume called 'matters of fact'): the empiricist's fundamental thesis is that all these truths can only be known from experience. (And the fundamental thesis of the rationalist theory of knowledge, yet to be considered, is that some interesting truths about the world can be known independently of experience of the world.)

There is a further very simple objection to the idea that the principle of induction can be known to be true – the objection is that the principle is false. It is just not true that the future resembles the past in all respects, that nature is uniform in all respects, or that unobserved cases always resemble observed cases. Russell illustrates the point nicely:

Domestic animals expect food when they see the person who usually feeds them. We know that all these rather crude expectations of uniformity are liable to be misleading. The man who has fed the chicken every day throughout its life at last wrings its neck instead, showing that more refined views as to the uniformity of nature would have been useful to the chicken. (1912: 63)

As a second example we can add that people have actually been poisoned and have died as a result of eating bread from the local bakery (the flour was made from wheat infected with the fungal disease ergotism which secretes a chemical lethal to humans).

Is this not cheap criticism? Did anyone ever seriously maintain that unobserved cases always resemble observed cases, or that nature is uniform in every respect? Perhaps not. But the cheap criticism does point to a real problem. Those who appeal to inductive principles need to find a principle which is strong enough to validate inductive arguments but not so strong that it is false. This problem will not easily be solved. Suppose we weaken 'Nature is uniform' to 'Nature is uniform in some respects' (or equivalently, 'There are some laws of nature'). Adding this weaker principle to our standard example about bread nourishing me tomorrow fails to validate the argument. (What we need to validate it, one might think, is something like: Nature is uniform in some respects and bread always nourishing is one of those respects. But then we might as well simply assume that bread always nourishes and deduce the prediction that it will nourish me tomorrow. This line of thought leads to the deductivist answer to Hume, to be discussed in due course.) There have been several attempts to formulate 'more refined views as to the uniformity of nature', inductive principles just strong enough but not too strong. None has been wholly successful. And none has really succeeded in meeting Hume's objection that such 'refined views' cannot be known from experience and cannot be known independently of experience either. We will mention one such attempt later. (Actually, the most refined views as to the uniformity of nature are the laws of nature proposed by scientists. Hume's objection applies with equal force to those laws, however.)

PROBABILISM

Let us pass on to the most popular and most appealing answer to Hume, probabilism. Probabilism begins with a concession to Hume. Inductive arguments as we have presented them so far are invalid (and appealing to inductive principles does not help). It does *not* follow from the fact that bread has always nourished me in the past that it will nourish me tomorrow (or always). Hence we cannot be absolutely sure that bread will nourish us tomorrow (or always). On all these points Hume is simply right. But, the probabilist claims, we can 'validate' inductive arguments if we weaken their conclusions to statements of probability. It does follow from the fact that bread has always nourished me in the past that it will probably nourish me tomorrow (or always). Moreover, probabilities rather than certainties are all we need to avoid Hume's charge of irrationalism. Past experience may not make it certain that tomorrow's bread will nourish me. But if past experience makes it probable that it will, then it is perfectly reasonable for me to eat the sandwich offered me and not the plate on which it is offered.

The rational person adjusts belief and behaviour to the probabilities – or as the slogan has it: 'Probability is the guide of life'.

Hume had little time for this approach. (Indeed, he had so little time for it that some say he did not consider it at all.) He simply denied (or we can deny on his behalf) that weakening the conclusion by inserting the word 'probably' could render an inductive argument valid. He claimed (or we can claim on his behalf) that you will still need to strengthen the premises with a probabilistic inductive principle such as 'Nature is probably uniform' or 'The future probably resembles the past' or 'Unobserved cases probably resemble observed cases'. And he said (or we can say on his behalf) that his old arguments apply with equal force against such principles: they cannot be known from experience on pain of infinite regress; they cannot be known independently of experience, for their negations are not contradictory; so they cannot be known at all, and we use them out of habit.

Most philosophers remain unconvinced by this Humean argument. It is obvious that 'Bread nourished me from Monday to Saturday, therefore it will nourish me on Sunday' is invalid – if Sunday's bread poisons me, as it might, then the invalidity of this argument becomes very apparent (its true premises have led to a false conclusion). But it is not obvious that 'Bread nourished me from Monday to Saturday, therefore it will probably nourish me on Sunday' is invalid – if Sunday's bread poisons me, as it might, it is not apparent that true premises have led to a false conclusion. This is because 'Bread will probably nourish me on Sunday' is consistent with Sunday's bread poisoning me, just as 'The next throw with this dice will probably not be a six' is consistent with a six turning up.

Encouraged by such reflections, probabilists did not give up. They sought to develop the theory of probability in such a way that it could show that probabilistic inductive arguments are valid. The theory of probability is a well-defined branch of mathematics. Its simplest applications are to chance set-ups like coin-tossing, dice-throwing, spinning a roulette wheel, or drawing a card from a well-shuffled pack of cards. In each chance set-up there are a certain number of possible outcomes which are assumed (in the simplest case) to be equally probable: the tossed coin can land heads or tails, the thrown dice can show one, two, three, four, five, or six, and so forth. The probability of any event can be defined as the number of possible outcomes in which it occurs (the number of 'favourable outcomes') divided by the number of all possible outcomes. Thus the probability of the tossed coin landing heads is $\frac{1}{2}$, the probability of the thrown dice showing less than five is $\frac{2}{3}$, and so on. The maximum probability is clearly 1 and the minimum probability 0. The mathematical theory of probability enables you to calculate, from the initial probabilities of the outcomes in a chance set-up, the probabilities of complicated events such as getting three successive heads with the tossed coin (this is $\frac{1}{8}$) or of getting dealt all the cards of one suit from a well-shuffled pack of cards (I do not know what this is).

How does all this help with the problem of induction? The probabilists dreamt of a different type of probability, logical probability, in which statements would have certain probabilities of being true. More precisely, they dreamt of developing this theory so that a hypothesis would have a certain probability given some evidence. Thus '$p(h, e) = r$' was to be read: 'The (logical) probability of hypothesis h given evidence e is r.' That such a concept of probability could be developed was suggested by the extreme cases. Suppose that e logically implies h, so that if e is true then h has to be true also – in this case, $p(h, e) = 1$. Or suppose that e contradicts h, so that if e is true then h cannot also be true – in this case, $p(h, e) = 0$. In between these extremes, probabilists thought, there must be intermediate cases where e neither entails nor contradicts h, but rather makes it more probable than not – in such cases $p(h, e) > \frac{1}{2}$. If such cases could be shown to exist, then inductive reasoning might be justified after all. For example, if e is evidence to the effect that all the bread I have eaten has nourished me, and h the hypothesis that the next piece will nourish me (or that all bread nourishes), then the result that $p(h, e) > \frac{1}{2}$ would justify the intuition that inductions are valid if their conclusions are weakened with the word 'probably'.

This, then, is the probabilist programme. Intuitively appealing though it is, it proved enormously difficult to carry out, and came to involve many logical subtleties which we cannot enter into here. For one thing, the theory was worked out for artificial or symbolic languages. This was because, just as in applying probability theory to chance set-ups we have to know (or to guess) all the possible outcomes, so also in applying it to hypotheses we have to know all the possible hypotheses. For natural languages this is not only infinite, but it is also sometimes unclear what is to count as a possible hypothesis. To manage this task, attention was focused on artificial languages each of which can be regarded as a precise though impoverished portion of a natural language. (Some object that these artificial languages are so impoverished that most of our interesting hypotheses cannot be expressed in them – to which probabilists reply, not unreasonably, that if the theory can be worked out for such simple languages first, it can later be extended.)

Now when we apply the probability calculus to such things as throwing a dice, we not only identify the possible outcomes but we also assign probabilities to them. If we think the dice a 'fair dice', we will assign equal probabilities of $\frac{1}{6}$ to each of the six outcomes. If we think the dice is not a 'fair dice', our initial assignment will not be so simple. The crucial point is that some initial assignment is necessary if the theory is to enable us to calculate the probabilities of more complicated events. Similarly with the theory of logical probability: we have to identify a collection of statements which will, so to speak, describe the 'possible outcomes' of investigating the world, and assign probabilities to them. And we should note that this initial assignment is based upon no experience of the world whatsoever.

Rudolf Carnap, the chief champion of this approach, succeeded in constructing some artificial languages, identifying a collection of statements in those languages which represent the 'possible outcomes' for each, and assigning equal probabilities to them on no experience (or evidence) whatever. He then achieved some interesting results regarding inductive reasoning. It turned out that he was able to validate singular predictive inference, but was not able to validate inductive generalisation. Intuitively speaking, in Carnap's system the more nourishing pieces of bread you have eaten (representing the evidence), the more probable it is that the next piece you eat will also nourish you. However, the probability that every piece of bread you eat will nourish you is initially zero and it remains zero no matter how much experience you have had of nourishing bread. (Other probabilists did not like this second result of Carnap's and sought to avoid it: and they did succeed in getting non-zero probabilities for generalisations provided some generalisations are assigned non-zero probabilities to begin with on no evidence whatsoever.)

Do these results, which I have merely sketched dogmatically, provide an answer to Hume? If Hume had been aware of them, he might have objected (as others certainly have objected on his behalf) that the initial probability distributions to statements on no evidence whatsoever represent a substantive assumption about the world. This assumption is not so simple as the statement 'Nature is probably uniform', which Hume claimed was necessary to validate probabilistic inductive arguments. But it is an assumption of the same kind: it is not based on experience, and it cannot be known independently of experience because its denial leads to no contradiction (as is shown by the existence of alternative consistent initial distributions). In short, it cannot be known at all, and probabilistic reasoning based upon it is therefore irrational.

This is all I will say about probabilism. An adequate treatment of this attempt to answer Hume would require a book in itself. But I hope I have been able to convey, albeit rather dogmatically, an indication of the successes and failures of this approach so far.

One may wonder whether it is really necessary, in order to answer Hume, to be able to produce precise numerical probabilities for statements which obey the rules of the mathematical calculus of probability. The person who says 'Bread always nourished me in the past, so it will probably nourish me tomorrow' may have no technical sense of the term 'probably' in mind. His statement may equally well be rendered

'Bread always nourished me in the past, so it is reasonable to believe (or to anticipate) that it will nourish me tomorrow'. Of course, if we could show that the probability that bread will nourish me tomorrow on the evidence is 0·9, then this would entail that it was reasonable to believe (or anticipate) that bread will nourish me tomorrow. But perhaps the failure to show the former does not entail that we cannot show the latter. Hume, of course, thought the latter false: he said that the fact that bread has always nourished us in the past gives us no reason to believe or anticipate that it will nourish us tomorrow, so that it is not reasonable to believe or anticipate that it will. Is there a possible answer to Hume which denies this claim of his without attempting to validate inductive arguments or probabilistic inductive arguments? The possibility might seem bizarre and a solution based upon it pretty desperate: but Hume's problem drives philosophers to desperate measures!

THE 'NO TRUE SCOTSMAN' PLOY

The third argument against Hume that we have to consider has been remarkably popular. I find this odd, for I think the argument is simply a red herring. It is not, however, easy to say why it is a red herring, which is the main reason for the popularity of the argument.

The argument goes something like this. Hume says that we cannot be sure that the next piece of bread we eat will nourish us, or that the next fire into which we thrust our hand will burn us. But this is absurd. If our next slice of bread did not nourish us, it would not be real bread or true bread but rather poisoned bread. If we were to thrust our hand into a fire and not get burned, this would only show that it was not a real fire or a true fire at all. Despite what Hume says, we can be quite sure that the next piece of bread (true bread) will nourish us and that the next fire (true fire) will burn us.

This has been called the 'No true Scotsman' ploy (Flew 1971: 393). Somebody announces: 'The Scots are all mean.' Anxious to disabuse him of his prejudices, we point to a generous Scot, say, Andrew Carnegie. To which the reply is: 'Ah, but Andrew

Carnegie is not a true Scot!' What is going on here? When we were told 'The Scots are all mean', it looked as though we were being told something interesting, something nasty about the Scots, to be sure, but something interesting. If we accepted what we were told, then we should not, for example, expect a big birthday present from our Scottish grandfather. But then it emerges, after we point out that there are generous Scots, that a generous Scot is not going to count as a 'true Scot' simply because he is generous. So what we were really being told was 'The true Scots are all mean', where a 'true Scot' is a mean Scot. What we were really being told was 'All mean Scots are mean', which was not telling us much and which was not very interesting at all. (Actually, it tells us nothing and is totally uninteresting: for example, we can accept it and still live in hope of our Scottish grandfather, who might, if we are lucky, not be a 'true Scot'.) We thought we had an interesting proposition about the Scots to consider, and it turned out to be a (rather idiosyncratic) analytic truth (like 'Bachelors are unmarried').

It is amazing how ready people are to resort to the 'No true Scotsman' ploy. Somebody proposes an interesting generalisation. Somebody else refutes it by producing a counterexample. And straightaway the first person disarms the counterexample by turning his hypothesis into an analytic truth, by declaring that he uses words in such a way that the counterexample (and any other counterexample) does not count. It is also amazing how often the ploy succeeds in diverting attention from the real issue into a verbal issue. The real issue is whether or not Scots are mean. Somebody proposes to use the word 'Scot' (or 'true Scot') in such a way that they must be mean, in the same way that bachelors must be unmarried. What typically happens next is that attention is focused upon whether the word 'Scot' really means (in part) somebody who is mean, or whether what it really means is simply somebody born in Scotland or some such thing. A quarrel ensues about the real meaning of the word 'Scot', leaving the original question behind. The way to avoid this diversion is obvious. One should simply accept that the word 'Scot' can be used (or defined) in such a way as to make 'Scots are all mean' an analytic truth. Instead of quarrelling with this use (or definition), one should introduce a new term (say 'Caledonian') to do the work that the word 'Scot' did before, to stand for people born in Scotland or some such thing. And then one should simply say 'I agree that as you use words, it is true that the Scots are all mean. But let us use the word "Caledonian" to refer to people born in Scotland. Tell me, do you also think that Caledonians are all mean? If so, what about Andrew Carnegie? He is not a (true) Scot, agreed. But he is a Caledonian and he is generous.' (More could be said about this matter of the meanings or 'real meanings' of words, but we have digressed long enough.)

Returning to Hume, if we use (or define) the word 'bread' in such a way that something which fails to nourish us does not count as bread (or as 'true bread'), then of course we can be sure that the next piece of bread we eat will nourish us. We can be sure of this because what looked like a prediction has been turned into an analytic truth. Moreover, our inductive argument has been turned into a valid argument. Now it cannot be the case that the premises are true and the conclusion false, because it cannot be the case that the conclusion is false. We have 'validated' the argument by weakening the conclusion – by weakening it to nothing (for an analytic truth says nothing about the world).

Hume did not actually consider the 'No true Scotsman' ploy (was it beneath his contempt, I wonder?), but it is easy to see what he might have said about it – and what we ought to say about it. First, we should not quarrel with the person who wants to use the word 'bread' in this fashion. (Such a person is simply using the term 'bread' as a dispositional term.) We should insist, however, that the epistemological situation remains precisely the same, but must now be differently described. We can now be sure that the next piece of bread we eat will nourish us, but that is to be sure of nothing because that is (in part) how we are using the term 'bread'. What we now cannot be sure of is that it is a piece of bread that we are eating! It may look like bread, have been bought from the bread shop, have been manufactured in the normal way by the baker, but it will not be bread if it fails to nourish us. If we define 'bread' (in part) by its effects on humans who eat it, then humans cannot be sure that it is bread they are eating until those effects have happened. We need a new term, say 'cread', to refer to what looks like bread, tastes like bread and so forth. We can be sure from observation (we are assuming) that something is a piece of cread. But now our original inductive inference must be expressed using this new term:

> Cread nourished me on Monday (and so turned out to be bread).
>
> Cread nourished me on Tuesday (and so turned out to be bread).
>
> Cread nourished me on Wednesday (and so turned out to be bread).
>
> Cread nourished me on Thursday (and so turned out to be bread).
>
> Cread nourished me on Friday (and so turned out to be bread).
>
> Therefore, cread will nourish me tomorrow (and turn out to be bread).

Hume's original conclusion about the invalidity of this argument stands.

NON-DEDUCTIVISM

The third premise of Hume's argument for irrationalism was 'To reason invalidly is unreasonable'. There are those who deny this premise – and, by implication, Hume's second premise ('Inductive reasoning is invalid') as well. Yet these philosophers do not attempt to validate induction by strengthening the premise of inductive arguments (as believers in the 'principle of induction' do), nor do they attempt to validate induction by weakening the conclusions of inductive arguments (as probabilists do). No, for these philosophers inductive arguments are perfectly valid as they stand. How can all this be? I will try to explain.

Hume pointed out that inductive arguments are not deductively valid – the truth of their premises does not guarantee that their conclusions are also true. This is perfectly correct. It is useless (as Hume also correctly observed) to try to turn invalid inductive arguments into valid deductive arguments by strengthening their premises or by weakening their conclusions. Inductive arguments just are not deductive arguments, and we should not try to make them so. Hume says that to reason in a deductively invalid way is unreasonable (premise 3 of his argument). But this is to overlook the fact that as well as deductive validity (and invalidity), there is also inductive validity (and invalidity). We may reason in an inductively valid way, and this is a perfectly valid way to reason.

The obvious difficulty with this response centres upon the notion of 'inductive validity (and invalidity)'. Which are the inductively valid, and the inductively invalid, ways of arguing? Surely, not every deductive fallacy is going to count as an 'inductively valid' way of arguing. 'If A then B, and B, therefore A' is counted as a deductive fallacy (it is called the fallacy of affirming the consequent). Is this inductively valid or is it not? On the matter of what inductive validity consists in, adherents of this approach adopt what John Watkins calls a 'sealed-lips policy' (see Watkins 1984: 32–6, or Musgrave 1989). They insist that inductive reasoning is inductively (but not, of course, deductively) valid, yet do not tell us what inductive validity is. (In this they are to be contrasted with the probabilists, who do take great pains to tell us what inductive validity is – it is deductive validity in the probability calculus.) They talk about 'courts of appeal', and insist that in the matter of 'inductive validity' there is no higher court of appeal than the inductive reasoners themselves. In the matter of witch-hunting, is there no higher court of appeal than the witch-hunters themselves?

DEDUCTIVISM

All of the answers to Hume which we have considered so far accept his first premise (that we must reason inductively) and try in different ways to show that his second premise (inductive reasoning is invalid) is mistaken. The solution we have now to consider, that of Karl Popper, begins from a denial that we reason inductively, from which it follows that the invalidity of inductive reasoning (concerning which Hume was perfectly right) does not matter!

Now in Chapter 4 we have already considered arguments to the effect that as a matter of fact we do not learn from experience (or form beliefs or habits) by inductive repetition. What we typically do is jump to conclusions and use these conclusions to regulate our future behaviour. (The 'we' here included animals, ordinary people in the common affairs of life and scientists.) Let us suppose for the sake of argument that this non-inductive view of belief-formation is correct. How will it help with Hume's problem?

Well, Popper argues, having formed beliefs or expectations in this non-inductive way, we employ them in perfectly valid deductive arguments in order to anticipate the future. Returning to the simple example of the nourishing bread, what happens is that I jump to the conclusion that bread always nourishes (perhaps on the basis of few, one, or no experiences with nourishing bread), and thereafter deduce from this hypothesis that the next piece of bread will nourish me.

Nobody is convinced, and rightly so. Is it reasonable to proceed in this fashion? Granted, for the sake of the argument, that we employ no invalid inductive arguments: we do not come to the hypothesis that bread always nourishes by argument, but dream it up, or postulate it, or freely conjecture it, and we get the prediction that bread will nourish tomorrow by deductive argument. (Actually, the factual thesis that people never reason inductively is not really essential to this solution. A person might as a matter of fact obtain the hypothesis that bread nourishes by inductive generalisation. That person has just argued invalidly to a hypothesis, as Hume said.) But what if somebody else jumps to the conclusion that bread never nourishes and deduces from his hypothesis that bread will not nourish him tomorrow? Is my hypothesis any more reasonable than his? Is my prediction any more reasonable than his? If not, then we are merely endorsing Hume's irrationalist conclusion that no belief or prediction about the unobserved is any more reasonable than any other. Merely to avoid the use of inductive arguments is hardly a way of avoiding this conclusion.

But there is an obvious difference between our two hypotheses. Suppose that, as in our simple story, bread has in fact nourished us from Monday to Friday. Then the hypothesis that bread never nourishes has been shown to be false, while the hypothesis that bread always nourishes has not been shown to be false. (And notice that the argument from experience to the falsity of the hypothesis is a perfectly valid deductive argument: If bread never nourishes then it does not nourish on Monday. But bread did nourish on Monday. Hence it is not true that bread never nourishes.) Suppose we say that it is reasonable to believe to be true (or to prefer, or to accept tentatively) hypotheses which have not been shown to be false, and unreasonable to believe hypotheses which have been shown to be false. It will follow that it is reasonable to believe that bread always nourishes and not reasonable to believe that bread never nourishes, given, of course, our experience with nourishing bread from Monday to Friday. (Notice again that this will follow deductively, thus: It is reasonable to believe unrefuted rather than refuted hypotheses. The hypothesis that bread nourishes is unrefuted and the hypothesis that bread never nourishes is refuted. Hence, it is reasonable to believe that bread nourishes and unreasonable to believe that it does not.)

More generally, suppose we say that it is reasonable to believe or prefer or tentatively accept hypotheses which have withstood criticism to hypotheses which have not withstood criticism. Here we acknowledge that refuting a hypothesis in the light of past experience is an important way of criticising it, perhaps the most important, but that it may not be the only way to criticise a hypothesis. Again, if we accept this, it will follow deductively that some hypotheses or general beliefs are more reasonable than others.

But what of the predictions about future or unobserved cases that we might deduce from general hypotheses: is any such prediction more reasonable than any other? Well, suppose we add a further principle to the effect that if it is reasonable to believe *H*, and *H* logically implies *P*, then it is also reasonable to believe *P*. It will then follow (deductively) that, in our simple little example, it is reasonable to believe that the next piece of bread will nourish us.

At this point, objections crowd in upon us. The first objection is that this is inductive reasoning in disguise, or that an inductive argument has been smuggled into the account. The evidence makes it 'reasonable to believe' the hypothesis, and the 'reasonably believed' hypothesis in turn makes it 'reasonable to believe' a prediction. Either there is an inductive argument from the evidence to the hypothesis (from which the prediction then follows deductively), or there is an inductive argument straight from the evidence to the prediction. Either inductive generalisation or singular predictive inference has been smuggled into the account. Popper may reply (should reply) that this is simply not true. There is an argument from the evidence to the conclusion that it is reasonable to believe the hypothesis (not to the hypothesis); but it is a deductive argument which has a principle about reasonable belief as an extra premise. There is also an argument from the premise that it is reasonable to believe a hypothesis to the conclusion that it is reasonable to believe a prediction (not to the prediction); but again this is a deductive argument which has a second principle about reasonable belief as an extra premise. But there are no inductive generalisations or singular predictive inferences. Indeed, there are no inductive arguments as we have been defining them so far at all.

This reply may be conceded (actually it seldom is conceded) and two further objections urged. Are not these 'principles of reasonable belief' inductivist principles? Would not Hume simple reject them out of hand? As to the first question, if a principle about reasonable belief counts as 'inductivist' if it says that it is reasonable to adjust our belief to the available evidence, then our first principle is 'inductivist'. (The second principle is simply a piece of what might be called 'applied deductive logic'.) Anyone who takes evidence seriously in any way at all in deciding what to believe, or tentatively to accept as true, or to 'prefer', is an inductivist in this broad sense.

Inductivism in this broad sense is more or less equivalent to empiricism, where 'empiricism' is defined as the incredibly weak thesis that there are non-conclusive reasons for belief (tentative acceptance, preference, or whatever) and that empirical evidence can sometimes be such a reason. And Popper the arch anti-inductivist is certainly an empiricist of sorts.

As to the second question, I think that Hume would reject our principles of reasonable belief out of hand. Hume would say that it is not reasonable to believe a hypothesis which is unrefuted by the evidence (or which, more generally, has withstood criticism), because such a hypothesis has not been shown to be true nor even shown to be probably true. And Hume would say that it is not reasonable to believe a prediction about the unobserved unless (what is not the case here) that prediction can be shown to be true or be shown to be highly probable. Let us say that a proposition has been justified if it has either been shown to be true or been shown to be probable (more likely to be true than not). Then Hume would insist that it is only reasonable to believe justified propositions. He would insist, further, that the invalidity of induction means that we cannot justify general hypotheses or propositions about unobserved cases. It follows that we cannot reasonably believe any general hypothesis or proposition about the unobserved.

It is at this point that Popper and Hume part company. Popper thinks that it is reasonable to believe (tentatively accept, prefer) some unjustified propositions, some propositions which have neither been shown to be true nor shown to be probable. It is reasonable to believe those unjustified propositions which have withstood serious attempts to show them to be false. We can justify our believing (tentatively accepting, preferring) a proposition without justifying that proposition itself. Hence Popper's position has been described as a non-justificationist theory of rationality.

I shall say no more now about this fundamental clash between this non-justificationist view of rationality and Hume's view (which is the traditional view). I shall say no more, either, about many other features of Popper's writings on this subject.

Nor shall I ask whether Popper himself would accept the foregoing reconstruction of his answer to Hume (I suspect that he would not accept all the details of it). I shall return to the matter in Chapter 15. (There is also more on this issue in Musgrave 1991a.)

CHAPTER 10

The rationalist alternative

So far we have been considering the empiricist attempt to defeat scepticism and show that certain knowledge is possible. But empiricism was not the only attempt to do this. We now turn to consider the rationalist or intellectualist alternative.

Return again to the sceptical infinite regress of proofs or justifications. Empiricists sought to stop the regress by saying that the senses were a source of immediate and certain knowledge about the world. The rationalist response to the regress is structurally similar: they seek to stop the regress by saying that the reason or intellect is a source of immediate and certain knowledge about the world. The rationalist first principles are not seen to be true in the light of sense-experience – rather they can be seen to be true by the 'natural light of reason'. And from these self-evident first principles we can prove many other things which at first sight may be very far from self-evident.

Rationalism or intellectualism is a far less plausible doctrine, at least initially, than empiricism. How can pure thought, the so-called 'natural light of reason', give us certain knowledge about the world? But we have seen how empiricism, despite its initial plausibility, is plagued with difficulties and was developed by the empiricists in some strange directions indeed. Perhaps some form of rationalism is the only way out of empiricism's difficulties. Several empiricists have thought so. We have only to recall Russell's desperate view that in order to validate inductive arguments and provide an answer to Hume, we must suppose that some general inductive principle is knowable independently of experience. Arguments from experience can only be legitimate, thought Russell, if we have some knowledge which is not based on any argument from experience!

Still, Russell gave no convincing account of how such knowledge is possible. The difficulties of empiricism were not the only reason, or even the main reason, why philosophers thought that such knowledge must be possible. The main reason for thinking that was that such knowledge actually existed (the best argument that something might exist is that it actually does exist). Which brings me to the rationalist paradigm.

THE RATIONALIST PARADIGM — EUCLID

Down the ages the rationalist paradigm for knowledge was mathematical knowledge in general, and Euclidean geometry in particular. Philosophers were incredibly impressed with Euclid. John Aubrey tells a nice story about the political philosopher Thomas Hobbes:

[Hobbes] was 40 years old before he looked on geometry; which happened accidentally. Being in a gentleman's library...Euclid's Elements lay open, and 'twas the [Pythagoras theorem]. He read the proposition. 'By G...' sayd he, (He would now and then sweare, by way of emphasis), 'this is impossible!' So he read the demonstration of it which referred him back to such a proposition; which proposition he read. That referred him back to another, which he also read. [And so to the beginning, and] at last he was demonstratively convinced of that truth. This made him in love with geometry. (Aubrey 1898, 1: 332)

In love with geometry Hobbes certainly became. He declared that it was 'the only science that it has hitherto pleased God to bestow upon mankind'. And he spent the rest of his life trying to do for political science what Euclid had done for geometry, to develop it 'in the geometrical manner' (his most famous work, *Leviathan*, was the result).

What impressed Hobbes so much? Pythagoras' theorem, on which his eye accidentally fell, says that the square on the hypotenuse of a right-angled triangle is equal to the sum of the squares on the other two sides. It is far from obvious or self-evident that this is true – indeed, Hobbes first thought it was impossible. Now Euclid does not try to convince us of its truth by exhibiting right-angled triangles of various shapes and sizes, erecting squares on their sides and measuring the areas of those squares. Such a method would give us no assurance that the theorem holds for all triangles, or that the next triangle we examine will not falsify the theorem; remember the problem of induction. Euclid's method is quite different: he proves the theorem, by showing that if you accept certain other simpler geometrical propositions as true, then you must also accept Pythagoras' theorem as true. Now these other propositions to which Euclid appeals in the proof, although generally simpler, are also not obvious or self-evident. So Euclid proves them, too. We know, from sceptical infinite regress arguments, that Euclid must start with unproved propositions or first principles or axioms. And so he does. But the unproved propositions or axioms upon which all of Euclid's subsequent proofs depend are obviously or self-evidently true. There are actually just ten of them:

> If equals be added to equals, equals result.
> If equals be subtracted from equals, equals result.
> Things equal to the same thing are equal to each other.
> Figures which coincide are equal.
> The whole is greater than the part.
> Any two points lie on a straight line.
> A straight line can be extended indefinitely in either direction.
> Given a point, and a length, there is a circle whose centre is
>   the point and whose radius is the length.
> All right angles are equal.

(I have modernised Euclid's wording. I have ignored the fact that Euclid called the first five 'common notions' rather than axioms, because they were not peculiar to geometry. The attentive reader will have noted that I announced ten axioms and have listed only nine; the reason for this deliberate mistake will become apparent in due course.)

What impressed Hobbes was this. Euclid's axioms are self-evident: once you understand them you can just see by the 'natural light of reason' that they are true. Yet by virtue of long and equally self-evident processes of reasoning Euclid is able to prove from them lots of other propositions which are far from self-evident or obvious. The example which Hobbes encountered was Pythagoras' theorem which he thought impossible at first. Another example occurs at the end of the *Elements*, where Euclid proves that there are exactly five perfect solids, no more, no less. (A perfect solid is a solid all of whose faces are identical, such as a cube.) And all this is achieved by pure reasoning, with no appeal to sense-experience at all.

Hobbes was not the only one to be impressed. Listen to just one more example, as Albert Einstein tells us what a great impression Euclid made upon him when he was twelve:

Here were assertions, as for example the intersection of the three altitudes of a triangle in one point, which – though by no means evident – could nevertheless be proved with such certainty that doubt appeared to be out of the question. This lucidity and certainty made an indescribable impression upon me. That the axioms had to be accepted unproved did not disturb me. In any case it was quite sufficient for me if I could peg proofs on propositions the validity of which did not seem to me to be dubious...it appeared that it was possible to get certain knowledge of the objects of experience by means of pure thinking. (Einstein 1949: 9–11)

Einstein puts his finger precisely on the rationalist dream: 'certain knowledge of the objects of experience by means of pure thinking'. Euclid seemed to have made the dream come true as far as knowledge of space was concerned. Rationalists hoped to make it come true for other disciplines, too, by doing for them what Euclid had done for geometry: begin with self-evident axioms appropriate to that discipline, and by self-evident processes of reasoning establish the truth of theorems in that same discipline.

There were several attempts. I have already mentioned Hobbes's *Leviathan*. Descartes's *Principles of Philosophy* was written in the geometrical manner, with axioms, theorems and proofs. So was Spinoza's *Ethics Demonstrated in the Geometrical Manner*. So was the most important scientific book ever written, Isaac Newton's *Mathematical Principles of Natural Philosophy* (the

title was a deliberate play on that of Descartes). James Mill's
Essay on Government also began with a few allegedly self-evident
axioms about human nature and tried to deduce political doctrines from them. These Euclidean projects were not inspired
solely by Euclid. There are many isolated examples of apparently
'self-evident first principles': 'Every physical object takes up
space', 'Nothing can be in two places at the same time', 'Two
things cannot be in the same place at the same time', 'Nothing
can be red and blue all over', 'If one thing causes another, then
the first thing cannot happen later than the second', 'The
more money you have, the less an extra dollar matters to you',
'Everybody prefers more of what they like to less of it' and so on.
But Euclid was the inspiration for the idea that such things
might be welded into a system of physics or economics or ethics.

Since the advent of the 'new maths', schoolchildren are not
taught geometry in the traditional axiomatic fashion. Today's
children are, therefore, denied the sort of intellectual experience
which so delighted Hobbes, Einstein and countless others.

As well as the sceptical infinite regress of proofs, which
rationalists stop at self-evident axioms, there was the sceptical
infinite regress of definitions. Some rationalists stopped this
regress, too, by appeal to the 'natural light of reason': reason
enables us to grasp certain concepts independently of experience. Again, Euclid was the chief inspiration for this view.
Because of the regress, Euclid operates with certain undefined
or primitive terms, such as 'point' or 'line' or 'plane'. Could
the meanings of these terms be learned from experience?
Rationalists think not, because the terms stand for things which
are not accessible to the senses at all. A geometrical point takes
up no room, and a geometrical line has no width. The 'points'
and 'lines' we draw on paper or on blackboards are relatively
small but extended blobs, and relatively thin and elongated
worms – more or less adequate approximations to proper
geometrical points and lines. I can only recognise one blob or
worm as a better approximation than another blob or worm to
a genuine point or line, because I am in possession of the
geometrical concepts of a point and line. The source of these
latter concepts, by which we judge what we experience, cannot

be experience. The point was extended to other concepts which do not stand for experienced items: God, justice, substance. These are all innate concepts or innate ideas, meaning that pure reason yields them.

Empiricists were not convinced, and devoted much energy to showing that all concepts or ideas were derived from experience. They postulated a faculty of abstraction: we perceive bigger and smaller blobs, abstract from size, and arrive at the concept of a geometrical point; we perceive limited and imperfect beings, abstract from the limitations and imperfections, and arrive at the concept of God. Empiricists like Locke also attacked the theory of innate ideas, which Locke took to be the absurd view that certain ideas (geometrical point, God, substance) are present to and in the mind of a new-born baby. Rationalists did not hold this absurd view.

Concepts and truths are to be distinguished. One can think that experience is the source of all concepts and all truths (as radical empiricists did). One can think that experience is the source of all concepts but not of all truths (as Locke did). One can think that experience is the source of all truths but not of all concepts (as Einstein did). One can think that experience is the source neither of all concepts nor of all truths (as Plato and Descartes did). The real dispute between the rationalists and the empiricists concerned the truths and the knowledge, not the concepts in which it was expressed. Let us, therefore, focus on the real dispute.

WHY MATHEMATICAL KNOWLEDGE IS A PROBLEM FOR EMPIRICISTS

While mathematical knowledge was the chief inspiration for the rationalists, it was a thorn in the flesh of the empiricists. In order to see the difficulties the empiricists had with mathematics, it is useful to begin with a pair of distinctions which were first sharply formulated by the German philosopher Immanuel Kant. The first distinction is that between a priori and a posteriori knowledge: a priori knowledge is that which can be gained independently of experience, a posteriori knowledge is that which can only be gained from experience. Two comments on the definition of a priori knowledge are necessary. First, a piece of knowledge can be a priori even though as a matter of psychological fact some person gained this knowledge as a result of experience – if the knowledge could have been obtained independently of experience, then it is a priori. Thus a person may as a matter of psychological fact come to believe that seven plus five equal twelve by counting objects, that is, as a result of experience. But if this truth can be known independently of experience, it remains an a priori truth. Second, a piece of a priori knowledge may depend upon a person's grasp of language, and that person may have learned language from experience. But if a person, having learned a language, can come to know a truth without any further experience, then that truth is known a priori.

Kant's first distinction is an epistemological distinction, a distinction between two types of knowledge. The second distinction is logical or semantical: it is the distinction between analytic and synthetic truths. (This is a distinction which has, in effect, already surfaced several times in our discussions.) Analytic truths are traditionally defined as those which are true by virtue of the meanings of the words they contain. Kant gave a special case of this same idea: a statement is analytic if its predicate is 'contained in' its subject. The favourite example, 'All bachelors are unmarried', conforms to both these accounts: once we understand the subject to mean 'unmarried men', we see that its predicate 'unmarried' is contained in it as a part. ('Contained in' must be interpreted broadly to include 'is the same as', so that 'All bachelors are bachelors' also qualifies as analytic.) This Kantian account, apart from its metaphorical nature, is restricted to subject–predicate propositions. But not all propositions are subject–predicate propositions. Perhaps because he realised this, Kant also gave another account of analyticity: a truth is analytic if its truth follows from the law of contradiction alone. We can take this to mean that a truth is analytic if its negation involves a contradiction (that is, if it can be proved by *reductio ad absurdum*). We can define synthetic truths simply as truths which are not analytic.

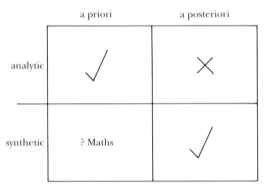

Figure 8. Kant's box

We can also speak of analytic and non-analytic falsehoods, defined in ways that are obvious given the foregoing. In this way the realm of the analytic in general is those statements whose truth or falsehood follows from the meanings of the words they contain. In what follows, as is customary, a statement described as analytic will be being described as analytically true.

These two distinctions, one epistemological and the other logical, give us four possibilities which can be set out in Kant's box (see Figure 8). Which of the four compartments of Kant's box are empty and which not? Empiricists and rationalists are agreed that the analytic a posteriori compartment is empty: if a statement's truth (or falsity) follows from the meanings of the words it contains, then we need not learn from experience whether or not it is true (or false). Empiricists and rationalists are also agreed that the analytic a priori compartment is not empty: analytic truths are knowable independently of ex-perience. Empiricists and rationalists are also agreed (though this is less obvious) that the synthetic a posteriori compartment is not empty. Empiricists think that all synthetic knowledge is a posteriori. Most rationalists, without accepting this universal claim, concede that some synthetic knowledge is a posteriori: even the most rabid rationalist concedes that the only way to find out how many hairs I have on my head at the moment is to count them. (The rabid rationalist might well say, however, that the synthetic a posteriori compartment does not really contain knowledge but only mere beliefs, since everything in it is uncertain.)

The issue comes down to the synthetic a priori compartment. The fundamental thesis of empiricism is that it is empty. Empiricists are adamant about a co-extensiveness thesis: the analytical is co-extensive with the a priori, or equivalently, the synthetic is co-extensive with the a posteriori. (Hume insisted upon it in his discussions of the general principle of induction: such a principle must either be analytic and knowable a priori, or synthetic and knowable a posteriori. Hume argued, as we have seen, that it was neither.) The fundamental thesis of rationalism, on the other hand, is that synthetic a priori knowledge exists. This is what Einstein was talking about when he talked of 'certain knowledge of the objects of experience by means of pure thinking'. The rationalist paradigm is mathematical knowledge in general, and Euclidean geometry in particular.

As well as the epistemological and logical distinctions we have discussed, there is a metaphysical distinction between necessary and contingent truths. Contingent truths are true in virtue of the way the world happens to be; had the world been otherwise, they would be false; or to put it another way, though true of the actual world they are false of some other possible world. Necessary truths are true no matter how the world happens to be; had the world been otherwise, they would still be true; or to put it another way, they are true of all possible worlds.

Empiricists tend to take a dim view of this third distinction, regarding it as no more than a confusing verbal variant on the logical distinction between analytic and synthetic truths. If empiricists traffic in the distinction at all, it is only to extend their co-extensiveness thesis: the analytic is co-extensive with the a priori and with the necessary. The rationalist view is less straightforward. They regard the analytic a priori as necessary, and the synthetic a posteriori as contingent. But is the synthetic a priori necessary or contingent? Kant regarded it as contingent (I think); others (such as Leibniz) regarded it as necessary. (The empiricist's extended co-extensiveness thesis has come under heavy attack in recent times from those who think there are a priori contingencies as well as a posteriori necessities. To discuss that attack would take us too far afield.)

What are the empiricists to make of the rationalist paradigm, mathematical knowledge? Given their co-extensiveness thesis, there are only two things they can make of it: they must locate it either in the analytic a priori compartment of Kant's box, or in the synthetic a posteriori compartment. Neither view is plausible.

It is, of course, trivial that some mathematical statements are analytic and a priori: 'All prime numbers are numbers' and 'Two is identical to two' seem to be examples. But is it plausible to suppose that they all are? Statements like '$7+5=12$' or Pythagoras' theorem or 'There is no biggest prime number' do not seem to be true by virtue of the meanings of the words they contain. A person can understand these statements perfectly well, and hence know what the words in them mean, without knowing whether or not they are true. In arithmetic, the simplest mathematical theory, there are famous unsolved problems which have been known for centuries and which are quite simple to state. Goldbach's conjecture says that every even number is the sum of two prime numbers. The twin primes conjecture says that there are infinitely many 'twin primes', that is, pairs of prime numbers the second of which is two bigger than the first. Arithmeticians have not been able to prove or disprove either of these conjectures, despite centuries of effort. Arithmeticians know perfectly well what these statements mean – how else could they set about trying to prove or disprove them? It is implausible to think that they are either analytically true or analytically false, but we have not yet found out which.

Known truths in mathematics do not seem to be analytic either. Mathematicians know that there is no biggest prime number (this is not an unsolved problem). But they know this, not by inspecting the meanings of the words, but by proving it. Nor does any contradiction seem to arise if we assume the negation of such a proven statement (or theorem). Here a subtle point has to be made. It is true that a mathematician might give a *reductio* proof of some theorem. But (and this is the subtle point) in deriving a contradiction from the negation of the theorem, the mathematician would appeal to other mathematical principles as premises. Careful analysis of all such proofs in arithmetic, say, will reveal that a small number of principles need to be assumed so that we can prove (either directly or by *reductio*) the theorems of arithmetic. These principles are, in effect, the axioms of arithmetic. So what can be shown is that the negation of '$7+5=12$' or 'There is no biggest prime number' leads to a contradiction given the axioms of arithmetic. (This is, in effect, just to show that the statements '$7+5=12$' and 'There is no biggest prime number' follow from the axioms of arithmetic.) And similarly for statements from other mathematical theories than arithmetic. Such mathematical propositions cannot be demonstrated from the law of contradiction alone: you cannot deduce contradictions from their negations by themselves. In short, they are not analytic truths.

The only way empiricists can resist this conclusion is to say that mathematical axioms themselves are analytic, so that anything proved from them (directly or by *reductio*) is also analytic. They might add that analytic truths need not be trivial or obvious truths, since they can get quite complicated. This is extremely implausible. Many mathematical axioms do not seem to be analytic. None of them can be proved by *reductio*, because none of them are proved at all, since they are axioms.

The second horn of the empiricist dilemma is to try to locate mathematics in the synthetic a posteriori compartment of Kant's box. The most famous advocate of this approach was John Stuart Mill. Mill said that (non-analytic) mathematical truths were 'generalisations from experience'. He added that we were apt to lose sight of this fact because mathematics contains some of our 'first and most familiar' generalisations from experience. Mill did not, of course, deny that having learned some mathematical truths from experience, mathematicians can prove other mathematical truths from them. But we cannot prove all mathematical truths from other mathematical truths, on pain of infinite regress. The chain of mathematical proofs must come to an end with mathematical truths which are proved, not from other mathematical truths, but from experience. Mathematical axioms must be generalisations from experience (Mill 1843, II: v–vi).

Kant had already criticised and rejected this view. Kant took Hume to have shown, in his critique of inductive reasoning, that no conclusion reached by inductive generalisation could be absolutely certain. So if '2 + 2 = 4' or 'The angles of any triangle add up to 180°' were the conclusions of inductive generalisations, as Mill was to maintain, then we would have to admit that we are not absolutely sure of their truth. But, Kant insisted, we are sure of their truth, and so they cannot be mere inductive generalisations.

Mill rejected this argument because he rejected Hume's critique of inductive generalisation. Mill validated inductive generalisation by appeal to the general inductive principle that nature is uniform. And he claimed that we know that principle to be true because it is also one of our 'first and most familiar generalisations from experience'. Mill took the first step down Hume's infinite regress of inductive principles, without seeming to realise that a regress threatened.

We can reinforce Kant's argument with a different one. It is a feature of truths known a posteriori that, no matter how certain we are of their truth, we can at least imagine how we might learn from experience that they are false. With such statements we can, in other words, specify a possible state of affairs which is such that, if we were to encounter it, we would regard the statement in question as having been falsified. I think it true that all ravens are black. I am, we can suppose, absolutely certain that it is true. (I am not certain of its truth because I think it analytic, because I think that being black is part of the 'definition' of the word 'raven'. We are here dealing with synthetic truths.) But certain as I am, I can tell you what would make me give up my belief – for example, seeing a pink raven fly in through the window. I am certain that this will not happen, but I have to concede that it might, that it is possible.

Can we do the same with '2 + 2 = 4' or 'The angles of any triangle add up to 180°'? People have tried, but the stories they tell are not plausible ones. I count two rabbits, and two more, put them all together, wait a year, and – lo and behold – I do not have four rabbits but hundreds of them. Or I count two drops of water, and two more, put them all together, and lo and behold, I do not have four drops of water but one big drop. Even Mill dismissed such 'possible refutations' of '2 + 2 = 4' as ridiculous misunderstandings: '2 + 2 = 4' is not a generalisation about what will happen if you count two things, and two more, then physically amalgamate them, then perhaps wait a while, and then count what you have. Nor do those physicists who talk about types of sub-atomic particles which mutually annihilate one another if brought together think that when this happens one and one had failed to equal two – rather, they say that some particles have disappeared.

Or consider a geometrical example. (This, it will emerge in due course, is not merely to labour the point.) What would be a possible refutation of 'The angles of any triangle add up to 180°'? We would have to find a triangle, measure its angles, and find that they do not add up to 180°. Now a triangle is formed by three intersecting straight lines. So to find a triangle, I have first to find three intersecting straight lines. Let us set aside worries about geometrical straight lines being inaccessible to the senses at all. Geometrical optics tells us that light travels in straight lines in homogeneous media. So we can imagine forming a 'light triangle', say by having three flashlights arranged in such a way that at each location of a flashlight the other two are visible. So at each location of a flashlight, we could measure the angle between the other two lights. If we then add up these angles, we have the sum of the angles in our 'light triangle'. Suppose the angles add up to 190°. Have we here imagined refuting our geometrical proposition?

Of course not. We would say that our measurement must have been wrong. Or we would say that the medium through which the light-rays from our flashlights travelled was not homogenous after all. And if neither of these would work, we would be forced to pin the blame on geometrical optics, and say that light does not always travel in straight lines in homogenous media. What we would never do is pin the blame on geometry.

It is worth dwelling on the logical situation here. Euclid gives us our geometrical proposition. Geometrical optics tells us that light travels in straight lines. These two together tell us that the angles of any 'light triangle' add up to 180°, as follows:

Euclid: The angles of any triangle add up to 180°.
Geometrical optics: Light travels in straight lines.
Conclusion: The angles of any 'light triangle' add up to 180°.

(Here, of course, I simplify by omitting qualifications about homogeneity of media.) Now our imagined measurements, supposing they are correct, certainly refute the conclusion of this argument. If we reject that conclusion, then we must also reject one of the premises. And what we have been saying is that we would not hesitate to pin the blame upon geometrical optics.

But why? The answer, in a nutshell, is that we need Euclid, not just in optics, but in the sciences generally, not to mention everyday life. To renounce Euclid would be to throw the whole of our knowledge into confusion, by leaving us without geometry. In contrast, giving up the idea that light travels in straight lines means that we only have to modify our optics. That would be serious but it would not be catastrophic. So while it is logically possible to pin the blame on Euclid, as our little argument shows, it is not really practically possible. One might say that Euclid is practically irrefutable or practically a priori.

The preceding argument tacitly operated with a new account of the a priori/a posteriori distinction. We tacitly assumed that a posteriori knowledge, rather than being knowledge which can be gained from (possible) experience, is knowledge which can be refuted by (possible) experience. It was because Euclid was (practically) irrefutable by experience that we said it was (practically) a priori. It is important to realise that the irrefutable/refutable distinction, like the old a priori/a posteriori distinction, is an epistemological distinction. There is no suggestion that the synthetic is to be identified with the refutable, still less that the metaphysical category of the contingent is to be identified with the refutable. To get these further claims, we need the empiricist co-extensiveness thesis as well.

Our little argument shows something else. It shows the way in which Euclidean geometry (and mathematics in general) is useful to us. Both premises of that little argument are needed to obtain its conclusion: geometrical optics alone could not give us the conclusion about the angles of light triangles, we need Euclid's proposition, too. If we omit the Euclidean proposition, the argument obviously becomes invalid. But if the Euclidean proposition were analytic, it could be omitted without affecting the validity of the argument. So as well as being 'practically a priori' our Euclidean proposition is synthetic: we need it to get substantive conclusions about the world (in our little example, about 'light triangles'). In fact, we use mathematical truths every day of our lives, and extremely useful truths they are. For example, how without knowing arithmetic could we check that we have been given the correct change at the grocery store? It is hard to see how mere analytic truths could be so useful to us. Mathematics must be synthetic in order to play the important role in everyday life and in the sciences that it does play.

So the empiricist dilemma is hopeless. Neither of the two possible empiricist theories of mathematics seems even slightly plausible. Perhaps the rationalist dream of synthetic a priori knowledge is not so foolish after all.

THREE SCEPTICAL OBJECTIONS

We have talked of the Euclidean achievement, of the rationalist dream of extending it to other spheres and of the difficulties empiricists had in accommodating it. What can the sceptic say of all this?

The most important sceptical objection strikes at the heart of the rationalist (or Euclidean) position. Rationalists say that their axioms are known to be true because they are 'self-evident', because their truth is obvious or indubitable to the 'natural light of reason', because (anticipating the view of Descartes) they are 'clearly and distinctly perceived to be true'. But what guarantee has the rationalist that a falsehood will not be self-evident, obvious, indubitable, clearly and distinctly perceived? The rationalist needs to establish that self-evidence (or whatever) guarantees truth. And this, the sceptic claims, cannot be established.

The basic objection can be expressed in various ways and supported by various considerations. Sceptics like to support it by pointing to things that our ancestors thought self-evident or obviously true, but which we think false ('The earth is flat' and 'The whole is greater than the part' are favourite examples). They also support it by pointing to extreme cases which seem entirely possible: what if A finds it self-evident that P, while B finds it self-evident that not-P? (For a possible example, see p. 213). A and B cannot both be right – so self-evidence cannot guarantee truth. How can the rationalist show that extreme cases of this type are impossible?

A second sceptical objection concerns the rationalist notion of proof. The rationalist claim was that truths which are not self-evident at first sight can be shown to be self-evidently true by proving them from self-evident axioms. But errors of reasoning are possible, especially where the trains of demonstration are long. If such an error occurs, we may actually 'prove' or 'demonstrate' a falsehood. Hence some uncertainty must surround any 'demonstrated' truth. Even if we were to grant that the axioms are known for certain, the same honorific cannot be extended to the theorems.

A third sceptical objection concerns the rationalist dream of extending the Euclidean project. What guarantee is there that this can be done? It is just a pious hope, says the sceptic, that self-evident axioms will be found which will be adequate to establish the truths of physics or ethics or political science. (Attempts to extend the Euclidean project beyond mathematics have been widespread and notoriously unsuccessful: Spinoza's *Ethics* is not a patch on Euclid's *Elements* in terms of logical rigour.)

The most important of these objections is the first one. To appreciate its force, let us consider a possible response to it. The sceptic claims that it is possible for one person to find some proposition self-evident (or obvious or indubitable) while another person finds the negation of that proposition self-evident (or obvious or indubitable). It may be objected that this is to misunderstand the nature of self-evidence. The sceptic is assuming that a proposition is not self-evident in itself, but only self-evident to some person or persons. The sceptic is regarding self-evidence as a psychological or epistemological relation which certain propositions bear to certain people. This is how she can suppose that a proposition might bear the relation to one person and not to another. But this is a misunderstanding: self-evidence is an intrinsic feature of some propositions, and is quite independent of what people think. Similarly, to say that a proposition is indubitable is not to say that this or that person cannot as a matter of psychological fact bring herself to doubt it. Rather, it is to say that as well as being true the proposition has a further feature – indubitability. It makes as little sense to speak of a proposition being self-evident or indubitable for one person and not for another, as it makes to speak of a proposition being true for one person and not for another. For self-evidence and indubitability, like truth, are intrinsic features of propositions.

How might the sceptic respond to this? She might first point out that if self-evidence or indubitability are intrinsic features of propositions, not to be analysed in relation to human knowers, then they are wholly mysterious features. What feature must a true proposition have, over and above being true, to qualify as self-evident or indubitable? (Here we assume that self-evidence or indubitability are not the same as truth. To deny this is to go in for a self-evidence or indubitability theory of truth. These and other theories of truth will be discussed in Chapter 14.) One answer to this question can be couched in terms of the 'ideally rational inquirer'. A proposition is self-evidently true, not if you or I find it obvious, but if an 'ideally rational inquirer' would find it obvious. A proposition is indubitably true, not if you or I cannot doubt it, but if an 'ideally rational inquirer' could not doubt it. And who is an 'ideally rational inquirer'? The favourite candidate is God.

But our problem is whether humans can know anything by pure reason, not whether God can. If rationalism is to be a positive theory of human knowledge, then it must traffic in self-evidence and the rest as humans see them, not as God sees them.

Of course, if truth is made a defining condition of self-evidence or indubitability, then the sceptic cannot talk coherently of a false proposition being self-evident or indubitable to a person. The sceptic must now talk of a false proposition appearing self-evident or indubitable to a person. Once the sceptic talks this way, her original arguments retain all their force.

Actually, some rationalist philosophers do not consistently make self-evidence (or indubitability or obviousness) mysterious intrinsic features of propositions akin to truth and involving it. Instead, they try to confuse the sceptic by flitting backwards and forwards between the intrinsic conception and the relational one. To beat the sceptic they draw attention to the undisputed psychological fact that people occasionally find certain propositions self-evident or obvious. The sceptic asks for a guarantee that no falsehood will be found self-evident. Straightaway she is told that it is absurd and contradictory to suppose that a proposition might be self-evident and false or indubitable and false. And after the sceptic has withdrawn in confusion, they fall back into the relational conception again, since only this can give them the certainty that they need. But the sceptic should not withdraw in confusion. She should expose this verbal game for what it is.

CHAPTER 11

Rationalism defended: Descartes

An elaborate defence of the rationalist theory of knowledge was provided by René Descartes (1596–1650). His impetus for this was not purely philosophical. In defending rationalism, Descartes was also seeking to defend the great contributions which he had made to mathematics and the sciences. Like many rationalists, he admired mathematics and sought to model all knowledge upon it. Unlike many rationalists, Descartes contributed to mathematics as well as admiring it. He is an inventor of analytic geometry, in which geometrical entities such as lines and curves are represented by algebraic equations, and in which geometric problems can then be solved by algebraic means. Cartesian co-ordinates, which make possible the algebraic representation of geometric entities, are named after him. Armed with analytic geometry, Descartes was able to solve geometrical problems that had lain unsolved for centuries. He also made important contributions to other sciences. He gave the first clear formulation of the law of inertia. He proposed a law of the conservation of motion, akin to the Newtonian law of conservation of momentum, and the first conservation law ever proposed. He discovered the law of refraction of light and used it to explain rainbows (it also explains our old friend, the bent oar in water). He wrote a pioneering work, which was not published in his lifetime, on physiology.

Descartes was, then, an important mathematician and scientist as well as an important philosopher. He would not have understood or accepted the distinctions implicit in saying this – for him philosophy, mathematics and the sciences were inextricably linked. His most famous work, *Discourse on the Method of Rightly Conducting the Reason and Seeking for Truth in the Sciences*, was first published (in 1637) as a sort of preface to three scientific books (*Dioptrics, Meteors, Geometry*). Descartes sets out his rationalist method, then he puts it into practice. Since then the *Discourse on Method* has been torn from the mathematical and scientific context in which it was written, and presented to generations of philosophy students as if it were a work of 'pure philosophy'. I shall, perforce, be guilty of the same thing. However, one can criticise Descartes's theory of knowledge (as I will), while applauding his contributions to knowledge (which I do). Descartes attempts to defeat scepticism in order to preserve his own contributions to knowledge. But we can see at the outset that something must be wrong somewhere with the Cartesian method – for Descartes proves too much. He claimed to have proved that his soul is distinct from his body, that his soul is immortal, that God exists, that there is no empty space, that light travels instantaneously from one place to another, and many other things. Since some of these things are false, and others doubtful at best, Descartes's claim cannot be right. The question is, where does he go wrong?

SYSTEMATIC DOUBT AND THE *COGITO*

Descartes's first philosophical work was a little book called *Rules for the Direction of the Mind*, which was never finished and never published in his lifetime (see 1984, 1: 9–77). In it he describes the method he has used in making his mathematical discoveries. It is a thoroughly Euclidean method. We start with a problem, a statement whose truth or falsehood we do not know. We 'split' the problem up into simpler and simpler 'parts', continuing to do so until we reach simple truths which are self-evident to our faculty of intuition. These simple truths are our Euclidean axioms and we discover them by this process of analysis. (Descartes claims, with some justice, that Euclid and the Greek geometers kept this process of analysis, by which axioms are discovered, a secret.) Having found our axioms, we retrace our steps and solve our problem, either by proving that the statement with which we started is true or by proving that it is false. This is called the synthesis.

Described in the abstract like this, the method of analysis and synthesis seems alternately trite and mysterious. The best way to appreciate it is to see it in action. The best example I know of the method in action is Euler's proof of the Descartes–Euler conjecture, as described at the outset of Imre Lakatos's *Proofs and Refutations*. A polyhedron is a solid whose faces are polygons, such as a cube or pyramid. (In Chapter 10, p. 179, we encountered Euclid's proof that there are only five perfect solids or regular polyhedra.) The Descartes–Euler conjecture (the problem) is that for all polyhedra the number of vertices ('points') V, minus the number of edges E, plus the number of faces F, is equal to 2 – or for short, $V - E + F = 2$. This holds for all the regular polyhedra – the reader may wish to check the two simplest, the cube and the regular pyramid. Euler's proof of this conjecture, by analysis and synthesis, is as follows:

Let us imagine the polyhedron to be hollow, with a surface made of thin rubber. If we cut out one of the faces, we can stretch the remaining surface flat on the blackboard, without tearing it. The faces and edges will be deformed, the edges may become curved, but V and E will not alter, so that if and only if $V - E + F = 2$ for the original polyhedron, $V - E + F = 1$ for this flat network – remember that we have removed one face. Now we triangulate our map. We draw (possibly curvilinear) diagonals in those (possibly curvilinear) polygons which are not already (possibly curvilinear) triangles. By drawing each diagonal we increase both E and F by one, so that the total $V - E + F$ will not be altered ... From the triangulated network we now remove the triangles one by one. To remove a triangle we either remove an edge – upon which one face and one edge disappear, or we remove two edges and a vertex – upon which one face, two edges and one vertex disappear. Thus if $V - E + F = 1$ before a triangle is removed, it remains so after the triangle is removed. At the end of this procedure we get a single triangle. For this $V - E + F = 1$ holds true. Thus we have proved our conjecture. (Lakatos 1976: 7–8)

Only the analysis is given here, resulting in the 'axiom' that for a single triangle $V - E + F = 1$. The synthesis reverses the process described, building up various polyhedra which (when the face which was removed first is restored) satisfy $V - E + F = 2$.

(In case you are wondering whether the Descartes–Euler conjecture holds for all polyhedra, I should tell you that it does not. In which case you will also be wondering how mathematicians can 'prove' a falsehood. All this, and more, is explained in Lakatos's fascinating and funny book, which takes the form of a classroom dialogue between the teacher, who proposes the above 'proof', and some very clever students who refute it.)

Returning to Descartes, in the *Rules for the Direction of the Mind* he raises and tries to answer the second sceptical objection to rationalism, the objection that we may make logical errors in proving theorems from axioms. Descartes's answer is that by going over the proof again and again, we can come to see that the axioms yield the theorem in a single act of intuition, just as we see that the axioms are true in single acts of intuition. There is some sense in this. When we suspect an error of reasoning the thing to do is to go over the reasoning again and again, until we have a direct (or more direct) 'intuition' that if our assumptions are correct so is the theorem we get from them. But this answer serves only to highlight the first sceptical objection to rationalism, the objection that we can never rely upon intellectual 'intuition' in the first place. Descartes shows that if we can rely upon intuition regarding the axioms, then there is no special problem regarding the proofs. But can we rely upon intuition regarding the axioms? I suspect that Descartes left his *Rules for the Direction of the Mind* unfinished because he saw this objection and did not yet know how to answer it.

He tries to answer it in his next book, the *Discourse on Method*. He begins by reviewing the various branches of learning and his reactions to them:

I knew that…oratory has incomparable powers and beauties; that poetry has quite ravishing delicacy and sweetness; that mathematics contains some very subtle devices which serve as much to satisfy the curious as to further all the arts and lessen man's labours; that writings on morals contain many very useful teachings and exhortations to virtue; that theology instructs us how to reach heaven; that philosophy gives us the means of speaking plausibly about any subject and of winning the admiration of the less learned. (*Discourse*, Part 1; 1984, 1: 112)

Cautionary words for students of philosophy! The trouble is, Descartes continues, that the sceptic casts doubt on the securest things in all branches of learning. He resolves to remedy the situation.

He does this, curiously, by adopting the method of systematic doubt. He becomes an extreme sceptic and resolves to reject as false anything which he finds the least bit doubtful. His aim is to show that we have some knowledge which cannot be shaken by any of the sceptic's arguments. Having found a secure starting-point, he hopes to retrace his steps and show that other things he had previously doubted and rejected as false could be shown to be true also. He likens his stock of beliefs to a basket of apples, some of which are rotten (false), all of which are infected with the suspicion of being rotten (false). We must empty the basket, examine the apples one by one, rejecting all the suspicious ones, until we find an apple that we know to be sound. Then using this sound apple as a touchstone, we can show that other previously suspect apples are also sound. The upshot will be a basket of apples (stock of beliefs) which may be less full than the one we started with, but which will contain only sound apples (justified true beliefs).

So Descartes adopts the mantle of an extreme sceptic, and some of the reasons to doubt things that he invokes are quite incredible:

Thus, because our senses sometimes deceive us, I decided to suppose that nothing was such as they led us to imagine. And since there are men who make mistakes in reasoning, committing logical fallacies concerning the simplest questions in geometry, and because I judged that I was as prone to error as anyone else, I rejected as unsound all the arguments I had previously taken as demonstrative proofs. Lastly, considering that the very thoughts we have while awake may also occur while we sleep without any of them being at that time true, I resolved to pretend that all the things that had ever entered my mind were no more true than the illusions of my dreams.

Radical scepticism indeed! Descartes adds that whenever there is a conflict of opinion, we should doubt both sides of the question. (So we should doubt that the earth is round because a flat-earth society still exists!) It might seem that nothing could survive the fires of so radical a scepticism. Descartes thinks otherwise:

> But immediately I noticed that while I was trying thus to think everything false, it was necessary that I, who was thinking this, was something. And observing that this truth '*I am thinking, therefore I exist*' was so firm and sure that all the most extravagant suppositions of the sceptics were incapable of shaking it, I decided that I could accept it without scruple as the first principle of the philosophy I was seeking. (*Discourse*, Part IV; 1984, I: 127)

Thus Descartes arrives at the famous *Cogito, ergo sum* (I think, therefore I am). Subsequent philosophers have spilled much ink on the *Cogito*. Some ask whether it is a single statement, or an argument from the premise 'I think' to the conclusion 'I am' (or 'I exist'). Descartes would have refused the question, given his view that even a long train of reasoning or arguing from a premise to a conclusion can be grasped in a single act of intuition just as a single statement can. Others object that neither 'I think' nor 'I exist' (where the 'I' refers to Descartes) is a necessary truth, since it is a contingent fact that Descartes thought and existed. Quite so. But this is no objection, because the rationalist need not think (as the empiricists who make this objection think) that synthetic a priori truths are all necessary. Others object that there is nothing special about the *Cogito*: 'I walk, therefore I exist' or 'I scratch my ear, therefore I exist' will do just as well. To which Descartes correctly replies that to walk or scratch your ear you must have a body, that the sceptical critique of the senses makes it doubtful that you have a body, and that it is therefore also doubtful that you walk or scratch your ear. There is no doubt that you might think that you are walking or scratching your ear – but this leads back to the *Cogito*. You cannot doubt that you think (whatever it is that you are thinking, including thinking that you are walking), for thinking includes all mental activity, including doubting.

Is there any good sceptical objection to Descartes's claim that he knows for certain that the *Cogito* is true? There is really only one objection, due to Bertrand Russell (1912: 19 or 1927: 171–3), which seems bizarre but which is actually of some importance. Russell objects to the use of the word 'I' in 'I think', because it assumes that there is an *I*, a single self which does all the thinking. All that Descartes is entitled to assume, all that he knows for certain, is 'There are thoughts' or 'Thinking is now going on'. This is of some importance because Descartes reads a lot into the little word 'I'. He asks what this *I* is, and answers 'a thinking substance'. He argues that since he cannot doubt that this thinking substance exists, while he can doubt that his body exists, his mind (the thinking substance) must be different from his body and able to exist without it. And thus, out of the little word 'I', Descartes spins a metaphysical theory known as Cartesian mind–body dualism.

Our chief concerns are epistemic rather than metaphysical. So, with Russellian caveats about how much is to be read into the term 'I', let us press on. The sceptic must grant Descartes his *Cogito*. She can hardly persuade someone that he does not exist – to be persuaded he must exist. A confused person may say 'I do not exist' – but the act of saying this 'contradicts' what is said (compare other self-refuting pronouncements like 'I never say anything'). If this is right, then Descartes has succeeded in refuting the extreme sceptical view that nothing at all can be known for certain. (Russellian caveats about the 'I' do not alter this verdict: if 'there are thoughts' is known for certain, then something is known for certain.) This victory is achieved at a price. Like the empiricists and their retreat into idea-ism, the price is a retreat into the subject.

Descartes would not agree. For him the *Cogito* was only the beginning, only the first of many sound apples or bits of certainty. He is aware that knowing 'I think, therefore I am' is not knowing much, and he tries to go further. Scepticism really gets a grip when Descartes tries to establish other truths on the basis of the *Cogito*. He continues:

After this I considered in general what is required of a proposition in order for it to be true and certain; for since I had just found one that I knew to be such, I thought that I ought to know what this certainty consists in. I observed that there is nothing at all in the proposition '*I am thinking, therefore I exist*' to assure me that I am speaking the truth, except that I see very clearly that in order to think it is necessary to exist. So I decided that I could take it as a general rule that the things we conceive very clearly and very distinctly are all true. (*Discourse*, Part IV; 1984, I: 127)

Here we get Descartes's general rationalist criterion of truth: anything clearly and distinctly conceived is true. It is a variant on the rationalist or Euclidean idea that anything self-evident is true.

Sceptical worries crowd in upon us. For one thing, Descartes seems to arrive at this general criterion by arguing thus: 'The *Cogito* is clearly and distinctly conceived and true and certain. Therefore, *anything* clearly and distinctly conceived is true and certain.' This is a patently invalid inductive argument. Can Descartes guarantee that he will never clearly and distinctly conceive a falsehood? Can he guarantee that what he clearly and distinctly conceives will be clearly and distinctly conceived by the next person? Can he rule out the possibility that A clearly and distinctly conceives that P, while B clearly and distinctly conceives that not-P?

These old sceptical worries are heightened by Descartes's immediate admission that 'there is some difficulty in ascertaining which [things] are those that we distinctly conceive'. This suggests that we might erroneously think that we clearly and distinctly conceive something when we do not. It suggests that clarity and distinctness are not a feature of our conceivings of things but rather a feature of the things conceived, a feature which incorporates their truth (to use a distinction introduced at the end of the last chapter). If so, sceptical worries remain but must be differently expressed. One cannot now clearly and distinctly conceive a falsehood, since clarity and distinctness entail truth. One can mistakenly think that you clearly and distinctly conceive something which you do not because it is a falsehood.

In the *Discourse* Descartes does not raise or answer this old sceptical objection to his new-found criterion of truth. Instead, he uses that criterion to establish (or so he thinks) further metaphysical truths: the difference between the soul and the body, the immortality of the soul, the existence of other minds, the existence of God, the existence of the physical world and its true geometrical nature, and so forth. However, in his next work *Meditations on First Philosophy*, published in 1641, Descartes shows that he is aware of such objections and he tries to answer them – or so I believe. (What follows is one interpretation of the *Meditations* and it is not the only one. I will be mentioning the chief exegetical issue.)

METAPHYSICAL DOUBT AND THE EVIL GENIUS

In the *Meditations* Descartes employs the method of systematic doubt once again. But he introduces a new and justly famous source of doubt, the hypothesis of the evil genius. He imagines that he has been created not by the supremely good god that good catholics like Descartes believe in, but by 'an evil genius, as clever and deceitful as he is powerful, who has directed his entire effort to misleading me'. This blighter feeds Descartes with 'perceptions' of an external world populated with tables and chairs, other people, animals and so forth – all is illusion and there is no such external world. This blighter also feeds Descartes with 'perceptions' of his own body, including the 'bodily sensations' – this is all illusion, too, and Descartes has no body. (In case you are thinking that Descartes's evil genius is Bishop Berkeley's benevolent deity, I think you are right.) Can the hypothesis of the evil genius cast a blight on everything? No:

> But there is a deceiver of supreme power and cunning, who is deliberately and constantly deceiving me. In that case I too undoubtedly exist, if he is deceiving me; and let him deceive me as much as he can, he will never bring it about that I am nothing so long as I think that I am something. So... I must finally conclude that this proposition, *I am, I exist*, is necessarily true whenever it is put forward by me or conceived in my mind. (*Second Meditation*, 1984: 17)

The *Cogito* survives even this extreme doubt. Descartes proceeds as before. What is this *I*? – A thinking substance. What is special about the *Cogito*? – That it is clearly and distinctly perceived. How to get beyond it? Here there is a new caution:

I am certain that I am a thinking thing. Do I not therefore also know what is required for my being certain about anything? In this first item of knowledge there is simply a clear and distinct perception of what I am asserting; this would not be enough to make me certain of the truth of the matter if it could ever turn out that something which I perceived with such clarity and distinctness was false. So I now seem to be able to lay it down as a general rule that whatever I perceive very clearly and distinctly is true. (*Third Meditation*, 1984: 24)

Once again we have the general criterion of truth. But now Descartes says only 'I now *seem* to be able to lay it down as a general rule'.

The caution is prompted by the thought that an evil genius might make Descartes clearly and distinctly perceive something false. He considers an extreme case, his clear and distinct perception that two plus three make five. For Descartes, this is an 'eternal truth', one whose denial involves a contradiction. Surely he knows this for certain – not even a deceiving God can bring it about that two plus three do not make five:

For whether I be awake or asleep, two and three added together are five, and a square has no more than four sides. It seems impossible that such transparent truths should incur any suspicion of being false.

And yet firmly rooted in my mind is the long-standing opinion that there is an omnipotent God who made me the kind of creature that I am. How do I know that he has not brought it about that there is no earth, no sky, no extended thing, no shape, no size, no place, while at the same time ensuring that all these things appear to me to exist just as they do now? What is more, since I sometimes believe that others go astray in cases where they think they have the most perfect knowledge, may I not similarly go wrong every time I add two and three or count the sides of a square, or in some even simpler matter, if that is imaginable? (*First Meditation*, 1984: 14)

Let us be clear about what Descartes is imagining here. He is not supposing that an evil genius or deceiving deity can make an eternal truth false, bring it about that two plus three do not make five or that a square does not have four sides. There is a contradiction in supposing that two plus three do not make five, and even the evil genius is bound by the law of contradiction. Descartes is imagining, not that the evil genius makes an eternal truth false, but that the evil genius makes Descartes err as to what the eternal truths are. Descartes sees clearly and distinctly that two plus three make five, deduces a contradiction from the contrary supposition. But might he have made a logical error in deducing this contradiction, might his clear and distinct perception be erroneous? Doubt is being cast, not on the eternal truths, but on Descartes's capacity to know them. The sceptical supposition is not 'It might be the case that two plus three do not make five', but rather 'It might be the case that I do not know for certain that two plus three make five'. (Besides, we argued in pp. 185–6 of the previous chapter that one cannot deduce a contradiction from the negation of 'Two plus three make five' alone.)

So the hypothesis of the evil genius (which says, not that the evil genius exists, but rather that the evil genius might exist) casts doubt upon everything that Descartes believes except the *Cogito*. It is his way of raising the basic sceptical objection against his rationalist criterion of truth (that everything clearly and distinctly perceived by him or self-evident to him is true). Descartes emphasises that the doubt induced by this hypothesis is a very weak one:

And since I have no cause to think that there is a deceiving God ... any reason for doubt which depends simply on this supposition is a very slight and, so to speak, metaphysical one. But in order to remove even this slight reason for doubt ... I must examine whether there is a God, and, if there is, whether he can be a deceiver. For if I do not know this, it seems that I can never be quite certain about anything else. (*Third Meditation*, 1984: 25)

The way out of the sceptical nightmare induced by the evil genius hypothesis becomes plain. Suppose Descartes can prove that there is a God and this God cannot be a deceiver. Then Descartes's rational powers, the 'natural light of reason' by which he clearly and distinctly perceives certain truths, will have been given to him by this benevolent deity who would not wish him to err. And so his general criterion of truth will be trustworthy after all. This is Descartes's strategy.

Before seeing how he implements it, we should note that the

hypothesis of the evil genius is the precursor of several similar sceptical hypotheses proposed more recently. The recent hypotheses have a more materialist flavour. Cornman and Lehrer (1974: 81–97) imagine a machine called 'The Braino' which can be attached to our heads and which, by artificially stimulating our sensory nerve-endings, gives us systematic hallucinations indistinguishable from our so-called 'perceptions'. Can we be sure that we are not victims of a Braino machine? Putnam (1981: 7) imagines that we are all disembodied brains kept alive in a vat of nutrient and hooked up to a super-computer which gives us 'experiences of the world' just like the experiences we do have (including the experiences we call 'talking to one another'). Can we be sure that we are not disembodied brains in a vat? These modern 'evil genius hypotheses' are children of their times and reflect contemporary suspicions about minds or souls. Descartes's evil genius hypothesis was also a child of its times and reflected then contemporary suspicions about bodies or brains. Descartes's hypothesis is better: the Braino hypothesis uncritically assumes that we have bodies, or at least heads, for the machine to be attached to; the brains-in-a-vat hypothesis uncritically assumes that we have brains for the super-computer to stimulate. Descartes's theologically inspired evil genius assumes none of this: we might just be disembodied 'thinking substances' certain of nothing except the *Cogito*. (The victim of the Braino or the brain in a vat could also satisfy himself of the truth of the *Cogito*.)

GOD AND THE CARTESIAN CIRCLE

Descartes gives three different proofs of the existence of God. The first is the so-called 'ontological argument' and it may be summarised as follows:

(1) I think, therefore I am.
(2) I have an idea of God, an idea of a perfect being, of 'a substance that is infinite, independent, supremely intelligent, supremely powerful, and which created both myself

and everything else...that exists' (*Tenth Objection*, 1984: 130–1).

(3) A perfect being can lack no perfection.
(4) Existence is a perfection.
(5) Therefore, a perfect being cannot lack existence, God must exist. (*Discourse*, Part IV; 1984: 129; *Fifth Meditation*, 1984: 46–8)

Descartes's second proof of the existence of God is called the 'cosmological argument' (goodness knows why!), and it may be summarised as follows:

(1) I think, therefore I am.
(2) I have an idea of God, an idea of a perfect being.
(3) '...it is manifest by the natural light that there must be at least as much reality in the efficient and total cause as in the effect of that cause' (*Third Meditation*, 1984: 28).
(4) I doubt, doubt is an imperfection, therefore I am imperfect.
(5) I cannot have created my idea of a perfect being [from (3) and (4)].
(6) My idea of a perfect being must have been created by a perfect being [from (3)].
(7) Therefore, a perfect being, God, must exist (*Discourse*, Part IV; 1984: 128–9; *Third Meditation*, 1984: 29–32).

Descartes's third proof of the existence of God is called the 'First Cause argument', is often regarded as a variant of the second proof and may be summarised as follows:

(1) I think, therefore I am.
(2) I am not 'self-caused', I do not have the power of existing in my own right.
(3) Some other being must have caused or created me.
(4) That other being is either self-caused or caused by yet another being.
(5) There cannot be an infinite sequence of causes.
(6) Therefore, a first cause must exist, a being which has the power of existing in its own right, God (*Third Meditation*, 1984: 32–5).

These proofs or arguments raise a host of interesting questions. Before entering into any of these questions, let us see how Descartes puts God to work.

God's first task is to provide a divine guarantee that Descartes's 'natural light of reason' will never lead him astray, that his general criterion of truth can be trusted after all:

And now, from this contemplation of the true God, in whom all the treasures of wisdom and the sciences lie hidden, I think I can see a way forward to the knowledge of other things.

To begin with, I recognize that it is impossible that God should ever deceive me. For in every case of trickery or deception some imperfection is to be found... and so cannot apply to God.

Next, I know by experience that there is in me a faculty of judgement which, like everything else which is in me, I certainly received from God. And since God does not wish to deceive me, he surely did not give me the kind of faculty which would ever enable me to go wrong while using it correctly. (*Fourth Meditation*, 1984: 37–8)

So we can, after all, be certain that two plus three makes five and that a square has four sides. We can also be certain that the external world exists, for our God-given senses tell us about it, and God would deceive if there were no external objects. (The senses can, however, lead us astray as to the nature of external objects, or rather, we can be prompted by sense-experience to make erroneous judgements as to their nature. It is actually the 'natural light of reason' which, reflecting on the fact that we have sense-experience, convinces us of the existence of material things. It is also reason which teaches us about the true mathematical or geometrical nature of material things, and the fact that they lack secondary qualities such as colours or smells.) We can also be certain that other people exist, because certain external objects are capable of conversing rationally with us and it is manifest that only other 'thinking substances' could do that. (Descartes says that it is the rational use of language which shows that other bodies are not just complicated machines, and are animated by minds and souls like our own. Animals are just complicated machines, since they cannot hold sensible conversations with us.)

According to Descartes, our knowledge of all these things

depends ultimately upon our knowledge of God. For all are known by intellectual intuition, the 'natural light of reason', and we cannot rely upon intuition unless we know that it is God-given. This even applies to our knowledge of the 'eternal truths' of mathematics. Descartes makes this abundantly clear by asking whether an agnostic mathematician (who does not know whether or not God exists) or an atheistic mathematician (who denies that God exists) can really know any mathematics. Descartes answers that they cannot, because they cannot trust their mathematical intuition. An atheist or agnostic can only know that he exists – all his other beliefs are infected with the 'metaphysical doubt' created by the hypothesis of the evil genius.

Clearly, everything hinges upon Descartes's proofs of the existence of God. Are the proofs valid? Are their premises true? Philosophers have devoted much attention to the proofs and many criticisms have been proposed, some denying their validity, others disputing some premise or other. The criticism I want to consider first is of a different kind.

Before Descartes's *Meditations* was published it was circulated in manuscript to various philosophers, who wrote objections to it. These objections, and Descartes's replies to them, were printed along with the *Meditations*. One of the philosophers who wrote objections was Antoine Arnauld and one of his objections (the *Fourth Objection*) was as follows. Even if Descartes's proofs are valid, and even if all of their premises are true, they are not proofs which Descartes is entitled on his own principles to pro-pose. Each proof contains premises other than the *Cogito*. Descartes accepts these other premises because he perceives them clearly and distinctly to be true. But before the existence of a benevolent God is proved, Descartes is not entitled to make use of his general criterion of truth. Before the existence of a benevolent God is proved, only the *Cogito* can be known and the hypothesis of the evil genius casts doubt upon everything else. So in a curious way Descartes argues in a circle: he uses his general criterion of truth to prove the existence of God, and then he uses the existence of God to guarantee the reliability of his general criterion of truth. This is called the 'Cartesian circle'.

If Arnauld is right, then we have a devastating objection to Descartes's attempt to defeat the sceptical objection to the appeal to self-evidence or clear and distinct perception. Some scholars try to rescue Descartes by saying that Arnauld and his followers (such as me) have misunderstood: Descartes was not even trying to give a theological guarantee of the reliability of his criterion of truth, for the evil genius hypothesis casts no doubt upon it. What, on this view, does the evil genius hypothesis call into doubt? Some say the evidence of the senses, others say demonstrated as opposed to intuited truths, some say both. I do not think that the texts taken as a whole support this interpretation, though I admit that particular passages can be found which do support it. Nor, it seems to me, does the interpretation really help. If the evil genius hypothesis casts doubt upon all demonstrated truths, then it casts doubt upon the existence of God and the reliability of the criterion of truth, since both of these are demonstrated truths. A circle remains: particular demonstrated truths are invoked to remove a metaphysical doubt which attaches to all demonstrated truths. Or suppose the evil genius hypothesis casts doubt only upon what we learn from the senses. Provided that none of the premises of Descartes's proofs of the existence of God are learned from sense-experience (a matter which might be disputed), we have no Cartesian circle. But nor do we have any response to the sceptical critique of reason or self-evidence or clear and distinct perception. The upshot seems to be, then, that we have only a circular response to the sceptic or no response at all.

There are other objections to some of the premises of Descartes's proofs. A famous one concerns the assumption, in the ontological argument, that existence is a 'perfection', that is, a desirable property that things may or may not possess. Is existence a property or feature that a thing may lack? We might examine a thing and find out that it is not red or heavy or square. But can we examine a thing and find out that it does not exist? (If we can, then as well as all the existent things there will be all the non-existent ones, too. The latter will be but they will not exist. How can that be?) No, when we say 'Horses exist' or

'Unicorns do not exist', what we mean is that some of the things that exist are horses, while none of the things that exist are unicorns. All things exist. Existence is a second-order property, not of things, but of properties of things (or of predicates applicable to things). To say that a property (or predicate) exists is just to say that something has that property (or that the predicate applies to something). If this objection (which is due originally to Kant) is correct, then the ontological argument is marred by a basic logical or semantical flaw.

There are many other objections. Some objected that it was impious to suppose that we had an 'idea' of God (a clear and distinct idea to boot) – can finite and imperfect human spirits really comprehend (clearly and distinctly comprehend to boot) the infinite and the perfect? Others objected to the principle that there must be as much reality in the cause as in the effect. One critic did not accept this principle at all, citing the spontaneous generation of flies from rotting meat as a case where the 'effect' has more 'reality' (since it is alive) than the 'cause' (which is dead). Another critic wondered whether the principle was true of ideas, and suggested that an imperfect being might itself create or cause an idea of a perfect being by reflecting upon its own imperfections and imagining them absent. Yet another critic wondered whether a chain of causes and effects might not stretch back into infinity. Another who accepted that there had to be a 'First Cause' wondered whether it had to be the benevolent Christian deity that Descartes needed.

Some of these objections are good ones, some not so good. I mention them, not so much to discuss them, as to discuss Descartes's response to them. It does not matter whether these various critics are right (the believer in the spontaneous generation of flies from rotten meat clearly was not right). What matters is that these critics quite sincerely do not find some of Descartes's premises self-evident or clear and distinct or indubitable. What can Descartes say to them? He cannot admit that they might be right in this. That would be to admit that what was indubitable to him might not be indubitable to the next person. And that would raise the awful prospect that the next person might be right, and he himself wrong, about the indubitability or clarity and distinctness or self-evidence of some premise. No, Descartes has to insist that his premises just are indubitable or self-evident despite what his critics say. But then, why do his critics not see this? Descartes has to say that they are wilfully refusing to see it because of their prejudices – or that their 'natural light' is somehow deficient or defective. This is exactly what he does say: people who do not find self-evident what I find self-evident are either prejudiced or mentally defective (1984, II: 97). It is a bankrupt epistemology that has to treat perfectly sincere critics in this way.

The point leads to a deeper one. Descartes's theory of knowledge proves too much and necessitates a conspiracy theory of error. Suppose a benevolent God has given us rational powers which will enable us to achieve certainty. Why are we ignorant of so many things and uncertain of so many others? It must be that we are not using our God-given powers properly: error is our fault, ignorance is sin. Descartes actually raises the so-called 'problem of error' and gives such a solution to it. (I say 'so-called "problem of error"' because error and ignorance are only a problem for those who think we have an infallible method for achieving certain knowledge.) Descartes says that as well as a God-given faculty of understanding, we also have a God-given faculty of judging and a God-given freedom of the will. Error arises when we exercise our freedom and make judgements where we do not properly understand. (This solution to the problem of error is structurally identical to the orthodox Christian solution to the problem of evil. Evil and error both result from the wrongful exercise of human freedom.)

Descartes's rationalist epistemology fails. Self-evidence or indubitability or clear and distinct perception are not infallible guides to truth. Descartes's attempt to show that they are breaks down, above all, because of the Cartesian circle. Sceptical doubts about rationalism remain: that something is self-evident to you, that you clearly and distinctly conceive it, that you cannot doubt it, do not establish that you know it.

CHAPTER 12

Kant and the synthetic a priori

Descartes's attempt to rescue rationalism from sceptical criticisms has been deemed a failure. But this failure did not mark the end of rationalism. Rationalism persisted largely because of the failure of the alternative theory of knowledge, empiricism, to give any convincing account of mathematical knowledge. This was to impress Immanuel Kant, who developed a radically new version of the rationalist theory in the late eighteenth century. These will be the topics of this chapter.

KANT'S QUESTION

We have already seen (in pp. 181–90 of Chapter 10) why mathematics was a problem for empiricism. It was Kant above all who drove this point home. It was he who distinguished the a priori from the a posteriori, and the analytic from the synthetic. And it was he who argued that empiricists must either regard mathematics as analytic a priori or as synthetic a posteriori, and that neither view is plausible. We reviewed his chief arguments in our earlier discussion, so I will say no more about them here.

Throughout his discussion Kant took it for granted that we know the truths of mathematics. We know for sure that seven and five add up to twelve. We know for sure that the angles of a triangle add up to 180°. But it is not just mathematical truths that we know for certain – the same applies to the fundamental truths of mathematical physics. We know for sure that the law of the conservation of matter is true, that 'in all changes in the corporeal world the quantity of matter remains unchanged' (*Prolegomena*: 22). And we know for sure that the fundamental laws of mechanics are true.

The fundamental laws of mechanics had been proposed, about a century before Kant, by Isaac Newton. Newton's theory consisted of three laws of mechanics and a law of gravitation:

(1) Law of inertia: Every body continues in its state of rest or uniform motion unless compelled to change that state by some force impressed upon it.

(2) Law of motion: Any change of motion is proportional to the impressed force and in the same direction.

(3) Law of action and reaction: To every action there is opposed an equal and opposite reaction.

(4) Law of gravitation: Between any two bodies there is an attractive force which is directly proportional to the product of the masses of the bodies and inversely pro-portional to the square of the distance between them.

These statements, with the possible exception of the last, might seem intuitively obvious, even self-evident. (In the 2,000 years before Newton a principle quite opposed to Newton's law of inertia was regarded as intuitively obvious, even self-evident: Newton's law says that change of motion requires a force or 'mover'; before Newton it seemed obvious or self-evident that motion required a force or 'mover'. Once again, so much the worse for obviousness or self-evidence.) Newton's laws added together formed the most successful scientific theory ever proposed. When applied to all kinds of physical situations, they yielded many surprising predictions. And when Kant wrote, all of these predictions had turned out to be correct. The theory explained Kepler's laws of planetary motion; it also predicted slight deviations from those laws, caused by the gravitational effects of the planets upon each other, which were observed. It also explained Galileo's law of falling bodies; and predicted slight deviations from that law when bodies fall from a great height, which were observed. It explained the tides in the

oceans as resulting from the gravitational attractions of the sun
and moon upon the oceans. It predicted that because the earth
spins on its axis, it is not exactly spherical, so that pendulum
clocks should run slower at the equator than at the north pole
– which they do. It predicted the return of Halley's comet
(Halley was a disciple of Newton), and Halley's comet returned
at the appointed time. In these and many other ways Newton's
theory had turned out to give correct results. We can perhaps
forgive Kant for thinking that it was something that we knew for
sure to be true.

Kant later described himself as being in a 'dogmatic slumber'
when he took for granted that he simply knew all of these things
to be true. (Kant scholars talk, more pompously, of his 'pre-
critical period'.) And Kant says that he was aroused from this
dogmatic slumber by Hume. Hume's critique of induction had
shown that no general law could be established as true on the
basis of experience. (One can put Hume's point like this: no
matter how many true predictions a theory makes, this does not
establish the truth of the theory.) How could our certain
knowledge of these things be reconciled with Humean scepticism?

Kant argued as follows:

We know the fundamental laws of mathematics and of
  mathematical physics.
These laws are synthetic rather than analytic.
Our knowledge of them is either a priori or a posteriori.
Hume has shown that we cannot know them a posteriori.
Therefore, we must know them a priori – that is, they must
  represent synthetic a priori knowledge.

This argument, which is perfectly valid, led Kant to his
fundamental question: How is synthetic a priori knowledge
possible?

KANT'S ANSWER

Kant's answer to this question is very ingenious, but it is also
very difficult to understand. He had to invent lots of special
terminology in order to explain it. Mastering this terminology,

and the ideas expressed with it, is a huge task. What follows is little more than a gesture in the direction of understanding Kant – but limitations of space and time prevent anything more substantial. (And I make all due apologies to Kant scholars for what is to come.)

We have seen that it is a feature of things known a posteriori that we can at least imagine experiences which would show them to be false. Let us begin by considering the law of conservation of matter, and asking whether any possible experiment might show it to be wrong. What might such an experiment be like? We would take some material substances, weigh them carefully, perform some experiment with them, and then weigh the materials left at the end of the experiment. Conservation of matter would be violated if at the end of the experiment the materials weigh more or less than they did at the beginning. But what would happen if a student of chemistry actually did such an experiment, and announced to his teacher that he had refuted the law of conservation? The teacher would simply say that the experiment was faulty, that some material had been lost or gained in the course of it, and direct the student to do it again more carefully. It is a condition of a properly conducted chemical experiment that the quantity of matter is conserved in it. Hence no properly conducted chemical experiment could show that the law of the conservation of matter is mistaken. The law is synthetic rather than analytic. But we know a priori that no experiment will refute it because we impose it as a condition upon proper experimentation.

(It will be objected that something must be wrong with this example, since scientists now think that the law of conservation of matter is false, and talk instead of the law of conservation of mass-energy. Quite so. Yet no experiment or group of experiments by themselves convinced scientists of this. What did convince them of it were various theoretical developments, which we shall not enter into here.)

We can get a little closer to Kant's big idea by considering the following story. (I should make it clear that this story was not told by Kant himself – Kant was a very serious philosopher who did not tell stories. The story is due to Russell (1946: 680).)

Imagine a group of people who are all born wearing rose-coloured spectacles. They cannot remove these spectacles, nor can they see (or otherwise experience) that they have them. Because of the spectacles, they see everything with a rosy tinge. They all come to believe that the world is rosy. And this proposition is true of the world as they see it or of the world of appearance. The way things appear to such beings is brought about partly by the world itself and partly by the rose-coloured spectacles through which they view the world. They cannot remove their spectacles and get through to the world as it is in itself. If one of them claimed to have seen something without a rosy tinge to it, he would be dismissed as suffering from an illusion or hallucination.

Now consider our imaginary people's knowledge that the world is rosy. We have assumed so far that this piece of knowledge was acquired from experience. But suppose that our people could somehow study not the world but the way in which they experience the world. And suppose that they can undertake this study before they embark upon studying the world. They would (somehow) find out about their immovable rose-coloured spectacles. They would find out that 'The world is rosy' would hold true of the world they were about to experience. They would gain a priori knowledge of this proposition. Yet the proposition is not analytically true (nor is it necessarily true). Assuming that this self-study could be undertaken, it would yield synthetic a priori knowledge of the world – or rather, of the world-as-experienced by these people.

Before commenting on this story, let me tell another one. This second story is actually told by Sir Arthur Eddington, a twentieth-century philosopher-scientist and a follower of Kant. Eddington (1939: 16–18) imagines a student of fishes gaining knowledge of them by casting a net (the net has a 2″ mesh):

Surveying his catch, he proceeds in the usual manner of the scientist to systematise what it reveals. He arrives at two generalisations:
(1) No sea-creature is less than two inches long.
(2) All sea-creatures have gills.
These are both true of his catch, and he assumes tentatively that they will remain true however often he repeats it.

Eddington explains that this is an analogy:

In applying this analogy, the catch stands for the body of knowledge which constitutes physical science, and the net for the sensory and intellectual equipment which we use in obtaining it. The casting of the net corresponds to observation; for knowledge which has not been or could not be obtained by observation is not admitted into physical science.

Eddington's story continues. Somebody objects that the first generalisation is wrong: 'There are plenty of sea-creatures under two inches long, only your net is not adapted to catch them.' The student of fishes dismisses this: he is interested in catchable fish, that is what his theory of fishes is about, what his net cannot catch does not count as a fish. Similarly, if someone objects that the real world, the things-in-themselves, cannot be captured by the methods of science, he too will be dismissed:

If you are not simply guessing, you are claiming a knowledge of the physical universe discovered in some other way than by the methods of physical science, and admittedly unverifiable by such methods. You are a metaphysician. Bah!

Someone else makes a different suggestion about the first generalisation.

You arrived at your generalisation in the traditional way, by examining the fish. May I point out that you could have arrived at the same generalisation more easily by examining the net and the method of using it?

Before going fishing (before observing the world), we might examine the fishing-net (our sensory and intellectual equipment) and find out that no sea-creature (more precisely, no catchable sea-creature) is less than two inches long. This would represent synthetic a priori knowledge about (catchable) fishes. And we could be absolutely sure of its truth. It is different with the second generalisation. It could not be discovered by examining the net. It can only be learned from experience (from casting the net), and it might be refuted the very next time that we go fishing. It is synthetic a posteriori and it cannot be known for certain to be true.

These two stories are meant to give some inkling of Kant's big idea. According to Kant, our experiences of the world depend upon two things: they depend upon stimuli proceeding from external objects; and they depend upon a structure which we impose upon those stimuli. We structure incoming stimuli according to certain categories (corresponding to the rose-coloured spectacles and the fishing-net in the stories). We impose a temporal structure on incoming stimuli, so that all our experiences are located in time, occur before or after one another. We also impose a spatial structure, so that what we experience has a spatial location. And we impose a causal structure, so that the things we experience stand in causal relations to one another. Nothing counts as an experience of the world which is not structured in this way. (Just as the person with rose-coloured spectacles would regard a non-rosy perception as hallucinatory, or the student of fishes would not regard a sea-creature less than two inches long as a catchable fish at all.) Now according to Kant, this structuring of our experience proceeds according to certain laws: the temporal structuring is governed by the laws of arithmetic, the spatial structuring by the laws of geometry, and the causal structuring by the laws of mechanics. (These correspond to the laws that the world is rosy, or that no sea-creature is less than two inches long, in the stories.) All experiences of the world conform to these laws, and no experience of the world could refute them. Yet they are not analytic truths (nor are they necessary truths). Moreover, by studying the way in which we structure experience we can come to know a priori that they are true. They represent, then, synthetic a priori knowledge.

These are very difficult ideas. One difficulty is to see how it is possible to study the categories, and their laws, which we impose upon our experience. Here our stories do not help us much: it seems that we could only find out about the rose-coloured spectacles, or the two-inch mesh on the fishing net, from experience. But Kant insists that we do not find out how we experience the world from experience; instead we engage in what he calls a 'transcendental analysis of human reason'. Kant enumerates the 'categories of the understanding' and tries to prove that anything brought under those categories (anything we experience) must conform to the laws of arithmetic, geometry and pure natural science. This is the most difficult part of Kant's theory, one which students of Kant labour long and hard to get to grips with.

Kant's question was 'How is synthetic a priori knowledge possible?' His answer, in a nutshell, is that it is possible because it consists of laws which we impose upon sensory stimuli to create the world of experience (which Kant calls 'nature'). In this way Kant saved the laws of arithmetic, geometry and 'pure natural science' both from the charge of analyticity and from the Humean scepticism which he thought infected all knowledge gained from experience. Here is a passage from Kant in which his central doctrine is summarised:

The main proposition ... that universal laws of nature can be known *a priori*, leads of itself to the proposition that the highest legislation of nature must lie in ourselves, i.e. in our understanding, and that we must not seek the universal laws of nature from nature by means of experience but conversely, must seek nature, as to its universal conformity to law, merely from the conditions of the possibility of experience which lie in our sensibility and in the understanding. For how would it otherwise be possible to know these laws *a priori*, as they are not ... analytical knowledge, but genuine synthetic [knowledge]? ... either these laws are borrowed from nature by means of experience, or conversely nature is deduced from the laws of the possibility of experience in general ... The former is self-contradictory, for the universal laws of nature can and must be known *a priori* (i.e. independently of all experience) ... thus only the second is left ... nature and possible experience are exactly the same ... *the understanding does not draw its laws from nature, but prescribes them to nature.* (*Prolegomena*: 80–2)

KANT'S IDEALISM

I shall say nothing of the details of Kant's theory. I will merely say that if the theory is accepted, we must pay a heavy price. For the theory lands us in a form of idealism. It yields synthetic a priori knowledge but this knowledge does not concern 'things-in-themselves' (as Kant calls them), rather it concerns 'things-as-experienced-by-humans', the 'world of appearance' or 'nature'. That we have a form of idealism here is apparent to anyone who reflects upon the extraordinary claims (in the passage just quoted) that 'nature and possible experience are exactly the same' and that 'the understanding does not draw its laws from nature, but prescribes them to nature'. We should pause over this. Kant's a priori laws of nature are actually laws about something which is partly of our own making, a 'world of appearance' which our 'sensibility and understanding' help to create. Indeed, all synthetic propositions concern this 'world of appearance' or 'world of (human) experience'.

Kant tried hard to distinguish his idealism from that of Berkeley. His writings contain several different versions of a 'Refutation of [Berkeley's] idealism'. In the following passage he compares his view with the view that colours exist only in the minds of perceivers:

> A man who will not allow colours to be attached to the object in itself as qualities, but only to the sense of sight as modifications, cannot be called an idealist for that; equally little can my doctrine be called idealistic merely because I find that more of, *indeed all, the qualities that make up the intuition of a body* belong merely to its appearance; for the existence of the thing which appears is not thereby cancelled, as with real idealism, but it is only shown that we cannot know it at all through the senses as it is in itself. (*Prolegomena*: 46)

According to Kant, then, all of the apparent or perceived qualities of bodies are subjective and exist only in the minds of perceivers: this applies to shapes and sizes just as much as colours and smells. This is not Berkeleyan idealism because it is still asserted that things-in-themselves, or bodies, exist. But we cannot know them 'through the senses' – sense-experience teaches us only about the 'appearances' that they produce. (Kant therefore subscribes to what we earlier called idea-ism, the view that the immediate objects of perception are 'appearances' or 'ideas' in the minds of perceivers.)

Kant admitted that his theory was a form of idealism – he called it 'transcendental idealism'. It is a new form of idealism, and it is not easy to get to grips with. Kant is no solipsist: he thinks that things-in-themselves exist and so do other people. The world of appearance or nature is common to all people, since the categorical apparatus which structures it is common to all people. The world of appearance is therefore inter-subjective and in this sense objective.

Kantian things-in-themselves are most peculiar things. The only thing we can say truly of them is that they exist. They possess none of the qualities or properties that they appear to possess: no shapes, sizes, weights, motions, colours, tastes, or smells. These are all qualities of their 'appearances', as we have seen. Nor do 'things-in-themselves' exist in space or time, since space and time are 'forms of sensibility' and only things-as-experienced-by-us ('appearances') exist in space and time. Nor (contrary to what was suggested two paragraphs back) do things-in-themselves cause experiences, since causality is a category which applies only to things-as-experienced-by-us, too. The idea that objects or things-in-themselves are nowhere, at no time and do nothing is very odd. It is perhaps no accident that some of Kant's immediate followers did away with them altogether, and turned Kantian idealism into something resembling Berkeleyan idealism – Berkeleyan idealism supplemented with a good Kantian emphasis on the structure imposed by the understanding on the raw data of perception.

Kant retained things-in-themselves. But he was very critical of any attempt to say anything positive about their nature. We can never penetrate the 'veil of appearance' and get through to them. Philosophers who try are metaphysicians and Kant wanted to bring metaphysics (that kind of metaphysics anyway) to a stop. This explains the titles of his *Prolegomena* and of his major work *A Critique of Pure Reason*. The only good metaphysics was Kant's own, which showed that the office of reason is to structure appearances, not to try to get beyond them.

We have called Kant a rationalist, since he accepts the basic rationalist thesis that synthetic a priori knowledge exists. But his is a new form of rationalism, too. It involves no appeal to self-evidence or anything akin to it as a criterion of truth. Kant denied that any such criterion existed and said that those who search for one present 'the ludicrous spectacle of one man milking a he-goat and the other holding a sieve underneath' (*Critique*, 1929: 97). (This is the only joke in the *Critique of Pure*

Reason!) Kantian rationalism involves no appeal to self-evidence for a sceptic to attack.

But although Kant is a rationalist of sorts, his position is often regarded, and rightly so, as a compromise between rationalism and empiricism. He thinks that our synthetic a priori knowledge, though very important, is also very limited. Most of what we believe, indeed most of our general beliefs, can only be acquired from experience. (Remember the fisherman's generalisation 'All sea-creatures have gills'.) Hume regarded any such general belief as rationally unfounded – and it is a nice question whether Kant had any answer to Hume on that point.

Kant's philosophy has been enormously influential, not just in philosophy but in the sciences also. Perhaps his most important idea, and the one which has received the widest acceptance, is the idea that in perception incoming 'data' or 'stimuli' are structured in accordance with categories or concepts provided by the perceiver. We have urged something similar ourselves in earlier chapters. This Kantian idea has been accepted by many philosophers and psychologists who are sceptical of Kant's further claims that all human perceivings are structured in the same way by an immutable set of a priori concepts and that examination of the way this is done can yield synthetic a priori truths.

How might the sceptic respond to Kant? There are many particular sceptical objections which cannot be discussed without entering into the details of Kant's arguments. But some general sceptical worries are obvious enough. Kant is an idea-ist and the familiar sceptical questions regarding idea-ism can be asked of Kant, too. How can Kant prove, on the basis of his own ideas, that things-in-themselves and other minds exist? Other questions are peculiar to the Kantian system. How does Kant know that all humans 'structure appearances' in the same way so that they face a common 'world of appearance'? Even if we grant Kant that assumption, what about non-human animals? Do non-human perceivers possess all the Kantian categories of the understanding which are conditions for the possibility of all experience? It is biologically implausible to suppose that they do. It is biologically even more implausible to suppose that humans are the only creatures that can have experiences. The upshot seems to be that chimps or honeybees or flatworms can have experiences without deploying the Kantian categories. But if they can do without them, why can we not do without them, too? (The Kantian philosophy, like most philosophy, is profoundly pre-Darwinian. Which is not to refute Kant; chimps, honeybees, flatworms, even other humans, are parts of the Kantian 'world of appearance'; to ask whether they, as things-in-themselves, are perceivers, is to ask an illegitimate metaphysical question.) I shall pursue none of these sceptical worries here.

A final thought is that, like Descartes, Kant proved too much. Something must be wrong somewhere in the Kantian system. For, as mentioned above (p. 215), the law of conservation of matter, which Kant thought a synthetic a priori truth, has been superseded in physics. The same applies to Newton's laws. The next chapter will be devoted to an objection of a similar kind.

CHAPTER 13

Alternative geometries

Down the ages the chief inspiration for rationalism was Euclidean geometry. Descartes and Kant both, in their very different ways, tried to explain how a priori reasoning could yield absolutely certain knowledge of the structure of space. Many people had reservations about these two rationalist theories of synthetic a priori knowledge. Few people had reservations about the rationalist paradigm for such knowledge, Euclidean geometry. Around 1800, as before, there seemed to be no plausible alternative to the rationalist view of geometry. In particular, empiricist accounts of mathematical knowledge in general, and of geometrical knowledge in particular, continued to seem hopeless. But soon the mathematicians themselves took a hand in these debates, shattered the consensus about the synthetic a priori status of geometry, and gave the empiricists new hope that they might be able to account for mathematics after all. To explain how and why all this occurred is the task of this chapter.

HOW NON-EUCLIDEAN GEOMETRIES WERE INVENTED

The Euclidean success-story was marred by one apparently minor defect which had been noticed quite early in the piece. The reader may recall that back in Chapter 10 (see p. 178) I said that Euclid had ten self-evident axioms – but I listed only nine of them. The one I omitted is this:

> If two straight lines are crossed by a third in such a way that the interior angles on one side are less than two right angles, then the two lines will meet if produced on that side.

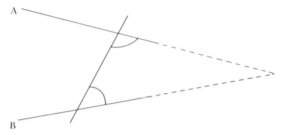

Figure 9. Euclid's axiom of parallels

This is a bit more complicated than Euclid's other axioms. To understand it fully you really need to see a picture (see Figure 9). This axiom says that lines A and B will intersect if produced to the right, since the marked angles sum to less than 180°. It is called the 'axiom of parallels', since it enables one to prove that when the two angles sum to exactly 180° the lines A and B are parallel. ('Parallel straight lines are straight lines which, being in the same plane and being produced indefinitely in both directions, do not meet one another in either direction' (Euclid 1956, I: 154).)

The early geometers did not seriously question the truth of Euclid's axiom of parallels, but several doubted that it was obviously or self-evidently true, as a genuine axiom ought to be. For example, Proclus, one of the earliest commentators on Euclid, said that 'we should expel from our body of doctrine this merely plausible and unreasoned hypothesis' (Euclid 1956, I: 203). In other words, we should not make an axiom out of a 'plausible hypothesis' about what will or will not happen when lines are produced 'indefinitely'. Such a hypothesis must be proved to be true. (Proclus' attitude reveals once again the weakness of appeals to self-evidence: what may have been self-evident to Euclid and others was certainly not self-evident to Proclus.)

Many geometers tried to do what Proclus had suggested, prove the axiom of parallels from the other nine axioms. Efforts to do this persisted for 2,000 years, but without success! Many alleged proofs were produced, but all turned out either to be mistaken or to smuggle in additional assumptions over and above the nine unproblematic Euclidean axioms. An important example of the latter kind was produced by the English mathematician Playfair, who showed that you can prove Euclid's axiom of parallels provided you assume that through a point not on a given line there is exactly one straight line in the same plane which is parallel to the given line. This statement, now known as 'Playfair's axiom', is equivalent to Euclid's axiom of parallels in the presence of the other axioms: Euclid had proved Playfair's axiom from his original axioms, and you can prove Euclid's axiom of parallels from his other nine axioms together with Playfair's axiom. In many discussions Playfair's axiom replaces Euclid's original one (sometimes it is wrongly attributed to Euclid himself). It will be our axiom of parallels from now on.

Is Playfair's axiom self-evident when Euclid's was not? Some said so, but were given pause by the equivalence result just mentioned. Equivalent axioms play the same logical and mathematical role in the system, so what does it matter if one of them seems more 'obvious' or 'self-evident' to some people?

So the 'Queen of the Sciences' had a skeleton in her cupboard, whose bones rattled ever more loudly down the ages. The list of failed attempts to prove the axiom of parallels grew and ran to twenty pages by the eighteenth century. In 1767 D'Alembert called it the 'scandal of geometry' (Bonola 1955: 52). Suspicion mounted that perhaps the axiom of parallels could not be (correctly) proved. But how on earth could one prove that? The fact that dozens of examined proofs all turned out to be incorrect does not show that a correct proof will not be discovered tomorrow. We cannot examine all possible proofs and find them all wanting.

One failed attempt is of special interest. In 1733 the Italian mathematician Saccheri published his *Euclid Vindicated from All Defects (Euclides ab Omni Naevo Vindicatus)*. In it he tried to prove the axiom of parallels by *reductio*: he assumed its negation and tried to derive a contradiction. Negating the axiom that there is exactly one parallel to a given line through a given point yields two possibilities: that there are no parallels, and that there is more than one parallel. Saccheri investigated both these possibilities and obtained some very peculiar results. For example, if you assume that there are no parallels, then you can prove that the angles of a triangle add up to more than 180° (and the bigger the triangle the bigger the angle-sum). If you assume that there is more than one parallel, then you can prove that the angles of a triangle add up to less than 180° (and the bigger the triangle the smaller the angle-sum). Saccheri thought these results were so absurd that Euclid's axiom of parallels had been vindicated. But he did not succeed in getting an explicit contradiction (a statement of the form '*P* and it is not the case that *P*') from the negation of Euclid's axiom of parallels, which is what would be needed for a genuine *reductio* proof. Saccheri is now regarded, not as Euclid's vindicator, but as the earliest investigator of non-Euclidean geometry.

Actually, the situation was a little more messy than this. Let E^* be the rest of Euclid's axioms, E Euclid's axiom of parallels, R the assumption that there are no parallels, and H the assumption that there is more than one parallel. Then the negation of E is 'Either R or H'. Saccheri got no contradiction from 'Either R or H'. He did, however, get a contradiction from R and E^*. Had he been able to get one from H and E^*, too, this would have shown that if E^* is true then 'Either R or H' must be false, that is, E must be true. This would have been a *reductio* proof of E from E^*.

A hundred years later others followed. In Hungary there lived an old man called Bolyai who had wasted his life on the 'scandal of geometry'. In 1804 he sent a new proof of Euclid's axiom of parallels to the most famous mathematician of the day, Gauss, who showed it to be yet another mistaken attempt. Undeterred, old Bolyai kept trying, and by the 1820s was assembling a book full of his failed attempts. At this point Bolyai's son, against the advice of his father, also set to work. He adopted Saccheri's method, though he knew nothing of Saccheri: he assumed that more than one parallel to a given line could be drawn through a given point, tried to derive a contradiction, and instead derived many of the crazy things that Saccheri had derived. Being a little crazy himself, young

Bolyai said that these results were not crazy at all, just different. He told his father that he had 'created a new universe from nothing' (Bonola 1955: 98).

Old Bolyai was not convinced and decided to show his son's work to Gauss. The 'Prince of Mathematicians', as he was called, sent a surprising reply:

> If I commenced by saying that I am unable to praise this work, you would certainly be surprised. But I cannot say otherwise. To praise it would be to praise myself. Indeed the whole contents of the work, the path taken by your son, the results to which he is led, coincide almost entirely with my meditations, which have occupied my mind partly for the last thirty or thirty-five years. (Bonola 1955: 100)

(Gauss always said this sort of thing when people sent him new results – and he was always right! That is why he was the prince of mathematicians.) Gauss goes on to explain that he has not published his results because they are so strange and because he fears for his reputation. But young Bolyai has no reputation to lose and is welcome to publish them. Young Bolyai did just that, in 1832 in an appendix to his father's book. Unknown to either the Bolyais or Gauss, in 1829 the Russian mathematician Lobatchevsky had already published similar results. (His work was quite independent, despite Tom Lehrer's 'Lobatchevsky Song', the chorus of which runs 'Plagiarise, plagiarise, all you gotta do is plagiarise'.) Saccheri, Gauss, young Bolyai and Lobatchevsky are now regarded as the co-inventors of hyperbolic geometry.

Gauss had been worried about how mathematicians would react to non-Euclidean geometry. His worries were justified: Bolyai's book was greeted with a storm of protest and its results dismissed as flippant and crazy. Some said that it was no wonder such crazy results were obtained, since the axioms of hyperbolic geometry were actually inconsistent, and would lead to contradictions. This was a grave charge. How could it be answered? How could one prove that no contradiction could be proved from Bolyai's axioms? The fact that no one had yet succeeded in deriving a contradiction from them did not show that a contradiction would not be derived tomorrow.

Actually, the assertion that non-Euclidean geometry is inconsistent is the same as the assertion that Euclid's axiom of parallels is provable. Using the same abbreviations as on p. 227, to say that non-Euclidean geometries are inconsistent is to say that neither 'E^* and H' nor 'E^* and R' can be true. Which is to say that if E^* is true, then H is false and R is false, and so is 'Either H or R'. But to say that 'Either H or R' is false is to say that E is true. So, to say that non-Euclidean geometries are inconsistent is to say that if E^* is true, then E must be true also. And this is to say that E follows from E^*. Contrariwise, to say that a non-Euclidean system is consistent is to say that E does not follow from E^*, and to prove the former is to prove the latter. The two logical problems 'How to prove that Euclid's axiom of parallels cannot be proved?' and 'How to prove that non-Euclidean geometry is consistent?' are actually the same problem. This paragraph has ignored a complication about Riemannian geometry which will be mentioned immediately, and a complication about the difference between validity and provability which will not be mentioned at all.

So far we have only talked of hyperbolic geometry. The other kind of non-Euclidean geometry results if we replace Euclid's axiom of parallels with the axiom that no parallels to a given line can be drawn through a given point. This geometry was investigated by Riemann in the late nineteenth century and is called elliptic or Riemannian geometry. Its development is not so straightforward as that of hyperbolic geometry. You cannot simply add the Riemannian axiom to the rest of Euclid's axioms, because the resulting system is inconsistent (as Saccheri had shown). You must also modify the Euclidean axiom which says that you can produce a straight line indefinitely in either direction. The Euclidean axiom yields infinitely long lines and infinite space. The modified axiom yields finite but unbounded lines and finite but unbounded space. A line is finite but unbounded if it has a finite length but no end points – a closed Euclidean curve, such as a circle, is finite but unbounded.

Riemann and others also laid to rest in the 1880s the serious charge that non-Euclidean geometries were inconsistent. They succeeded in showing that if Euclidean geometry itself is consistent, then so are non-Euclidean geometries. What this means is that we have three different possibly true descriptions of the structure of space.

It is very hard for us to imagine how non-Euclidean geometries might be true, because we are so familiar with the Euclidean conception of space extending infinitely in three dimensions. In fact, this conception of space (physical or real space) is of relatively recent vintage (it is only about 500 years old). For most of recorded history (the preceding 2,000 years) Western thinking was dominated by a different conception, due to Aristotle, according to which space or the universe was finite and spherical in shape. According to Aristotle, there is nothing, not even empty space, outside the spherical universe. For 2,000 years thinking people understood this conception perfectly well, and most of them accepted it as true. We find this very hard to understand. It is also very hard for us to understand how it could possibly be that there are no parallels or more than one parallel. However, one can give 'pictures' or 'models' of how the non-Euclidean axioms might be true, if one is prepared to set aside the Euclidean conception of space. Suppose there is a 'space' of only two dimensions all the points of which are confined within a circle. A straight line in this 'space' will be (a segment of) a chord of that circle. And through any point not on that straight line infinitely many other straight lines can be drawn which do not intersect the given line no matter how far they are produced in the space (see Figure 10). (How do we know that infinitely many 'parallels' exist? The Euclidean geometry of the inside of a circle tells us.) We are irresistibly tempted here to say that only one of these further lines is really parallel to the given line, since all of the others will intersect the given line if both are produced outside the circle. Quite so. But this is to fall back on the Euclidean picture. The 'space' of our model is bounded by the circle, all lines are finite in length, and no line can be extended outside the circle for there are no 'points of space' there. (In much the same way as in the Aristotelian system there are no points of space outside the spherical universe.)

One can also give a 'model' or 'picture' of a space in which

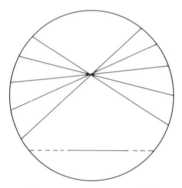

Figure 10. Infinite parallels

there are no parallels. Imagine a 'space' all the points of which are located on the surface of a sphere. A straight line on such a surface (the shortest distance between any two points upon it) is (a segment of) a 'great circle', a circle whose centre is the centre of the sphere. ('Great circles' are what planes fly along to get where they are going as quickly as possible.) Any two segments of great circles intersect (twice) if they are both produced. Hence there are no parallel straight lines in this space. (How do we know that any two segments of great circles intersect if produced? The Euclidean geometry of the surface of a sphere tells us.) Again, we are irresistibly tempted to say that segments of great circles are not really straight lines, and that the shortest distance between two points on the surface of a sphere is a straight line joining them up and passing through the inside of the sphere. Again, this is to fall back on the Euclidean picture, and to embed the sphere in Euclidean three-dimensional space. The 'space' of our model is confined to the surface of the sphere, all lines are finite but unbounded (have no end points), and there are no points of this space (and hence no lines either) inside the sphere at all.

The two simple 'models' just given are not models of the non-Euclidean geometries, in which all of the axioms of those geometries are true. Other axioms fail in our simple 'models'. (Inside the circle you cannot extend a line indefinitely in either direction. On the sphere two points opposite one another do not determine a unique straight line.) Our simple 'models' each depict a 'space' in which one of the two distinctive non-Euclidean axioms is true. Models in which all of the axioms of hyperbolic or Riemannian geometry are true are much harder to define. However, our simple models can also give us an inkling of how geometers were able to prove that if Euclidean geometry is consistent, then so is non-Euclidean geometry. For it is the Euclidean geometry of the circle and sphere which tells us that the non-Euclidean axioms are true of the 'spaces' we defined.

These consistency proofs were of the utmost importance. They showed that the 2,000-year programme of proving Euclid's axiom of parallels was attempting to do the logically impossible. They showed that doubts about the mathematical respectability of non-Euclidean geometries were unfounded. From a mathematical point of view, each of the three geometries is on a par, each is a possible description of the structure of space. (Some would say instead here, 'each is a description of a possible space' – but this is not to say the same thing.)

WHY NON-EUCLIDEAN GEOMETRIES ARE PHILOSOPHICALLY IMPORTANT

The discovery of non-Euclidean geometries, and the proofs of their consistency, are also of the utmost importance to philosophy. They deprived the rationalists of their paradigm of the synthetic a priori. And they gave the empiricists an important clue as to how they might after all accommodate mathematical knowledge within empiricism.

At the beginning of this chapter we said that around 1800 everybody thought that (Euclidean) geometry was a priori knowledge and a true description of the structure of space. Earlier we discussed the difficulties empiricists had with (Euclidean) geometry. We pointed out that, unlike ordinary a posteriori truths, the truths of Euclidean geometry seem to be practically irrefutable. We combined (see p. 189) Euclid with optics to obtain a refutable conclusion:

Euclid: The angles of any triangle add up to 180°.
Geometrical optics: Light travels in straight lines.
Conclusion: The angles of any 'light triangle' add up to 180°.

And we said that if measurements on some 'light triangle' were to contradict this conclusion, we should not pin the blame on Euclid since this would leave us in the catastrophic position of having no geometry to work with. The invention of non-Euclidean geometries completely changed this situation.

The first to appreciate this may have been Gauss (Carnap 1966: 135). Gauss is reported to have measured the angles of a 'light triangle' produced by three torches on three hill-tops in order to determine which geometry (Euclidean or hyperbolic) was true. If this report is correct, then Gauss was the first to see that once we have competing geometries which yield different results about the angle-sums of 'light triangles', it is up to experience or experiment to teach us which is true. We no longer know a priori that Euclid is true of real space. (Actually, we never knew this – the illusion that we did was brought about by the poverty of the then-current mathematics, which provided us with only one geometrical option.) We can now at least imagine how we might refute Euclid. What was previously unthinkable now becomes at least thinkable. If Gauss had found that the angle-sum of his 'light triangle' was less than 180°, he might just have pinned the blame on Euclid and said that space is hyperbolic. (If Gauss had found an angle-sum greater than 180°, he would have had a problem: unaware of the possibility of Riemannian geometry, he would probably have put the result down to errors of measurement or to some other source.) In fact, Gauss found neither of these things. The angles of his 'light triangle' (the report continues) added up to 180°. Did this prove that Euclid was correct after all? Hardly, for the very next triangle Gauss measured might have had a different angle-sum. Did Gauss's result at least refute non-Euclidean geometries? It did not do this either, and this for a subtle reason. Gauss's measurements could not have shown him that the angles of his 'light triangle' added up to exactly 180°. Every measurement involves some margin of error *e*. The most Gauss could say is that the angles of his 'light triangle' added up to 180° plus or minus *e*. The margin of error leaves a loophole for the non-Euclidean geometer to slip through. Hyperbolic geometry gives angle-sums less than 180°, and the bigger the triangle the less the sum. Riemannian geometry gives angle-sums more than 180°, and the bigger the triangle the greater the sum. But we do not know by how much the angle-sum of a given triangle of a given size will fall short of or exceed 180° until the value of a certain quantity (the 'coefficient of curvature') is fixed. With that value unfixed, the non-Euclidean geometer could always say that Gauss's 'light triangle' was not big enough for the deficit or excess in angle-sum to be measured, because the deficit or excess was less than the margin of error in the measurements.

In the respect just mentioned, and in many others, non-Euclidean geometries are more complicated than Euclidean geometry. This led the great French physicist-mathematician Henri Poincaré to argue that although it is logically possible to refute and reject Euclid, we will never actually do this because the resulting system of science will be too complicated. If things were to go wrong, it would always be simpler to stick with Euclid and pin the blame on something else (optics, perhaps). Kant was wrong to say that we must (logically must) structure our science on Euclidean principles – he was right to say that we always will. Poincaré said, in Kantian style, that we will always impose a Euclidean structure on our science: by refusing to take seriously a complicated science which does not incorporate Euclidean geometry, we make that geometry a priori true by convention or decision. Kant talked, of course, not of structuring our science on Euclidean principles, but of structuring our perceptions on Euclidean principles. Some Kantians distinguish 'perceptual space' from 'physical space' and say that Kant was right about the former. I do not know if they are right, because I do not know what 'perceptual space' is.

There is a final twist to our tale. We already mentioned the most successful scientific theory ever proposed, Newton's theory of mechanics and gravitation. This theory assumes and incorporates Euclidean geometry. (It is because all took Newton for granted that all took Euclid for granted, too.) However, in 1916 Albert Einstein proposed a new and radically different theory of mechanics and gravitation, which assumes and incorporates Riemannian geometry. The two theories yield different results for experiments involving very fast-moving and/or very massive bodies. And the experiments favour Einstein's theory over Newton's. Many physicists today, asked whether space is Euclidean or Riemannian, would answer that the evidence suggests it is Riemannian. They might add that for most everyday and scientific purposes we will not go far wrong, and certainly will not go detectably wrong, if we assume that it is Euclidean. Surveyors need not drop everything to learn non-Euclidean geometry! (On Poincaré's and Einstein's views, see Carnap 1966: Chapter 15.)

It does not matter for philosophical purposes whether such physicists are right. What matters for philosophical purposes is that the invention of non-Euclidean geometries taught us that the question of whether space is Euclidean or not is a question of physics to be settled, in the last analysis, by observation and experiment. That invention taught us that we do not have a priori knowledge of the structure of space. Hilary Putnam has said that the invention of non-Euclidean geometry 'is the most important event in the history of science for the epistemologist' (1975: x). We are beginning to see what he meant.

It would be too strong, and therefore wrong, to say that the invention of non-Euclidean geometries destroys rationalism. It would not be wrong to say that it destroys the most important argument for rationalism. That argument was a simple one: Euclidean geometry gives us synthetic a priori knowledge of the structure of space; therefore synthetic a priori knowledge exists. The invention of non-Euclidean geometries showed that the premise of this argument is false.

LOGICAL EMPIRICISTS TAKE COMFORT

It is one thing to destroy an argument for rationalism and quite another to vindicate the empiricist point of view. Could empiricists take comfort from the events we have related? Some empiricists, calling themselves 'logical empiricists' to distinguish themselves from their empiricist forebears, derived much comfort from them. Earlier empiricists had been undecided whether to put geometry into the analytic a priori or the synthetic a posteriori compartment of Kant's box. Logical empiricists say that we must first make an important distinction, the distinction between pure geometry and applied geometry. Pure geometry is what pure mathematicians engage in; Euclidean and non-Euclidean geometers engaged in it in the nineteenth century. Applied geometry arises, as its name suggests, when we try to apply a theory of pure geometry to the world. Questions like 'Is real space Euclidean or non-Euclidean?' or 'Do the angles of "light triangles" add up to less than 180°, exactly 180°, or more than 180°?' are questions of applied geometry. In fact, they are an abstract and difficult type of physics question. What the invention of non-Euclidean geometries taught us is that the assertions of applied geometry are synthetic a posteriori assertions: we have to try to learn from experience or experiment whether or not they are true.

Because applied geometry is a posteriori it is subject to all the sceptical arguments to the effect that no such belief or assertion can be known with certainty to be true. There are some special considerations that lead to the same conclusion. In order to apply geometry we must always combine it with some other theory. Remember our little example about 'light triangles', where we had to combine Euclidean geometry with geometrical optics to obtain a testable conclusion. When tests confirm such conclusions we cannot, of course, infer that the premises from which they follow are true, since false premises can yield true conclusions. When tests refute such conclusions we are not forced to conclude that our geometrical premise is false: we can always try to pin the blame on the non-geometrical premises (and Poincaré said that this is what we always should do in order to preserve Euclidean geometry). So experience or experiment cannot establish or prove either the truth or the falsity of a statement of applied geometry. Einstein understood this well when he famously remarked:

As far as the laws of [geometry] refer to reality, they are not certain; and as far as they are certain, they do not refer to reality. (Einstein 1921; 28)

Some logical empiricists tried to soften this conclusion by insisting that the 'other premises' with which geometrical statements have to be combined to yield testable conclusions are analytic or definitional truths. They are definitions or stipulations of what geometrical terms mean in applied geometry. So in our little example about 'light triangles' the second premise should really read: 'A straight line is, by definition, the path of a light-ray.' The effect of this is that when things go wrong we must pin the blame on the geometrical premise(s), since the remaining premises are true by stipulation or definition. I see no reason to accept this stipulation about stipulative definitions.

What can logical empiricists say of pure geometry, geometry 'in so far as it is not about the world'? What they would like to say about it will be obvious enough: that it belongs in the analytic a priori compartment of Kant's box, the only other compartment which empiricism allows. In our earlier discussions we found this an implausible position: geometrical axioms and theorems do not seem to be analytic, true by virtue of the meanings of the words they contain. But the logical empiricists found a way around this difficulty, in the form of a new account of the nature of pure geometry. What is the pure geometer really interested in doing? He is interested in finding 'interesting' sets of axioms and in proving 'interesting' theorems from those axioms. He is not interested in whether any set of geometrical axioms or any theorem proved from them is true – that is a question for the applied geometer. When the pure geometer, whether Euclidean or non-Euclidean, has done his work, the result established is always conditional in form:

If Euclid's axioms are true, then the angles of all triangles sum to 180°.

If Bolyai's axioms are true, then the angles of all triangles sum to less than 180°.

> If Riemann's axioms are true, then the angles of all triangles sum to more than 180°.

Now if the pure geometer has done his work well, a proved theorem will logically follow from the axioms used. But where this is the case, a conditional statement linking the axioms to the theorem (a statement like those just given) will be a logical truth. And the logical truths are the least problematic analytic truths. Pure geometry is analytic a priori after all. (For a logical empiricist taking comfort in this way, see Carnap 1966: Chapter 18.)

These are the bare bones of the logical empiricist view of pure geometry. In defence of it the empiricists can point out that it is easy to hide or disguise the conditional character of the assertions of pure mathematics. Geometers are apt to express the three results of the previous paragraph as follows:

> The angles of all Euclidean triangles sum to 180°.
> The angles of all hyperbolic triangles sum to less than 180°.
> The angles of all Riemannian triangles sum to more than 180°.

The empiricist insists, however, that if we unpack the adjectives here, we will be led back to conditional propositions. What is a Euclidean triangle? It is the sort of triangle you get if Euclid's axioms are true. If Euclid's axioms are true, then all triangles are Euclidean, that is, have angles which sum to 180°. Or in short, if Euclid's axioms are true, then the angles of all triangles sum to 180°.

So far we have talked only of geometry. Obviously, the logical empiricist is going to try to extend his view of geometry to the whole of mathematics. We must distinguish pure and applied mathematics. The former establishes conditional assertions which, if true, are logically true. The latter asks whether the axioms of the mathematical theory in question (and therefore also the theorems proved from those axioms) are true of anything in the world. The view that pure mathematics consists entirely of conditional assertions is called 'if-thenism' or 'postulationism'. Earlier we said that is was wildly implausible to suppose that pure mathematics consists entirely of analytic a priori truths. 'There is no biggest prime number' or 'The square on the hypotenuse of a right-angled triangle is equal to the sum of the squares on the other two sides' do not seem to be true by virtue of the meanings of the words they contain. But the logical empiricist is not saying that they are. (Actually, some did say this – they were the logicists and their followers, who will be mentioned in a moment.) What are analytic a priori (because logically true) are rather the statements:

> If the axioms of arithmetic are true, then there is no biggest prime number.
> If the axioms of Euclidean geometry are true, then the square on the hypotenuse of a right-angled triangle is equal to the sum of the squares on the other two sides.

Many would agree that such statements are logical truths. The really controversial claim is that pure mathematics, properly understood, consists entirely of such statements. Because of this, the if-thenist view of pure mathematics is still highly controversial.

One objection to it is that pure mathematicians are not just interested in establishing conditionals linking axioms to theorems, they are also interested in establishing the consistency of collections of axioms, and assertions of consistency are not conditional. Quite so. But this is a weak objection. An (unconditional) assertion of the form 'Axioms *A* are logically consistent' is also, if true, logically true. So the basic if-thenist thesis, that the truths of pure mathematics are all logical truths, can still be maintained, but will require slight reformulation to deal with unconditional assertions of consistency. (Pure mathematicians do not just assert consistency, they also prove it. But all proofs rest upon assumptions or axioms, which lead us to further conditionals: 'If axioms *A* are consistent, then axioms *B* are also consistent' in the case of relative consistency proofs', 'If axioms *A*, then axioms *B* are consistent' in the case of absolute consistency proofs. Such conditional statements are, once again, if true, logically true.)

Another objection to if-thenism is that pure mathematicians

do not just prove things from any old set of axioms, they are interested only in interesting axioms and interesting theorems. This is also a weak objection because the if-thenist can simply accept it and develop an account of what makes axioms or theorems interesting. Such an account might run something like this: a set of axioms is mathematically interesting if it is or might be scientifically interesting, that is, if it has or might have some interesting uses in applied mathematics. This ties 'mathematical interest' to 'scientific interest' and assumes that we can give an independent account of the latter. The qualifications 'or might be' and 'or might have' are meant to deal with notorious cases (like that of non-Euclidean geometry) in which a mathematical theory was worked out long before anyone had any inkling that it actually was of scientific interest.

A third objection to if-thenism is that, although it works for those parts of mathematics where alternative theories are available (such as geometry), it does not work at all for those parts of mathematics where no alternative theories are available (such as arithmetic). It works for the former because when we have alternatives, we see that the question of which alternative is true is a question of applied mathematics. It does not work for the latter: there are no 'alternative arithmetics'; (unconditional) arithmetic truths are still truths and synthetic a priori truths to boot. This is also a weak objection. It involves a massive concession to the if-thenist point of view for large parts of mathematics. The absence of available alternatives is a poor reason to confer synthetic a priori status on any theory; Euclidean geometry had no rival for centuries, yet was never a priori knowledge. Might not alternative arithmetics be devised tomorrow? (Some philosophers have even tried to devise them already – without much success.) Finally, even in the case of arithmetic we must distinguish pure arithmetic from applied arithmetic. The latter is synthetic a posteriori: for example, we learn from experience that '$2 + 2 = 4$' is false when the items added are drops of water and addition is seen as physical amalgamation.

This last point (and much of what preceded it) will be regarded as beside the point by the most strenuous critics of if-thenism. I refer to the mathematical Platonists. Their objections are so important that they deserve a section to themselves.

PLATONISM AND LOGICISM ABOUT MATHEMATICS

According to mathematical Platonism, mathematics deals with special abstract mathematical entities such as natural numbers, geometrical points, sets, or groups. The mathematician seeks to discover the truth about these entities. The natural numbers exist, there is a truth of the matter as to whether any of them is the biggest prime number, and the arithmetician wants to know what the truth of the matter is. Geometrical points and lines exist, there is a truth of the matter as to whether Euclid's axiom of parallels is true of them, and the geometer wants to know what the truth of the matter is. Sets exist, there is a truth of the matter as to whether the next largest set after the set of natural numbers is the set of real numbers, and the set theorist wants to know what the truth of the matter is.

From a Platonist point of view, if-thenism is absurd. The Platonist is not interested in conditionals linking axioms to theorems (he might even accept the if-thenist account of these). The Platonist is interested in the axioms and theorems themselves. These are also true or false statements, and the aim of pure mathematics is to find the true ones. Since '$2 + 2 = 4$' is a truth of arithmetic, the natural numbers two and four must exist for it to be true of. The idea that pure mathematics does not assert the truth of axioms or theorems amounts to the ludicrous idea that pure mathematicians are not interested in mathematical truth. What account can the if-thenist give, not of conditionals linking axioms to theorems, but of the axioms and theorems themselves?

If-thenists have two options here. The first is to deny that mathematical axioms and theorems are, when properly understood, true or false statements at all. This is hard to reconcile with the if-thenist thesis that conditionals linking axioms and theorems are true or false statements. Alternatively, the if-thenist can bite the bullet and say that the axioms and theorems are all false because there are no abstract mathematical entities.

For example, '$2 + 2 = 4$' is false, not because two and two add up to some other number than four, but because there are no numbers for the numerals '2' and '4' to be names of. What, then, is the difference between '$2 + 2 = 4$' and '$2 + 2 = 5$'? The if-thenist cannot, like the Platonist, give the obvious answer that the former is true and the latter false. The if-thenist will have to say that the former is better than the latter, not because it is true, but because it is more useful in applied arithmetic. Whether such an answer can be adequately worked out is still a moot point. (Hartrey Field bites the bullet in this way: see Field 1980 and 1989.)

If-thenism seems absurd. But the Platonist perspective from which it seems absurd is itself fraught with problems. Suppose mathematical objects do exist. They do not exist in space and time: it makes no sense to ask where the number three is at the moment, or when it began to be, or whether it will cease to be. Mathematical objects are abstract objects, eternal Platonic objects. That being so, they enter into no causal relations with objects that do exist in space and time like we do. We cannot experience them through the senses, for sense-experience involves causal transactions between the object experienced and the experiencer. It becomes wholly mysterious how we get to know about these abstract mathematical objects. A special case of this epistemic worry concerns alternative mathematical theories. We said 'Geometrical points and lines exist, there is a truth of the matter as to whether Euclid's axiom of parallels is true of them, and the geometer wants to know what the truth of the matter is.' How does the geometer set about finding this out? Geometers might agree that there is a truth of the matter as to which applied geometry is correct. But that is not the question here. I doubt that many pure mathematicians think that in the Platonic realm of 'mathematical objects' there is space which is either Euclidean or hyperbolic or Riemannian, or regard it as their task to find out which of these options is true. As with geometry, so with set theory. There are alternative, equally consistent, 'Cantorian' and 'non-Cantorian' set theories. The former has something called the continuum hypothesis as an axiom, the latter has the negation of the continuum hypothesis as an axiom. (The continuum hypothesis, in its simplest form, says that there is no infinite number between the infinite number of natural numbers and the bigger infinite number of real numbers. For an excellent non-technical account of non-Cantorian set theory see Cohen and Hersh 1967.) Do many set theorists believe that in the Platonic realm there is a single 'universe of sets' which is either Cantorian or non-Cantorian, or regard it as their task to find out which it is? It is completely unclear how the pure geometer or the pure set theorist would set about these Platonic tasks. They have no access to the Platonic realm. They cannot inspect this abstract 'space' or 'universe of sets' to see what it is like. (Most mathematicians give different accounts of these two examples, regarding the Platonist 'pure geometer' as absurd, and the Platonist 'pure set theorist' as far from absurd. But what is the difference between them?)

Early in the twentieth century these epistemic worries seemed for a while to have been laid to rest. The logicists (Frege and Russell) claimed that pure thought could teach us about mathematical objects because these objects are logical objects, and truths about them are logical truths. This was an incredibly bold thesis, carefully to be distinguished from its pallid if-thenist counterpart. The logicists were saying not just that 'If the axioms of arithmetic are true, then there are infinitely many prime numbers' was a logical truth, but that the axioms of arithmetic themselves or statements like 'There are infinitely many prime numbers' were also logical truths. (They did not, however, extend this view to geometry: Frege accepted Kant's view of geometry and denied that the alternative geometries were genuine geometries at all; Russell accepted the if-thenist view of geometry.) The attempt by Frege and Russell to demonstrate the logicist thesis is called the 'logicist programme'.

The logicist programme failed. Frege and Russell were not able to prove the axioms of arithmetic from admittedly logical truths. It turned out, in fact, that one of the things they thought logically true was actually logically false! What they were able to show was that if we can help ourselves to lots of sets or collections of things, then we can identify the natural numbers with certain sets and show that the axioms of arithmetic are true of them. The number o is the set of all those sets which are equinumerous with the sets of all those things which are not identical to themselves (the 'empty set'). The number 1 is the set of all those sets which are equinumerous with the set whose only member is the empty set. The number 2 is the set of all those sets which are equinumerous with the set whose only members are the empty set and the set whose only member is the empty set. And so on. One set is 'equinumerous' with another if their members can be placed in 'one–one correspondence', that is, if we can assign to each member of the first set exactly one member of the second and vice versa. (A maid laying a banquet table may know that the set of knives she laid is equinumerous with the set of forks she laid without counting the knives or forks: it is enough for her to know that every time she put down a knife she also put down its corresponding fork.) Natural numbers, the simplest mathematical objects, are actually logical objects, objects whose existence is guaranteed by logic.

All this is fine provided we have the sets. But how to get the sets? One way to 'get a set' is to list its members. For example, we might get or form the set consisting of Frege, Russell and Mount Everest (which set is, by the foregoing, a member of the number 3). But it is hard to list all the members of very big sets, and impossible to list all the members of the infinitely big sets with which mathematics deals. Another way to get a set is to specify some property or feature which things in the set possess and things outside it do not. Thus we might get, form or obtain the set of red things or the set of mathematicians or the set of one-legged piano players. But when we get sets this way we are assuming that every property determines a set (the set of things that have that property).

This is what turned out to be logically false! Russell asked the queer question whether a set can be a member of itself. Most sets are not members of themselves. The set of one-legged piano players is not itself a one-legged piano player. But the set of things which are not tea-spoons is not a tea-spoon (nobody stirred their tea with a set), so it does seem to be a member of itself. Call a set 'normal' if it is not a member of itself. We have now specified a property of sets, 'normality'. So, on the assumption that every property determines a set, there is a set of all the 'normal' sets. Now ask whether the set of all 'normal' sets is 'normal'. If it is 'normal', then it is not a member of itself, and so is a member of the set of all 'normal' sets, namely itself. If it is not 'normal', then it is a member of itself, namely, of the set of all 'normal' sets, and so is 'normal'. Either way, we have a contradiction. This is Russell's paradox.

This mind-spinning result (if you, the reader, are reading the preceding paragraph for the third time, do not worry!) – this mind-spinning result convinced Frege and Russell that they could not assume that every property determines (yields the existence of) a set. So less profligate 'set existence axioms' were assumed. And thus was set theory (as opposed to 'naive set theory') born.

Russell and Frege thought they were proving arithmetic from logic. They thought they were establishing an important philosophical result (that unconditional arithmetic truths are analytic a priori). What they actually established was an important mathematical result (that if the axioms of set theory are true, so are those of arithmetic). This result, like all the results of pure mathematics, is conditional in form – or so the if-thenist would insist. Russell resorted to if-thenism when he realised that the logicist programme had failed. Frege, on the other hand, tried to extend his Kantian view of geometry to the whole of mathematics. The logical empiricists fudged the issue, dodging between if-thenism and logicism as if they were the same thesis (for further details, see Musgrave 1977).

It is time to sum up. The invention of non-Euclidean geometries deprived rationalism of its paradigm. It also suggested to empiricists a new way to deal with mathematics: distinguish pure mathematics from applied mathematics, locate the latter in the synthetic a posteriori compartment of Kant's box, and the former in the analytic a priori compartment of Kant's box. One attempt to do the last, logicism, is generally admitted to have failed. Another attempt, if-thenism, is still hotly debated among philosophers. On the other hand, the logical empiricist view of applied mathematics has met with pretty wide acceptance. The rationalist dream, 'certain knowledge of the objects of experience by means of pure thinking', is shattered even though the nature of pure mathematics remains problematic indeed.

CHAPTER 14

Truth and truth-theories

We have been considering the battle between the sceptics and the two camps of dogmatists. Suppose for the sake of the argument that the sceptics have won (nothing in what follows will depend on that supposition). Suppose, in other words, that the sceptics are right, and that certain knowledge is unattainable. (We might want to qualify this by saying that nontrivial certain knowledge is unattainable.) There is a radical way out of this sceptical nightmare, if nightmare it be. That is the topic of the present chapter.

Dogmatists and sceptics alike accept a traditional account of what it would take to know something. Both accept the justified true belief account of knowledge, according to which knowledge requires truth. In our discussions so far we have assumed that we all know well enough what truth is, what it means to say of something that it is true. Perhaps this was a rather uncritical assumption. After all, Pontius Pilate asked famously 'What is truth?' Perhaps the concept of truth is not so unproblematic as we have been assuming. And perhaps an answer to the sceptic will emerge from a consideration of that concept. This brings us to the philosophical problem of truth.

THE PROBLEM OF TRUTH AND ITS COMMON-SENSE SOLUTION

What is the philosophical problem of truth? It is Pilate's question. But Pilate's question is ambiguous. There are actually two quite different questions which he might have been asking, which it is crucial to keep separate:

(1) What is truth? That is, what does it mean to say of something that it is true?

(2) What is true? That is, what is the truth about the matter in which we are interested (whatever that is)? And how do we find out the truth of that matter?

Perhaps when Pilate asked 'What is truth?', he was really asking a question of the second kind, asking what was the truth of the matter he had in hand. No matter. What is clear is that the second question is far more important than the first: it is actually the problem of knowledge in disguise, and our earlier discussions have all, in a way, been devoted to it.

Yet the first conceptual problem is in one respect more fundamental than the second. Until we know what truth is (what the word 'true' means), we cannot set about investigating the second, more important problem. Just as, until we know what the word 'unicorn' means, we cannot set about investigating whether there are any. (Everything is contentious in philosophy: there are those who contend that what goes for unicorns does not go for truth, and that the questions 'What is truth?' and 'What is true?' cannot be separated as we have separated them. We shall get to these philosophers soon.)

So far we have been taking for granted a simple, common-sense answer to the question 'What is truth?' We are interested in what it means for a sentence or statement or proposition to be true. Our simple answer, applied to a particular example, is:

(1) The statement 'Snow is white' is true if and only if snow is white.

This is the common-sense idea of truth. A Norwegian philosopher called Arne Naess actually presented non-philosophers with cases like (1) and asked them whether that was what they understood by the word 'true'. He reports that 90 per cent said 'Yes' (Naess 1938). I suspect that the other 10 per cent thought he was crazy to be asking such trite questions, and read more into the question than was intended. Philosophers have tried to capture this common-sense theory of truth in general formulations or slogans:

To say of what is that it is not, or of what is not that it is, is
false: while to say of what is that it is, or of what is not that
it is not, is true. (Aristotle, *Metaphysics*, 1908: 1011b26–9)

A statement is true if and only if what it states to be the case
really is the case.

A statement is true if and only if it corresponds to the facts.

Aristotle's formulation is fine, except that it tells us only about
what it takes for statements of the forms '*A* is' and '*A* is not' to
be true. The other two formulations are fine, too, except that
philosophers have found all sorts of 'difficulties' in them, and as
a result have come to think the common-sense idea of truth
highly problematic. These philosophers 'raise a dust and then
complain they cannot see' (as Berkeley said in another context).
But before seeing those 'difficulties' and making good that
claim, let us see the most important difficulty which the
common-sense idea of truth raises.

This difficulty is that the common-sense theory of truth makes
it difficult (sceptics say impossible) to know the truth. For it
makes of truth a relation between what we believe and the way
the world is, the facts. According to this view of truth, something
might be true even though nobody believes it, or false even
though everybody believes it. Operating with this view of truth,
sceptics are able to show (or so we are assuming) that certain
knowledge is unattainable.

SUBJECTIVE TRUTH-THEORIES

This suggests a new way to defeat the sceptic. Let us define truth
as consisting, not of a relation between belief and the outside
world, but of some 'internal' property of beliefs. Then, assuming
that the believer can know whether his beliefs possess this
'internal' property, the believer can also know the truth. We
might call any such theory of truth a subjective theory, since
any such theory identifies truth with some subjective property of
beliefs. Here are some examples:

The self-evidence theory: a belief is true if and only if it is self-
evident to me;

The indubitability theory: a belief is true if and only if I cannot doubt it;

The clear and distinct perception theory: a belief is true if and only if I perceive (conceive) it clearly and distinctly;

The coherence theory: a belief is true if and only if it coheres with the rest of my beliefs;

The pragmatist theory: a belief is true if and only if I find it useful to have it;

The verifiability theory: a belief is true if and only if it is confirmed by my experience;

The consensus theory: a belief is true if and only if my intellectual community agrees that it is.

Many of these formulations are vague (of which a little more later). All of them are unfamiliar: in particular, it is not customary to emphasise, as I have done, their subjective character. For example, the self-evidence theory would normally be expounded by saying that truth is self-evidence – not self-evidence to me (or anybody else), just self-evidence. But I formulate them as I do for a reason: the antisceptical virtues of these theories (if virtues they be) derive only from such formulations. I am an authority on what is self-evident to me, so if this is what 'true' means I am an authority on what is true also. If something could be self-evident to me without being genuinely self-evident (whatever that might be), then the sceptic remains undefeated and certainty remains as unattainable as ever. Similarly with the other theories. For example, if something could cohere with my beliefs without being genuinely coherent (whatever that means), then the coherence theory of truth would have no anti-sceptical virtues at all. So let us stick with my subjectivist formulations for a while. And let us emphasise that these are theories about the meaning of the word 'true': the connective on their right-hand sides is to be read 'if and only if (by definition)'.

There is a grain of truth in these subjective theories of truth. It is true that we use the various subjective properties of beliefs as fallible symptoms of truth, as fallible guides as to what we will believe to be true or accept as true. If a belief strikes us as self-evident or indubitable, we tend to accept it as true. If a belief 'coheres' with our other beliefs, we tend to accept it as true. Things which turn out to be 'expedient in the way of our thinking' (to use William James's phrase, see James 1907: 222) tend to be accepted as true. Things confirmed by our experience, or by others in our 'intellectual community', tend to be accepted as true also. But to say that X is a fallible symptom of truth or a fallible guide to truth is a long way from saying that 'true' means X. To obtain a subjective theory of truth, you first conflate the questions 'What is truth?' and 'What is true?' You then ask how to decide what is true (which is part of the second question). Next you convert some fallible symptom of truth into an infallible criterion of it. Finally, you invoke criterion philosophy: the meaning of a word is our criterion for applying it. Hey presto: 'true' means 'self-evident', or whatever! (This is not the only way to get a subjective theory of truth. Another is based upon Wittgenstein's later slogan that the meaning of a word is the use to which it is put. It is observed that people use phrases like 'That is true' to endorse some statement just made, or to emphasise it, or to express a liking for it, or try to get on the right side of the person who said it and so on. Meaning being use, we are then told that 'That's true' means 'I endorse that' or 'I emphasise that' or 'I like that' or 'I would like to get on the right side of whoever asserted that'. All such theories are also subjective: truth ceases to be a property of statements made and becomes instead a psychological feature of statement-makers.)

Every step might be disputed. The two questions are not to be conflated: we cannot ask how we decide what is true until we have first found out what the word 'true' means. Symptoms are not criteria, and in any case no general criterion of truth could possibly be known. For suppose someone says: (C) A belief's possessing property C is an infallible criterion that the belief is true. Sextus Empiricus asked how (C) itself could be known to be true. If you answer that (C) itself possesses property C, then you argue in a circle. If you answer that (C) does not possess property C, but some other property D which assures you of its truth, then you have admitted that possessing C is not an infallible criterion of truth (since (C) lacks C yet is true) and an infinite regress opens up when we ask how you know that (C)'s possessing D assures you of its truth.

The chief worry here concerns criterion philosophy itself. Suppose it is claimed that A is an infallible criterion for B. Such a claim is interesting only if A and B do not mean the same thing. It is interesting to be told that a man's being unhappy is an infallible criterion for his being a bachelor, that a person's having a high temperature is an infallible criterion for that person's having the flu, that an oil-slick on the water is an infallible criterion for a ship's having sunk. But these claims are interesting precisely because 'is unhappy' does not mean the same as 'is a bachelor', 'has a high temperature' does not mean the same as 'has the flu', and 'there is an oil-slick on the water' does not mean the same as 'a ship has sunk'. In contrast, it is not interesting to be told that a man's being unmarried is an infallible criterion of his being a bachelor. Criterion philosophy is self-defeating: once you identify the meaning of a word with our criterion for applying it, you rob the fact (or alleged fact) that we have a criterion for applying that word of any philosophical interest. (I am aware that in the three examples given here we do not really have infallible criteria, but rather highly fallible symptoms. Uninteresting analyticities aside, infallible criteria are hard to find.)

So the route to subjective theories of truth is highly suspect. Let us next see what follows from them. What was promised was a victory over the sceptic. But the victory is completely hollow and the tactic which achieves it entirely verbal. The sceptic says we know nothing, have no justified true beliefs, in one sense of the term 'true'. And the reply is that we do know things, do have justified true beliefs, in another sense of the term 'true'. You might as well refute scepticism about unicorns by turning the word 'unicorn' into a synonym for 'rabbit' and then insisting that there are some unicorns (rabbits).

An objection to subjective theories of truth is that they all lead to relativism. They all have the consequence that a statement may be true for me but not for you. For a statement may be self-evident to me but not to you, unable to be doubted by me but doubted by you, clearly and distinctly perceived by me but not by you, cohere with my beliefs but not with yours, be useful for me to believe but not for you, be confirmed by my experience but not by yours, be agreed upon by my 'intellectual community' but not by yours. Some think this is no real objection because relativism is right. The popularity of locutions like 'That's true for you but not for me' shows, it is said, that most people are relativists about truth. Relativist locutions are popular. But this is hardly decisive: 'That's true for you but not for me' may simply be an unclear way of saying 'You think that's true but I do not'. Thus construed, they are quite compatible with an absolutist view of truth.

What if we do not construe relativist locutions this way, but instead take them literally? Why is relativism about truth a bad thing? Suppose that A finds S self-evident, while B finds 'It is not the case that S' self-evident. (What goes for self-evidence here will also go for any other subjective property of beliefs.) So on the self-evidence theory of truth, S is true for A and 'It is not the case that S' is true for B. We like to think that A and B might have a rational discussion to resolve their disagreement. But this is now impossible because there is no real disagreement between A and B. They will not, or should not, argue about what they each find self-evident: A will, or should, accept that B finds Not-S self-evident, and B will, or should, accept that A finds S self-evident. (Remember, each person is supposed to be an authority on the subjective features of his beliefs.) What they should argue about, of course, is whether or not S is true. But we no longer have the common-sense notion of truth which would make this possible. A and B must simply 'agree to differ', not about what to believe, but about what is true for each of them. Sometimes having to 'agree to differ' in this way might not matter. But suppose A and B have to reach a consensus because they have to act either on S or on Not-S. Rational discussion having been foreclosed, force remains the only option: either A forces B to act on S, or B forces A to act on Not-S. In short, relativism about truth encourages the use of violence to achieve consensus in action (if not in belief).

Subjectivism about truth entails relativism about truth, and that flies in the face of two laws of truth. These are the law of excluded middle ('Either S is true or Not-S is true') and the law of contradiction ('S and Not-S are not both true'). Suppose that we make these laws adequacy conditions on any account of truth, that is, require that any account yield these laws if it is to be adequate. Then any subjective theory of truth must be deemed inadequate.

So we have a *reductio ad absurdum* argument against subjective truth-theories: they are to be rejected because they lead to the absurdities of relativism and violation of the laws of truth. But in philosophy one person's *reductio* argument is the next person's derivation of interesting consequences. The subjectivist might simply respond by saying: 'So much the worse for absolutism about truth and your so-called "laws" of truth.'

It is interesting, however, that adherents of these truth-theories tend not to tough it out in this way. Instead, they try to present the theories so that they do not have the relativistic consequences just mentioned. They would reject my narrowly subjectivist formulations of the various theories, in favour of formulations which 'go social' or 'go ideal' or 'go to the long run'. Here are some examples:

Self-evidence: a belief is true if and only if it would be self-evident to an ideally rational inquirer (or an ideally rational community of inquirers) in the long run.

Indubitability: a belief is true if and only if an ideally rational inquirer (or community of such) would be unable to doubt it even at the end of an ideally rational inquiry.

Clarity and distinctness: a belief is true if and only if an ideally rational inquirer (God?) would perceive it clearly and distinctly.

Coherence: a belief is true if and only if it coheres with the beliefs which an ideally rational inquirer would come to possess in the long run.

Pragmatism: a belief is true if and only if it proves useful right through to the end of an ideally rational inquiry.

Verifiability: a belief is true if and only if it is confirmed by all the experiences of an ideally rational community of inquirers.

Consensus: a belief is true if and only if an ideally rational community of inquirers would always agree that it was.

The hope is that by going social, ideal and to the long run in this kind of way relativism about truth will be avoided and the laws of truth preserved. Perhaps – and perhaps not. It is little more than a pious hope that going social, ideal and to the long run will deliver a single belief-system which contains one of P and not-P but never both of them. Why, for example, should not two ideally rational inquirers arrive in the long run at incompatible belief-systems?

Even if we set aside this question, the price paid for these devices will be obvious enough: they rid subjectivist theories of truth of any anti-sceptical virtues (if virtues they be). The sceptic is not interested in whether an ideally rational inquirer (God?) or community of such can know things in the long run. She is interested in whether we human beings can know things in the short run. (Human beings are always in the short run – in the long run, as Keynes said, we are all dead.) Social, ideal and in the long run qualifications to the subjective truth-definitions make truth just as inaccessible to human beings as does the common-sense or objective theory of truth. (In the same way, making self-evidence a semantic, rather than an epistemic or psychological, feature of statements also makes it inaccessible to us – as we saw in pp. 192–3 of Chapter 10.)

In fact, there is an unresolved tension among the subjectivists. When anti-sceptical motives are uppermost, they go subjective. When the desire to stay close to the ordinary conception of truth surfaces, they go social, ideal and to the long run. I think it would be better if we had never departed from the ordinary objective conception of truth in the first place. For I find it impossible to characterise what an ideally rational inquirer would in the long run come to believe in any other way than this: the truth.

Some particular subjective truth theories have difficulties

peculiar to themselves. The coherence theory, for example, seems seriously incomplete because it requires a stock of beliefs about whose truth or falsehood it says nothing, and 'tests' other beliefs for truth by seeing if they 'cohere' with that stock of beliefs. Again, what exactly is coherence? There are two logical accounts of it, but neither will do. If we say that a belief *b* coheres with a stock of beliefs *B* when it is consistent with *B*, then the law of contradiction fails: both *b* and not-*b* might be consistent with *B* and hence true. A stronger logical view is that a belief *b* coheres with a stock of beliefs *B* if it is derivable from them. But now the law of excluded middle fails: neither *b* nor not-*b* may be derivable from *B* and hence neither would be true. (To illustrate both, let *B* be the pretty impoverished stock of beliefs consisting of the single belief *Cogito ergo sum* – and let *b* be the belief that the moon is made of green cheese.)

The foregoing rests upon plausible assumptions about the nature of the stock of beliefs *B*. It may be objected that an ideally rational inquirer in the long run will have a stock of beliefs *B* which is consistent and complete: given any further belief *b*, either *b* or not-*b* will be derivable from *B* but not both. At the end of this chapter we will show that this ideal situation is not achievable. For the moment, let us simply remark that going ideal and to the long run with coherence gives only a God's-eye perspective on truth and is no use to beings whose stocks of beliefs do not have this ideal character.

It will be objected that all this uncritically and naively assumes that there is an unproblematic common-sense, objective conception of truth. And it will be pointed out that part of the reason why philosophers investigate alternative conceptions of truth (including the 'subjective' ones) is that this naive assumption is false. Let us investigate.

TARSKI'S T-SCHEME

So far all we have said about the ordinary conception of truth concerned a particular example and a few traditional slogans. The slogans included 'Truth is correspondence with the facts'. The example was:

(1) The statement 'Snow is white' is true if and only if snow is white.

Now (1) is not, of course, a general definition of truth for all the statements of the English language. But given any statement of the English language, we can explain what it means to say of that statement that it is true with a sentence like (1). The general form of such sentences is:

(T) The statement *S* is true if and only if *P*

where '*S*' is a name of the statement in question and '*P*' is a translation of that statement into the language in which the statement of the form (T) is formulated (more of 'translation' in a moment). This is the famous T-scheme formulated by Alfred Tarski (1956: 155–6 or 1944: 344).

According to Tarski, we could get a general definition of truth for all the statements of the English language if we could list them all and give a statement of the form (T) for each. But the number of statements of English (or of any other natural language) is infinite and we cannot make infinitely long lists. Moreover, it is sometimes not completely clear whether something is a statement of English (the same applies to any other natural language). Alfred Tarski solved (avoided?) these problems by switching his attention to artificial languages where it is clear whether a given expression counts as a genuine statement. Tarski proposed a Convention T to the effect that an adequate definition of truth for a language should entail a statement of the form (T) for each statement of the language. And he showed that it is possible to satisfy this convention for the artificial language(s) he considered. He also showed that his truth-definitions for these artificial languages entail the laws of truth. Finally, the expressive power of languages for which Tarski truth-definitions can be given is considerable: any statement of English (or any other natural language) can be expressed in (or translated into) one of those languages.

The technical details of Tarskian truth-definitions are considerable. Fortunately we need not enter into them, because most if not all of the philosophical worries do not concern the technical details, but rather Tarski's T-scheme.

One worry is that the T-scheme, and statements like (1) that are instances of it, are trivial. Sometimes it is said that (1) is trivial because it is circular: the same thing (the statement 'Snow is white') appears on both sides. This is a misunderstanding: on the left is a statement about a statement which contains the name of that statement: on the right is a statement about snow. The misunderstanding is enhanced by the fact that (1) uses a quotation-mark name of the statement, formed by putting the statement in quotes. We tend to read inside the quotation-marks, and when we do we read the same statement there as we find on the right. But the quotation-mark name is a unit and we should not read inside the quotes. In doing so we make the same mistake as he who says that 'Socrates is a rat' is analytically true because its predicate ('rat') is contained in its subject 'Socrates'. We can avoid this mistake, and the accusation of circularity to which it leads, by not using quotation-mark names. Christen the statement 'Snow is white' with the name 'Icabod' and say:

The statement Icabod is true if and only if snow is white.

Or number the statements of the language we are interested in and say (supposing 'Snow is white' is numbered 17):

The statement numbered 17 is true if and only if snow is white.

Or find out that 'Snow is white' is my favourite statement and say:

Alan Musgrave's favourite statement is true if and only if snow is white.

Or be systematic, if long-winded, and say:

The statement containing three words, the first word consisting of the letters 's', 'n', 'o', and 'w', in that order, the second consisting of the letters 'i' and 's' in that order, and the third consisting of the letters 'w', 'h', 'i', 't', and 'e' in that order, is true if and only if snow is white.

(Incidentally, the fact that not all the names of statements need be quotation-mark names shows that the current fashion of calling the T-scheme the 'disquotational scheme' is rather misleading.)

There is quite another way to dispel the accusation that (1) is trivial because circular. (1) speaks about a statement of English and it does so in English. Compare:

> (1*) The statement 'La neige est blanche' is true if and only if snow is white.

(1*) speaks in English about a statement of French. It is by no means necessary that the language we speak about truth in must be the same as the language whose truths we speak about. This is why, in explaining Convention T, I said that 'P' is a translation of statement S into the language in which the statement of form (T) is formulated. (Where the languages are the same, as in (1), we have a degenerate case of 'translation'.) Now even if we make the mistake of reading inside the quotation-marks in (1*), we will not think it trivial: it imparts the interesting piece of linguistic information that the French statement 'La neige est blanche' means that snow is white. (Disquotation applied to (1*) results, of course, in nonsense.)

Incidentally, Tarski is sometimes accused of having the mistaken view that sentences, viewed as meaningless sequences of inscriptions, have truth-values. The accusation is misguided. Any statement of the form (T) involves a translation of a sentence, which shows that it is not being treated as a meaningless sequence of inscriptions. Tarski himself makes it perfectly clear that his truth-bearers, and falsity-bearers, are meaningful sentences or statements. He even called his theory the semantic conception of truth, where semantics deals with meanings.

But perhaps the accusation of triviality is not based on the mistaken claim that statements like (1) are circular. Perhaps the thought is that (1) is trivial because it does not tell us whether or not 'Snow is white' is true, nor does it give us any indication how we might set about finding out whether or not 'Snow is white' is true. This thought stems from the idea that the question 'What is truth?' cannot be separated from the question 'What is true?': a theory of truth should tell us what is true and what not, or at least tell us how to find out. Should an account of what the word 'influenza' means tell us who has influenza and who does not, or at least tell us how to find this out? This is criterion philosophy once again. Tarski's theory of truth is trivial in this sense and so it should be. An account of what a word means should not be expected to solve epistemological problems: semantics or the theory of meaning cannot absorb the whole of philosophy.

Is Tarski's semantic conception of truth rightly regarded as a version of the classical objective or correspondence theory of truth? Tarski himself thought so (see, for example, Tarski 1944: 342–3). And we might make the thought explicit by rewriting the T-scheme thus:

> (T*) The statement *S* is true (or corresponds to the facts) if and only if *P*.

But many philosophers disagree with the thought and would reject (T*). Their reason takes us back to the earlier history of the correspondence theory. Earlier correspondence theorists tried to give an account of the correspondence relation (and of the 'facts' which are the second term of that relation). Such an account would tell us what all the truths have in common, what their 'essence' is. It would tell us how thought or language, and reality or the facts, match up with one another. But this search for a general account of correspondence (and of facts), this search for an essence of truth, led nowhere – or to be more precise, it led into a philosophical quagmire.

How exactly can a linguistic item correspond with something non-linguistic? Mathematicians talk of one–one correspondences between collections of things. Are true statements those whose separate words can be placed in one–one correspondence with things in the world? That seems hopeless: 'The cat is on the mat' and 'The mat is on the cat' contain the same words: if the first can be placed in one–one correspondence with things,

Figure 11. Stylised representation

then so can the second: but if the first is true, the second is not. The mathematical notion of correspondence will not help. Perhaps language and reality correspond in the same way that a picture 'corresponds' to what it is a picture of. Ludwig Wittgenstein explored this idea in his *Tractatus Logico-Philosophicus*. It is not completely crazy: there are hieroglyphic languages in which some sentences are little pictures, albeit highly stylised ones. Wittgenstein actually said at one point that all languages were hieroglyphic languages, only some were more stylised than others (1922: 4.016). Which is to say that Figure 11 is a pretty stylised picture of puss on the mat in the corner, and

'The cat is on the mat'

is a more stylised picture of the same thing. But Wittgenstein came to see that this would not work (for reasons we need not go into). And he concluded something much stronger: he concluded that there could be no theory of the way in which language and the world 'match up', that this was something ineffable, something which could be shown but could not be said. As a result, he dismissed his own attempt to say the unsayable, not merely as mistaken, but as meaningless. (See above, p. 22. Wittgenstein still published his meaningless book!) Wittgenstein's strong conclusion looks like (and is) a *non-sequitur*: 'My theory will not work – so no theory will work.'

And then there were troubles with the other term of the correspondence relation, the facts. Is there a fact in the world for every true statement to correspond to? If 'There is a typewriter on the table' is true, is there a fact for this to correspond to?

What sort of entity is this fact? Is it a third entity distinct from the typewriter and the table, yet somehow composed of them? Is it located in the same place as the typewriter and the table? And do true negative statements have facts to correspond to as well? If so, is the table-top cluttered up, not merely with the typewriter and the rest, but also with an infinite series of 'negative facts' for the following infinite series of true statements to correspond to:

> There is not one elephant on the desk.
> There are not two elephants on the desk.
> There are not three elephants on the desk.
> ...
> ...

The table-top will stay cluttered even if we insist that only positive facts exist, for the following are all true, too, and look 'positive':

> There are less than two typewriters on the desk.
> There are less than three typewriters on the desk.
> ...
> ...

Such was the sorry scholastic state of the correspondence theory when Tarski entered upon the scene. Tarski embarks upon none of these questions about the nature of the correspondence relation or of facts. His theory does capture 'the correspondence relation' as well as it can be captured: it tells us that what all true conjunctions have in common is the truth of each conjunct, that what all true existential statements have in common is that what follows the existential quantifier is satisfied by at least one object and so on. (An existential statement has the form 'There exists an x such that ... x ...', where the existential quantifier is the phrase 'There exists an x such that'.) It even tells us, if you like, what the simple truths 'Ronald Reagan is a man' and 'The Empire State Building is a building' have in common: what they have in common is that the objects referred to (Ronald Reagan and the Empire State Building) have the properties referred to (the properties of being a man and being a building). But none of this adds up to an account of the correspondence relation of the kind sought after by earlier correspondence theorists (see Levin 1984: 126). None of it adds up to an account of the essence which all truths share. According to Tarski, languages are many and various, and so are the truths expressible in each. Language is a human creation with a largely conventional component. The idea that all the truths in all the languages might share an essence, form a natural kind like hydrogen atoms or Bengal tigers, is utterly naive.

One might say that Tarski shows that we can have an objective or correspondence theory of truth without giving an account of 'the correspondence relation' or of the 'nature of facts'. Or one might say that Tarski shows the classical correspondence theory of truth to be utterly misguided. I prefer to say the former. But I am also quite happy to say the latter, and to drop the words 'correspondence' and 'fact' if they cause philosophical difficulties of the sort we have considered. The important thing is not these words, but the fact that Tarski's semantic theory captures the common-sense conception of truth, which makes of truth an objective relation between a statement and what that statement is about. I use the term 'objective' to contrast Tarski's theory with the various subjective theories considered earlier. If this term causes philosophical 'difficulties', I shall drop it, too.

CONCEPTUAL IDEALISM

Perhaps the foregoing discussion only scratches the surface of the philosophical 'difficulties' with the idea of correspondence. Here is a 'deeper' worry. We have just said that Tarski's semantic theory makes truth an objective relation between a statement and what that statement is about, a relation between a linguistic item and the world. But this suggests that we can 'get outside' language to see how it matches up with the world. We cannot do this, and Tarskian statements like (1) do not do it. (1) does not relate language to the world, rather it relates one bit of language to another bit of language. As Wittgenstein saw, the way language relates to the world cannot be said (for that is just more language). There cannot be a genuine correspondence theory of truth – so Tarski's theory of truth is not such a theory.

Where to begin? (1) does speak about both a linguistic item (the statement 'Snow is white') and the world (actually, snow). To speak about any item you must use a linguistic item to refer to it. But this does not mean that you only succeed in speaking about linguistic items, and never speak about non-linguistic ones. There is a difference between using a word to speak about the world, and mentioning a word (using a name of a word) to speak about that word. The idea that we are 'imprisoned in language', that all talk is about talk, simply overlooks the use–mention distinction. We are 'imprisoned' in language only in the trivial sense that we cannot talk without using some language. We are not 'imprisoned' in language in the serious sense that we can only talk about (mention) language.

The British empiricists analysed thinking in terms of having streams of 'impressions' and/or 'ideas'. They mistakenly concluded that all we can ever think about are our own impressions and ideas. For example, Hume writes:

Now since nothing is ever present to the mind but perceptions, and since all ideas are deriv'd from something antecedently present to the mind; it follows, that 'tis impossible for us so much as to conceive or form an idea of any thing specifically different from ideas and impressions. Let us fix our attention out of ourselves as much as possible: Let us chace our imagination to the heavens, or to the utmost limits of the universe; we never really advance a step beyond ourselves, nor can conceive any kind of existence, but those perceptions, which have appeared in that narrow compass. (*Treatise*, 1, ii, 6; 67–8)

The 'new way of ideas' is replaced with an even newer 'way of words', but the same mistakes are made. Instead of saying that all we can think about are our own ideas, we now say that all we can talk about are our own words. Pouring psychologistic wine into new linguistic bottles has not improved its flavour.

But 'deeper' still we can go. Is it really the world that we succeed in talking about, the world-in-itself, the world-as-it-is-independently-of-our-linguistic-or-conceptual-scheme? Or is it not rather only the world-as-categorised-by-us? The world-in-itself is not divided up or parcelled out according to any system of concepts. It is we who divide it up and parcel it out according to our system of concepts. The world-in-itself is not divided up into the stuff that is snow and the stuffs that are not snow, or into the things that are white and the things that are not. It is us, with our concepts of snow and of whiteness, who effect this division. Other beings with other interests and other concepts would carve up the world differently. Indeed, they do carve it up differently: Eskimos carve up the stuff we call 'snow' into seven different stuffs, Kalahari bushmen do not carve it into snow and not-snow at all. Again:

Nowadays we say 'it rains'. The old Orkneymen had a range of words for every kind and intensity of rain – a driv, a rug, a murr, a hagger, a dagg, a rev, a hellyiefer. (Brown 1972: 29)

(I do not vouch for the anthropological accuracy of the foregoing: it is enough for our purposes that it might be accurate.) We are imprisoned in our language in the deeper sense that the world we talk about, even talk truly about, is a world which is partly of our own linguistic making, a world-as-described (categorised, conceptualised)-by-us.

Again, where to begin? The foregoing expounds a kind of generalised Kantian conceptual idealism. It is trivially true that different conceptual or linguistic schemes carve up the world differently. It is also trivially true that we cannot conceptualise or talk about the world without using some scheme or other. It is trivially false (I think) that the invention and deployment of such a scheme somehow changes the world or brings into existence a new kind of world, a world-as-described (conceptualised)-by-that-scheme. If science is to be believed, before there were any beings with any schemes, the world contained rain, snow, the sun and the planets. It was just that there were no beings with schemes to note the facts. The moon did not pop into existence when the first being armed with the moon-concept said 'Lo, the moon'. The world (world-in-itself) was not a single undifferentiated blob of 'pure being' until the first concept-mongers started carving it at the joints. What has to be resisted (I think) are Kantian ersatz entities like the world-in-itself versus the world-as-described-by-English-speakers or the world-as-described-by-Eskimos. (Is 'ersatz' German for 'hyphenated', I wonder?) There is just the world and different schemes for describing it, suited to different purposes, and able to latch on to different differences.

Let us with that leave the 'deep' waters of conceptual idealism for shallower ones. It is objected that if Tarski's theory of truth is accepted, then we will be committed to a naive realism concerning lots of things we do not want to be realists about. This is because Convention T can be applied across the board:

(1) The statement 'Snow is white' is true if and only if snow is white.

(2) The statement 'Electrons are negatively charged' is true if and only if electrons are negatively charged.

(3) The statement 'Eating people is wrong' is true if and only if eating people is wrong.

(4) The statement 'The *Mona Lisa* is beautiful' is true if and only if the *Mona Lisa* is beautiful.

(5) The statement 'There are prime numbers greater than a million' is true if and only if there are prime numbers greater than a million.

(6) The statement 'Jack the Ripper gives me the creeps' is true if and only if Jack the Ripper gives me the creeps.

Suppose that (1) yields common-sense realism regarding snow. Then (2) yields scientific realism regarding electrons, (3) yields moral realism regarding wrongness and rightness, (4) yields aesthetic realism about beauty, (5) yields Platonic realism regarding natural numbers, and finally (6) yields realism regarding an entity (the creeps) which Jack the Ripper gives to me (and, no doubt, to others at the same time). This cannot be right. Nobody wants creeps-realism. And in between snow in (1) and the creeps in (6), there are lots of other realisms which many respectable philosophers would dispute. Tarski's scheme must be rejected, not because it is trivial and proves nothing, but because it proves too much.

This criticism is groundless because by itself Tarski's scheme has none of these alleged consequences. To get realism about X or X's (let X range from snow to the creeps) you must:

(a) take statements about X or X's at face-value for logico-philosophical purposes;
(b) apply Tarski's Convention T to those statements;
(c) accept some of those statements (appropriate ones) as true.

To explain. We all eschew realism about the creeps by regarding 'Jack the Ripper gives me the creeps' as an idiom which is not to be taken at face-value for logico-philosophical purposes. We do not say that if it is true (and it is true) then the giving-relation holds between Jack the Ripper, Alan Musgrave and the creeps. Instead, we insist that it be replaced by its non-idiomatic equivalent (say, 'Jack the Ripper makes me nervous'), and that this equivalent is what should be subjected to logico-philosophical analysis. Similarly, those sceptical of Platonic realism can either refuse to take statements about numbers at face-value or take them at face-value and say that any which entail the existence of numbers are false. (The latter is Field's view, as we saw on p. 242.) Those sceptical of realism about electrons can either refuse to take statements about them at face-value (as instrumentalists do) or take them at face-value and say that any which entail the existence of electrons are false (as positivists do) or take them at face-value, say some might be true, but refuse to accept any of them as true (as 'epistemological anti-realists' like Bas van Fraassen (1980) and Larry Laudan (1977) do). Those sceptical of moral or aesthetic realism can take similar courses. Even Bishop Berkeley could accept Tarski's scheme, but say first that statements about material objects taken at face-value are all false, and second (softening the former conclusion) that what they 'really mean' (that is, how Berkeley wants them taken for logico-philosophical purposes) does not involve the existence of material objects at all.

Tarski's Convention T by itself is philosophically neutral between realist and anti-realist views of any kind (Tarski himself said as much when he proposed it; see Tarski 1944, 361–2). What then is its importance for realism? Simply this: it makes realism about entities possible. Other theories of truth, in rather curious ways, do not. For other theories of truth identify it with some internal feature of belief-systems. This done, the semantic rug is pulled from under the realist's feet. The ardent realist about electrons (or whatever) tries to affirm his realism by saying 'But it is true that electrons exist'. The purveyor of the subjective truth-theory says to himself, smiling: 'All that means is that he cannot doubt it, it coheres with his other beliefs, it is expedient for him to think that, and so on.' Tarski's theory of truth does not beg the question in favour of realisms – rather, it is the only theory that does not beg the question against them.

There are many other objections to Tarski's theory of truth. I will confine myself to discussing just two of them. The first concerns the laws of truth which Tarski's theory preserves. It is objected that these laws break down for sentences containing 'egocentric' or 'token-reflexive' words. The sentence 'I am hungry' may be true if uttered by one person, false if uttered by another, contrary to the law of contradiction. 'It is raining here' may be true if uttered in one place, false if uttered in another. 'It is now night-time' may be true if uttered during the night, false if uttered during the day.

It is true that Tarski developed the theory for languages devoid of egocentric or token-reflexive words. The standard way to deal with such sentences is to distinguish sentence-types (e.g. 'I am hungry') from sentence-tokens (e.g. particular utterances of 'I am hungry' by particular people on particular occasions). Different things are said, different statements made, by different tokens of the same sentence-type if that sentence-type contains token-reflexive words. Hence the laws of truth hold only of meaningful sentence-tokens, or if you prefer, of the statements made by sentence-tokens. Each meaningful sentence-token (or each statement made by a sentence-token) is either true or false, and none is both, in conformity with the laws of truth.

THE LIAR PARADOX AND GÖDEL'S INCOMPLETENESS THEOREM

The last objection to Tarski's theory of truth leads into some interesting territory. Tarski's theory preserves the common-sense idea that a sentence is true if what it says is the case really is the case. And it preserves the laws of truth which say that each (declarative) sentence is either true or false but not both. But if we apply these simple ideas to the following sentence, we are in trouble.

> **The only sentence inside this rectangle is false.**

The sentence is either true or false. If it is true, then what it says is the case really is the case; but what it says is that it is false, so it is false. The supposition that it is true leads to a contradiction. Now we would ordinarily take this simply as a *reductio* proof that the sentence is false. But this is no ordinary case. For suppose that it is false; what it says is the case is really not the case; but what it says is that it is false; so it is not false; so it is true. The supposition that it is false leads to a contradiction, too. When we have a 'double contradiction' or a 'double *reductio*' like this, we have a logical paradox on our hands. This one is called the 'paradox of the liar'. So the objection is that Tarski's theory of truth is paradoxical.

Not surprisingly, Tarski was one of the first to take this paradox seriously (1944: 347–51). The paradoxical sentence is formulated in English. Tarski asked what features a language must possess in order for the paradox of the liar to be formulated in it. The liar paradox is a sentence about a sentence (namely itself), so to formulate it the language must contain ways of referring to its own sentences. And the liar paradox says of itself that it is false, so to formulate it the language must contain semantical terms, and in particular the terms 'true' and 'false'. Tarski calls the language whose sentences are being spoken about the 'object language', and the language in which the object language is being discussed the 'metalanguage'. In the case of the liar paradox, as we have formulated it, the object language and the metalanguage are the same, namely English. So it seems that any language which has the expressive power to be a metalanguage of itself (any language which is semantically closed, as Tarski calls this property) will be a language in which the liar paradox can be formulated. Tarski takes the liar paradox to be an objection not to his theory of truth, but rather to the idea that language can be semantically closed. Any language that is semantically closed will be paradoxical. The only way to solve (or better, avoid) the liar paradox is to introduce rules which prevent a semantically closed language. The simplest formulation of such a rule is 'No language can (directly or indirectly) be a metalanguage of itself'.

The effect of this (admittedly artificial) rule is to split a natural language such as English into a hierarchy of languages – or equivalently, into a hierarchy of levels. There is 'object-English' (the object-level of English) which talks of items other than the items of 'object-English'. Then there is 'meta-object-English' which talks about 'object-English' and in which we might define the predicate 'true in object-English'. We might also ascend to 'meta-meta-object-English', which talks about 'meta-object-English' and in which we might define the predicate 'true in meta-object-English'. And so on, in principle, indefinitely.

How does this solve the liar paradox? It solves it by avoiding it, by preventing us from formulating it. The first key point is that we always define 'true in L', for some L: a truth-definition is always a definition of truth for some particular language (or level of language). After all, it is possible for there to be different languages which happen to have some sentence in common, a sentence which is true in one of them and false in the other. The second key point is that Tarski's rule means that the definition of 'true in L' is not formulated in L but in meta-L, so that the same applies to any statement containing the expression 'true in L'. Tarski's rule means that the liar paradox must be formulated as follows:

The only sentence of L inside this rectangle is false in L.

This sentence contains the expression 'false in L'; therefore it is a sentence not of L but of meta-L; since it is the only sentence in the rectangle, there is no sentence of L in the rectangle. (Here L can stand either for a language or for a level of language.) This means that the sentence in the rectangle is no longer para-doxical. Precisely how it means this depends upon what view you take of sentences containing definite descriptions (phrases of the form 'the so-and-so') which fail to refer to anything (like the phrase 'The only sentence of L inside this rectangle'). The most popular theory is Russell's, according to which any sentence containing a definite description which fails to refer is false. On Russell's theory, the sentence in the rectangle is just false – and no contradiction arises from the idea that it is false. A rival theory of 'empty descriptions' is Strawson's, according to which any sentence containing a definite description which fails to refer is neither true nor false. On Strawson's theory, the sentence in the rectangle is neither true nor false – and no contradiction arises from this idea either.

Tarski's rule is artificial – but any way of solving (avoiding) the liar paradox involves artificialities of this kind. Tarski's rule bans a certain kind of self-referential sentence. A simpler rule would be to ban all self-referential sentences: 'No meaningful sentence can refer to itself.' But this rule, besides being artificial as well, is too sweeping: it bans sentences which are not merely non-paradoxical, but which seem unproblematically to be true (consider 'This sentence occurs in a philosophy book').

Tarski's discussion of the paradox of the liar actually led him to an extremely interesting and important conjecture. The subsequent proof of this conjecture (provided by Kurt Gödel in 1931) represents one of the most outstanding intellectual achievements of the twentieth century. And this achievement has important repercussions for our philosophical discussions of truth and truth-theories. Let me conclude this chapter by explaining the essentials of this – with the proviso that one of the essentials will be stated but not explained, since to explain it would require another book.

Reflection on the liar paradox led Tarski to conclude that if 'true in L' were definable in L, then the liar paradox could be formulated in *L*, and *L* would be inconsistent. So we have, in general, the following:

(1) If *L* is consistent, then 'true in *L*' is not definable in *L*.

Tarski next considered a language in which we could do arithmetic. In it we would have expressions for natural numbers and operations upon them. In it we would formulate axioms for arithmetic, and prove theorems of arithmetic. Calling this language *A*, the general result (1) entails:

(2) If *A* is consistent, then 'true in *A*' is not definable in *A*.

Now there is a property of sentences of arithmetic (sentences of *A*) which we can label 'provable in *A*': roughly, a sentence of *A* is provable in *A* if it can be obtained from the axioms of arithmetic by (correctly) applying the rules of proof for arithmetic. Tarski had a hunch to the effect that 'provable in *A*' is definable in *A*. This is the difficult essential, to explain and establish which would take a whole book. Forgoing any explanation or argument, let us simply record it:

(3) 'Provable in *A*' is definable in *A*.

Down the ages arithmeticians had thought (or hoped) that if an arithmetical sentence was true then it would be provable, and if an arithmetical sentence was provable then it would be true. They had thought (or hoped) that arithmetical truth and arithmetical provability might coincide. They had thought (or hoped) that they might formulate a set of axioms for arithmetic which would be complete: all and only arithmetical truths would be provable from them.

Tarski argued that this hope could not be fulfilled. For suppose a sentence is true in *A* if and only if it is provable in *A*. Then we could simply define 'true in *A*' as 'provable in *A*'. But then, since by the hunch (3) 'provable in *A*' is definable in *A*, 'true in *A*' would also be definable in *A*. But then, by (2), *A* would be inconsistent. So:

(4) If *A* is consistent, then *A* is not complete (it is not the case that a sentence is true in *A* if and only if it is provable in *A*).

Since (4) depends upon the hunch (3), it too is a hunch. But Gödel shortly afterwards showed that (3) is correct, and therefore that (4) is correct also (Gödel 1962). This is Gödel's (first) incompleteness theorem. (It is left open by (4) whether some provable arithmetical sentences are not true, or whether some true sentences are not provable. Gödel showed that the latter is the case, and actually exhibited a sentence G which is true in A but not provable in A. Why not, one might ask, add this 'Gödel sentence' G as an extra axiom to A, augmenting the axioms to A^*? Because Gödel's methods are quite general, and he will be able to show that there are truths in A^* which are not provable in A^*, and to exhibit a new Gödel sentence G^* which is true in A^* but not provable in A^*.)

These are remarkable results with wide-ranging significance. But what is their philosophical significance? Down the ages mathematics had been admired for the certainty that could be achieved in it. Mathematicians, above all, could know the truth of their statements. And what was the mathematicians' criterion for truth? Nothing else than provability from axioms: grant the mathematician knowledge of axioms, and the method of proof generates knowledge of theorems proved. But now it turns out that in the simplest part of mathematics, arithmetic, this criterion of truth is demonstrably incomplete: meta-arithmeticians can prove that the method of proof in arithmetic cannot ever capture all the arithmetic truths. The best 'criterion of truth' ever invented is not a complete criterion for the limited class of truths for which it was designed. And the same goes for 'provability from axioms' in any stronger mathematical theory than arithmetic. Given this situation in mathematics, where we came closer to having such a criterion than anywhere else, the prospects for finding a satisfactory criterion of truth elsewhere do not seem bright. (For more on this and on 'criterion philosophy', see Popper 1945, II: 369–74. For more on Tarski's T-scheme, which yields what he calls the 'minimalist conception of truth', see Paul Horwich 1990, which is excellent.)

CHAPTER 15

Fallibilist realism

We have examined the sceptical criticisms of both empiricism and rationalism. And in the last chapter we dismissed attempts to produce a defeat for scepticism by endorsing some subjective theory of truth. Where does this leave us? Are we forced to agree with the sceptic that certain knowledge is unattainable, that none of our (non-trivial) beliefs can be justified, that all such beliefs are therefore unreasonable? Have we made no progress towards a positive solution to the problem of knowledge?

I now want to set forth and discuss a third positive solution to our problem. It incorporates a large dose of scepticism. It also, being a positive solution, incorporates ingredients from both rationalism and empiricism. It is sometimes called 'mitigated scepticism', sometimes 'critical rationalism' (we could equally well have 'critical empiricism'), sometimes 'fallibilist realism', or for short 'fallibilism'. I shall usually prefer the last name, because it is the shortest. What is fallibilism? Is it acceptable? Let us begin with perception.

SOPHISTICATED INDIRECT REALISM ABOUT PERCEPTION

Early in this book we encountered a theory of perception which has come to be called 'naive' or 'direct realism': we perceive external objects directly or immediately and as they really are. Sceptical and scientific arguments (especially those considered in Chapter 5) demolished this view. Empiricists therefore replaced it with idea-ism or sense-data theory: we perceive ideas or sense-data directly or immediately and as they really are. This theory preserved the infallibility of the empirical basis for knowledge. But it did so, as we have seen, at a very heavy price: the problem of appearance and reality was intensified. More than that, idea-ism was a key premise in Berkeley's 'master argument' for his idealism or immaterialism (see p. 125), and it was also a key premise in Hume's argument for the irrationality of our 'natural belief' in the distinct and continued existence of external objects (see p. 150). Given the peculiar difficulties and doctrines to which idea-ism leads, it is natural to ask whether a third view of perception is possible. And it is perfectly clear what that third view should be. We might call it 'sophisticated indirect realism': we perceive external objects indirectly or 'mediately' and not necessarily as they really are. While naive realism and idea-ism both maintain the infallibility (and the 'directness') of perception (idea-ism abandons realism in order to do this), sophisticated realism does not: its perceptual reports or 'observation statements' are fallible. But the realism of naive realism is preserved: a perceptual report remains a report about external objects or the external world.

To see whether sophisticated realism is a viable alternative, we must first re-examine the arguments for the idea-ist point of view. Some of these arguments need not detain us long. One (see p. 88), assumed that the senses must give us certain knowledge about something (external objects or ideas). Another (see p. 92) assumed that the senses must give us direct or immediate information about something (external objects or ideas). The sophisticated realist will simply reject these key premises (and build their rejection into the very statement of her alternative view).

Other arguments (see pp. 90–1) led to the 'reification' of sense-data or ideas and to the view that they must be the immediate objects of perception. For example, we had:

When I view a straight oar half-immersed in water, I see something bent.
The straight oar is not bent.
Therefore, when I view a straight oar half-immersed in water, I do not see the oar.

This argument is valid, its second premise is obviously true, and its conclusion is something the perceptual realist will reject. So the perceptual realist must also reject the first premise. And reject it she will: it already reifies sense-data by saying 'I see something bent'. The perceptual realist will simply deny that when you view a straight oar (in whatever circumstances) you see something bent – what you see is always something which, by assumption, is straight. Similarly, when you view a round coin from whatever angle, what you see is always something which, by assumption, is round. The reifying premises are to be rejected in favour of the following:

> When I view a straight oar half-immersed in water, it (the straight oar) looks bent.
> When I view a round coin from the side, it (the round coin) looks elliptical.

We do not always perceive things as they really are (straight oars can look bent and round coins can look elliptical and so on) and that is all there is to it for the sophisticated realist.

Hallucinations are a special case to be distinguished from perceptions (whether illusory or not). The realist insists that the object perceived (when perception occurs) is always an external object. It follows that hallucination is not perception at all. The drunk who hallucinates pink rats does not see anything at all (though he may mistakenly think that he does). This is, admittedly, odd because we say of the hallucinating drunk that he is 'seeing things'. According to the perceptual realist, this is an idiomatic way of speaking which is not to be taken at face-value. In support of this we might return to our previous attempt to formulate for hallucination the sort of argument we had for illusion. We ended up with (see, pp. 90–1, above):

> When I hallucinate pink rats, I see pink rats.
> There are no pink rats.
> Therefore, when I hallucinate pink rats I do not see pink rats.

As noted previously, this is a very queer argument. To make it valid we have to add the premise 'If there are no pink rats, then

I do not see pink rats'. But now, if we suppose as well that I do hallucinate pink rats, the premises (there are now four of them) yield the contradiction that I both see pink rats and do not see pink rats. This is a *reductio* proof that the first premise is false, that when I hallucinate pink rats I do not see pink rats.

And then there was Joad's time-lapse argument. The key premise of that argument was (see p. 94, above): 'To say that one can see what may no longer exist is absurd.' Stuff and nonsense. Since seeing takes time, we always see what may no longer exist. Since seeing takes time, we always see into the past, see things as they were (or seemed to be) some time ago. All that the time-lapse argument really points to is another possible source of perceptual error. We look into the night-sky, spot Sirius, and confidently declare 'There is Sirius', meaning 'There is Sirius *now*'. In this we may be mistaken: Sirius may have exploded in the interval between emitting the light which causes us to see it and our seeing it. Similarly, I glance at the table and confidently declare 'The table is brown', meaning 'The table is brown *now*'. In this I might be mistaken: God (who might exist) might have changed the table's colour or zapped the table out of existence altogether (if He exists He can do anything), in the small interval between the table's reflecting the light which causes me to see it and my seeing it.

Similar points can be made about Russell's extraordinary contention (see p. 93, above) that 'The observer, when he seems to himself to be observing a stone, is really, if physics is to be believed, observing the effects of the stone upon himself'. Stuff and nonsense again. What, if physics (and physiology) are to be believed, are the effects of the stone upon the perceiver? Confining ourselves to vision, they are stimulations of retinal cells, productions of impulses in optic nerves, and neurological disturbances in the visual cortex. Physics does not teach us that such things are what are really observed when we look at a stone. On the contrary, physics assures us that such things cannot be observed. (Or at least, cannot be observed with the 'naked eye': special equipment is needed if we are to observe, or detect, such things as stimulations of retinal cells.) It is one thing to say (and physics says it) that seeing a stone requires such effects to occur. It is quite another thing to say (and only bad philosophy says it) that such effects are what is really seen.

We just spoke of the physiologist, armed with special equipment, observing or detecting retinal stimulations. On Russell's view, this cannot happen. On Russell's view, the physiologist can no more observe my retinae than I can observe a stone. On Russell's view, the physiologist is actually observing the remote effects that my retinae have (via the special equipment) on his brain. (Russell sees this implication of his position and endorses it.)

The fact is that ideas or sense-data do not exist. That sounds paradoxical, too. But what were ideas or sense-data supposed to be? They were supposed to be (a) what is produced in us or 'given' to us in our sensory interactions with the external world and (b) what we are immediately aware of in perception. But we are not aware of what is 'given' to us. We do not see visual experiences, hear auditory experiences, or touch tactile experiences. If seeing a tree is to be analysed as seeing a visual sense-datum of a tree, from which we infer that a tree is present, why is not seeing a visual sense-datum of a tree to be analysed as seeing a visual sense-datum of a visual sense-datum of a tree, and so on *ad infinitum*? Contrariwise, if this regress is to be stopped, why not stop it at the start and say that we can see trees?

To sum up. We began with naive or direct realism: we directly perceive external objects as they really are. Sceptical and scientific arguments demolish this view. Empiricists seek to retain the directness and infallibility of perception (the naivety of naive realism, if you like) and say: we directly perceive ideas or sense-data as they really are. But it is also possible to retain the realism of naive realism and say: we indirectly perceive external objects not necessarily as they really are.

It is important to realise that no anti-sceptical mileage is to be gained from the sophisticated indirect realist (or critical realist) view of perception. On the contrary, it endorses large parts of the sceptical critique of the senses, and is powerless against the rest. In particular, the argument from illusion is accepted and is the reason for the qualification 'not necessarily as they really are'. For the critical realist hallucinations and dreams are not cases of perception at all: hallucinators and dreamers may think that they are perceiving things but they are not. But the arguments from hallucinations and dreams remain intact. For example, if there is no sure way to tell dreams from waking life, then there is no sure way to tell when we are perceiving and when we are not.

It may be objected that the so-called 'critical realist' uncritically assumes that there are external objects which we sometimes perceive. Not really. Critical realism, properly understood, is merely an account of what it would take for us to perceive something. If we were disembodied Cartesian egos constantly tricked by an evil genius, we would never perceive anything but would instead always hallucinate. We would always hallucinate, too, if we were disembodied brains-in-a-vat hooked up to a super-computer. If either Berkeley's immaterialism or phenomenalism is the correct metaphysic, then once again the critical realist will say that we never perceive anything but always wrongly think that we do. An analysis of perception is one thing, the claim that perception occurs is quite another. We need both to overcome these extreme sceptical possibilities, and nothing has yet been said in defence of the latter.

The price we pay for remaining realists about perception is that we cease to have an infallible empirical basis for knowledge. Observation statements reporting what we perceive (or seem to perceive) become particular and pretty basic hypotheses or conjectures about the world, rather than certainly known truths. (Although we shall see in due course that they can be given some sort of privileged status despite this.) Fallibilist realism incorporates the critical realist view of perception. Thus far, then, fallibilism would seem to be just another name for scepticism. (For more on critical realism regarding perception see Maurice Mandelbaum 1964 – an excellent book.)

SCEPTICISM, IRRATIONALISM AND FALLIBILISM

The problem of knowledge was traditionally viewed by both dogmatists and sceptics as the problem of certain knowledge or of justified belief. Dogmatists thought we could achieve it, sceptics did not. Radical sceptics argued that since all (non-trivial) beliefs are uncertain and unjustifiable, they are all unreasonable or irrational also. Is radical scepticism correct?

Two sceptical theses need to be distinguished (compare Watkins 1984: 58–9):

(1) Certainty scepticism: Any (non-trivial) belief is uncertain and unjustifiable.
(2) Rationality scepticism: Any (non-trivial) belief is unreasonable.

Radical sceptics accept both: indeed, they claim that (2) follows from (1). But (2) follows not from (1) by itself, but from (1) together with the following principle:

(*R*) A belief is reasonable if and only if it is certain or justified.

Dogmatists and sceptics both accept *R* or something like it. Because dogmatists accept it, they pursue certainty to gain rationality. Because sceptics accept it, their denial of certainty (1) turns into a denial of rationality (2). But we can sever the link between scepticism and irrationalism if we reject *R*. Rejecting *R* leaves room for a mitigated scepticism, one which accepts certainty scepticism (1) but rejects rationality scepticism (2).

But it is not enough simply to reject *R* – that leaves us with no account of when a belief is reasonable. Not even the mitigated sceptic wants to take the absurd view that it is reasonable to believe anything. To say that all beliefs are equally reasonable is no different from saying that they are all equally *un*reasonable. We need an alternative principle of rationality, and the critical rationalist gives us one.

The basic idea behind this alternative theory is simple

enough. Suppose that I believe that *P*. There are two ways that I might set about establishing the rational credentials of my belief. I can try to show that it is true, and hence worthy of belief. Or I can try to show that it is false, and hence unworthy of belief. I might try to justify *P* or I might try to criticise *P*. The way of justification has been considered already. The critical rationalist adopts the way of criticism. Her basic idea is that if we succeed in criticising *P*, find a reason to think *P* false, then we are not justified in believing *P* – whereas if we do not succeed in criticising *P*, find no reason to think *P* false, then we are justified in believing *P*. It is the second view which provides the alternative principle of rationality:

(*R**) A belief is reasonable if and only if it has withstood serious criticism.

R* is programmatic: more needs to be said about how beliefs can be criticised, and about when a criticism is a 'serious' criticism and when not. We shall say a little more about these matters. But first an objection needs to be considered.

The objection is that there is nothing new in all this. The fact that a belief has 'withstood serious criticism' is itself an inconclusive justification of that belief. Critical rationalism, enshrined in *R**, is not an alternative to justificationism, but a species of it.

The critical rationalist simply denies that this is the case. The failure to show that *P* is false does not justify *P*. An important distinction must be drawn. Talk of 'justifying *A*'s belief that *P*' is ambiguous between justifying *P*, the proposition *A* believes, and justifying *A*'s believing that proposition. Traditional justificationism conflates the two, thinking that *A* is justified in believing *P* only if *A* can justify *P* (either conclusively or inconclusively). Critical rationalism separates the two, thinking that *A* may be justified in believing *P* even though *A* cannot justify *P* (either conclusively or inconclusively). In particular, the critical rationalist thinks that *P*'s having 'withstood serious criticism' justifies us in believing *P* but does not justify *P* (either conclusively or inconclusively). According to critical rationalism, it is reasonable to believe P if we are justified in believing P, not if P is justified. We should make this subtle distinction explicit in $R*$:

($R*$) It is reasonable to believe P (we are justified in believing P) if and only if P has withstood serious criticism.

Armed with this subtlety, the critical rationalist insists that her position is an alternative to traditional justificationism rather than a species of it. Let us grant the point. The important question is not whether critical rationalism is a new position but whether it is an acceptable position.

The subtle distinction between justifying belief in P and justifying P has one happy consequence which we should note immediately. It makes room for the possibility of having a justified belief in a falsehood. We should leave room for this possibility. Suppose we form some belief and make several serious attempts to show that belief to be false, all of which fail. Are we not then justified in believing the proposition in question? Critical rationalists say that we are. Yet that proposition might be false and we might subsequently find out that it is false. (Notice, however, that if we do find this out, we say that what we believed was wrong, not that we were wrong to believe it.)

Without the subtle distinction between justifying belief in P and justifying P it is less easy to make room for this possibility. Suppose we think that belief in P is justified only if P is. And suppose we also think that one cannot conclusively justify or prove a falsehood. It follows that one cannot have conclusively justified belief in a falsehood either. Suppose we think (though it is less plausible to think this) that one cannot even *in*conclusively justify a falsehood. It follow (again less plausibly) that one cannot have even (inconclusively) justified belief in a falsehood.

But if one can have a justified belief in a falsehood, what becomes of the justified true belief account of knowledge? The critical rationalist will modify that account, but not to the extent of thinking that one can know a falsehood. The modified account is this:

A knows that *P* if and only if

(1) *A* believes that *P*.
(2) *P* is true, and
(3) *A* is justified in believing that *P*.

Here only the third condition is modified, in the light of the subtle distinction whose consequences we are exploring. We shall return to this fallibilist account of knowledge in a while.

So far we have explained fallibilism and explored a few of its immediate consequences. How are we to evaluate it? One way to evaluate a philosophical theory (or any theory for that matter) is to compare it with its rivals and see how well it copes with objections to those rivals. So let us ask how well fallibilism copes with sceptical objections to empiricism and rationalism. This will also enable us to see how fallibilism incorporates features of both the traditional theories.

There was fundamentally only one sceptical objection to classical rationalism, that self-evidence and the like are not infallible criteria of truth. The fallibilist simply endorses that objection. Having endorsed it, the fallibilist will not seek to evade it by retreating into some subjective theory of truth. The fallibilist is an uncompromising adherent of the common-sense objective conception of truth.

There were fundamentally two sceptical objections to empiricism. The first was that the senses are not an infallible source of knowledge. As we have seen, the fallibilist simply endorses this objection and adopts the 'sophisticated indirect realist' or 'critical realist' view of perception. The fallibilist also naturally inclines to the Lockean view that the secondary qualities are objective.

On the positive side fallibilism can incorporate some features of empiricism. The senses are a source not of certain knowledge, but of reasonable beliefs. You seem to see a table. A natural explanation of your experience, one adopted unthinkingly on most such occasions, is that there is a table before you. If you are in any doubt about the matter, you can check out your explanation in various ways: reach out and touch the table, ask the person next to you whether they can also see it and so forth.

(Logically speaking, each of these 'checking outs' represents a test of the natural hypothesis that a table is before you. If you can touch the table as well as see it, or if the person next to you confirms your sighting, then you have tried to refute the hypothesis and failed. It is reasonable for you to believe that hypothesis.)

But most of the time we do not doubt our perceptual judgements and do not 'check them out' in any way at all. Are 'unchecked' perceptual beliefs reasonable beliefs in the fallibilist sense? The fallibilist can say so if she makes a further concession to the empiricist emphasis on the epistemological primacy of sense-experience. The concession is to say that the senses are to be trusted as a source of reasonable belief unless there is some specific reason not to trust them. In saying this the fallibilist places the burden of proof, so to speak, upon him who would discount the evidence of the senses: he must produce some specific criticism of the perceptual belief in question. This retains the epistemological primacy of the senses in the following way: perceptual beliefs are reasonable unless they fail to withstand criticism; other beliefs are reasonable because they succeed in withstanding criticism. (This will involve an obvious modification to the fallibilist theory of rationality, $R*$.)

The fallibilist position of the last paragraph is really no more than the common-sense view of the matter. And it can be defended by an evolutionary argument. If the theory of evolution is to be believed, the human sensory system has evolved to give us information about the world we inhabit. A sensory system which gave false information most of the time would be disadvantageous to its possessor and would be eliminated by natural selection. Hence if the theory of evolution is to be believed, we should also believe that the senses do not give us false information most of the time: it is reasonable to trust them unless we have a specific reason not to. The fallibilist needs to add, to complete the argument, that the theory of evolution is to be believed, that it is a reasonable belief in the fallibilist sense.

It may be objected that evolutionary theory has no such sanguine consequences about the general reliability of the human sensory apparatus. On the contrary, evolutionary theory entails that the human sensory apparatus is highly selective and species-specific: other species with other interests will perceive the world quite differently than we do. Quite so. But this is irrelevant to the argument being considered. That argument showed that what the human sensory apparatus tells us is by and large correct, not that the human sensory apparatus tells us everything there is to know. Our senses can be selective without being mistaken. (To think otherwise is to commit the 'no truth but the whole truth' fallacy: 'John is tall' is false because it leaves something out, because it does not tell us whether John is also fat, or bald.) Evolutionary theory can be used to show that there are more things in heaven and earth than are dreamt of in our philosophy of perception – that does not show that our philosophy of perception is wrong.

There is a deeper objection to our evolutionary argument: it is circular. The fallibilist thinks it reasonable to believe the theory of evolution. If so, it has withstood serious criticism, including observational or experimental tests. But we rely upon the senses to collect observational or experimental evidence. So we argue in a circle: the senses are by and large to be trusted, so it is reasonable to believe the theory of evolution; it is reasonable to believe the theory of evolution, so the senses are by and large to be trusted. This objection is quite just. The most that the argument from evolution shows is that evolutionary theory and the fallibilist attitude to sense-experience are mutually supporting or go hand-in-hand. But this is not a trivial point. For it can be shown that other, non-fallibilist attitudes to sense-experience are profoundly anti-evolutionary. Naive realism is obviously pre-Darwinian. Less obviously, so is the view that the senses always deceive. Less obviously still, perhaps, is any idealist metaphysic which would construct the real world out of the sense-data of humans (since Darwinism entails that the real world existed before any human sense-data did). This is only one example of the way in which science and the fallibilistic theory of knowledge go hand-in-hand – we shall see others.

So critical rationalism might equally be called 'critical empiricism', since it gives a kind of epistemological primacy to observation reports. But the critical empiricist does not agree with the classical empiricist that all our beliefs are derived from sense-experience. Beliefs typically transcend experience, though they are invented to account for it. They typically have an a priori component, in the form of freely invented explanatory concepts which cannot be reduced to experience. Thus the fallibilist accepts a kind of synthetic a priori. But this is not the monolithic system of synthetic a priori certain knowledge of the classical rationalist. Rather it is a multiplicity of competing systems of synthetic a priori conjectures or guesses, some of which experience will show to be mistaken, others of which will be rationally credible and even true. The fallibilist endorses Kant's dictum: 'The understanding does not draw its laws from nature, but prescribes them to nature.' But the fallibilist does not try to secure certainty for these laws, at the price of making them laws governing the 'world of appearance' only. They are laws (or purported laws) of nature proper.

The second big sceptical objection to empiricism lay in the problem of induction, which showed that the senses are not an adequate basis for knowledge. Enough has been said to make it clear that the fallibilist will be drawn to Popper's deductivist answer to Hume. (Indeed, fallibilism as here understood is based largely upon that answer.) The answer was, recall, that the invalidity of inductive reasoning does not matter, because all of our reasonings are deductive ones (or can be reconstructed as such). We jump to conclusions, form hypotheses about the world. Some of these general beliefs are reasonable beliefs in the fallibilist sense. We use such beliefs to anticipate the future by deducing predictions from them. Predictions deduced from reasonable beliefs are themselves reasonable. Hume is right that every prediction about the unobserved is uncertain; he is wrong that every such prediction is unreasonable. But even if all of this is accepted (a very big 'if', of course), a new objection must be considered.

FALLIBILISM AND THE GRUE PROBLEM

In considering this objection, let us return to the happy situation mentioned earlier (on p. 172), in which experience has refuted 'Bread never nourishes' and failed to refute 'Bread always nourishes'. We had rationally accepted the latter (albeit tentatively), and we had rationally predicted that the next piece of bread will nourish us (again tentatively, but rationally). We said that it would be unreasonable to predict that the next piece of bread will fail to nourish us, because the hypothesis 'Bread never nourishes' from which that prediction follows has been falsified. But wait! Consider the admittedly peculiar hypothesis 'Bread has nourished up to now but will fail to nourish after now'. This hypothesis is also unrefuted by the evidence. So it is as reasonable to accept it as it is to accept 'Bread always nourishes'. But this peculiar hypothesis predicts that the next piece of bread will not nourish me. So it is as reasonable to predict this as it is to predict that the next piece of bread will nourish me. So it is not more reasonable to predict the one thing than the other. Hume was right after all, and the deductivist cannot defeat him even if what the deductivist proposes is accepted.

This objection is due to Nelson Goodman. It is called the 'new riddle of induction'. It is also called the 'grue problem', because of Goodman's own example. Goodman asks us to imagine that we have observed lots of emeralds and all have been green. The 'natural' hypothesis is that all emeralds are green, and the 'natural' prediction is that the next emerald we observe will be green, too. The hypothesis that all emeralds are blue has been thoroughly refuted. But what of the hypothesis that all emeralds are grue, where 'grue' is a technical term which means 'green if observed before now and blue if observed after now'. This hypothesis is also unrefuted by the data. It is as reasonable to accept it as it is to accept 'All emeralds are green'. But 'All emeralds are grue' predicts that the next emerald we observe will be blue. So it is as reasonable to accept this prediction as it is to accept the prediction that the next emerald will be green. This example has enabled philosophers to indulge

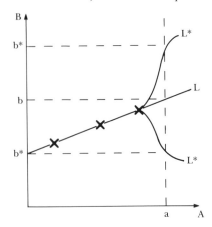

Figure 12. The curve-fitting problem

their sense of humour with articles entitled 'Goodman's gruesome emeralds', 'The very thought of "grue"', or 'Grue, bleen and oops-a-daisy' (you can guess what 'bleen' means).

Amusing titles aside, it is important to see that what is being claimed here is quite general. What is being claimed is that for any body of evidence E and any prediction p, I can concoct a hypothesis H which is consistent with the evidence E and which yields the prediction p. And the claim is, further, that it is as reasonable to accept H as it is to accept any other hypothesis, and hence as reasonable to predict p as to predict anything.

One way to see the generality of the problem is to consider curve-fitting. (Actually, Goodman's grue problem is an application to qualitative hypotheses of the old curve-fitting problem.) A scientist is interested in the relationship between two measurable quantities A and B. He makes some measurements, plots them on a graph, and finds that all the measured values lie on a straight line. The scientist quickly draws a straight line through his data points: this represents a hypothesis, and for any unobserved value of A it predicts a value of B (and vice versa). In Figure 12, the crosses represent the data points, and the 'natural' linear hypothesis L predicts that when A has the value a, B will have the value b. But suppose, for whatever reason (or for no reason at all), we would like to have a hypothesis which predicts that when A has the value a, B has a value b^* different from b. We can easily construct such hypotheses by drawing 'funny' curves through the data points and through the point (a, b^*), as the various L^* curves in Figure 12 show. No matter what pair of unobserved values of A and B we choose, there will be a hypothesis (a curve) which is consistent with the observations (passes through the data points) and which predicts those unobserved values.

What are we to do about the gruesome hypotheses and the funny curves? We do not, as a matter of fact, ever consider such hypotheses. Confronted with a thousand green emeralds we straightaway guess that they are all green or that the next one will be. Confronted with co-linear data points we straightaway draw the straight line which joins them up. This is the natural thing to do, and we all do it. But is it the reasonable thing to do? Hume did not deny that our ordinary 'inductive behaviour' was natural to us: he challenged us to show that what we naturally do is the reasonable thing to do.

The difficulty is especially acute for the deductivist because in explaining it we have accepted what the deductivist says: there are no inductive arguments: there are fallibilist principles about what it is reasonable to believe, which we have accepted. And the upshot seems to be that any prediction about the colour of the next emerald is as reasonable as any other, on the fallibilist's own grounds. Somehow the fallibilist has got to show that the gruesome hypotheses are not as reasonable as the natural ones. How might she try to do this?

She might first try to argue that the gruesome hypothesis is not so well supported by the evidence available as the natural hypothesis. In developing the objection, we said that we could concoct a gruesome hypothesis which was consistent with the evidence. But mere consistency with the evidence is not enough for the evidence to make it reasonable to accept the hypothesis (if it were, the observation of a hundred green emeralds would make it reasonable to believe that the moon is made of green cheese, since the two are consistent). The hypothesis that emeralds are green is not merely consistent with the evidence, it entails it. Does the hypothesis that all emeralds are grue also entail the evidence? It can be shown that, strictly speaking, it does not. If we label the emeralds we have observed 'Emerald$_1$', 'Emerald$_2$' and so on, then our evidence might be written 'Emerald$_1$ is green' 'Emerald$_2$ is green' and so on. 'All emeralds are green' certainly entails 'Emerald$_1$ is green'. But 'All emeralds are grue' does not, rather it entails 'Either emerald$_1$ is observed before now and is green or emerald$_1$ is observed after now and is blue'. It is easy to overlook this point because we take it for granted that emerald$_1$ (and all the others) have been observed before 'now'; after all, we cannot observe emeralds in the future. But if, in the gruesome hypothesis, we were to replace 'now' with a name of the time at which it was proposed (say '3 p.m. on 5 June 1940'), the point would be clearer to see. Another way to put it is this. Evidence supports a hypothesis only if it arises from an unsuccessful attempt to refute the hypothesis. To refute 'Emeralds are green' we must get hold of an emerald and note its colour. Hence 'Emerald$_1$ is green' reports an unsuccessful attempt to refute 'Emeralds are green' (for after all, emerald$_1$ might have turned out to be blue). Hence 'Emerald$_1$ is green' supports 'Emeralds are green' ('supports' does not mean 'proves' or 'makes more probable', it merely means 'fails to refute'). Now to refute 'Emeralds are grue', on the other hand, we must get hold of an emerald, note its colour, and note the time at which we are observing it. 'Emerald$_1$ is green' cannot really support 'Emeralds are grue' because 'Emerald$_1$ is green and observed after 3 p.m. on 5 June 1940' would have refuted it. The point is unconvincing as it stands because observing emerald$_1$ might have refuted 'Emeralds are grue' whether or not we note the time of observation: what if emerald$_1$ had turned out to be red? (It would be different if the gruesome hypothesis had been 'Emeralds are green if observed before 3 p.m. on 5 June 1940 and not green if observed after 3 p.m. on 5 June 1940'. Still, perhaps this line of thinking can be pursued, and a theory of evidential support worked out which will show that gruesome hypotheses are not so well supported as natural ones, so that it is not as reasonable to believe them.

Another possibility is that 'Emeralds are grue' can be criticised in a way that 'Emeralds are green' cannot, and is for this reason not so acceptable as 'Emeralds are green'. The criticism which immediately springs to mind is that 'Emeralds are grue' is not as simple as 'Emeralds are green'. This raises two problems. First, can we develop a way of assessing the simplicity of hypotheses which will enable us to justify our intuition about the relative simplicity of these two hypotheses (or our intuition that the linear hypothesis is simpler than the peculiar curves)? This problem has proved unexpectedly diffi- cult to solve in general terms, though some progress has been made. But even if we assume that the problem of defining simplicity has been completely solved, another problem faces us. Why should simplicity (in the sense defined) be a factor in hypothesis-selection? Why is it reasonable to believe (or to prefer) the simpler of two hypotheses?

In answer to this second question, some philosophers have postulated that 'Nature is simple', and justified the appeal to simplicity by saying that the simplest hypothesis is the true one, or by saying that the simpler of two hypotheses is more likely to be true or more probable. But postulating that nature is simple is not much different from postulating that nature is uniform. Like the latter postulate, it will enable us to validate inductive arguments, thus:

> Nature is simple, so that the simplest hypothesis consistent with the data is true.
> All observed emeralds are green.
> The simplest hypothesis consistent with the data is the hypothesis that all emeralds are green.
> Therefore, all emeralds are green.

And all of Hume's arguments against the inductive principle that nature is uniform can also be brought to bear upon the principle that nature is simple.

The fallibilist, however, will not want to show that the simpler hypothesis is the true one or the more probably true one (for she does not try to validate inductive arguments). The fallibilist will merely want to show that it is reasonable to accept or prefer the simpler of two hypotheses. Popper has actually proposed (1959: Chapter 7) one of the best accounts of simplicity that we have; it is not entirely adequate (there are some intuitive judgements of relative simplicity which it fails to capture), but no theory is entirely adequate. And he justifies the appeal to simplicity (in the sense he defines) by saying that the simpler hypothesis is preferable because, if it is false, it will be easier to show that it is false. This is not just different from the inductivist appeal to simplicity, it is quite the antithesis of it: the simpler hypothesis is not true or likely to be true, but easier to falsify.

Perhaps lack of simplicity is not the only ground on which the fallibilist might object to gruesome hypotheses. One of Popper's followers says that it is a criticism of a hypothesis that it does not solve the problem that it sets out to solve. And he says, further, that 'All emeralds are grue' is not proposed to solve any problem at all and may be criticised on this count. I wonder. Perhaps the problem solved by 'All emeralds are grue' is precisely the same as that solved by 'All emeralds are green', namely: 'What colour(s) are emeralds?' Or perhaps the problem solved (very successfully) by 'All emeralds are grue' is: 'How can I best embarrass the critical rationalists?'

The fallibilist still has work to do if she is to solve the grue problem on fallibilist grounds. But it is important to realise that although we have formulated this problem as a specific objection to fallibilism, versions of the same problem afflict other views also. The fallibilist seems to do better than the traditional empiricist in answering Hume – at least, she does no worse.

The overall conclusion seems to be that fallibilism stands up to old sceptical criticism better than either empiricism or rationalism. It is really quite obvious that this must be so: scepticism is parasitic upon dogmatism and perishes without it. As Pascal pointed out long ago:

What astonishes me most is to see that all the world is not astonished at its own weakness. Men act seriously, and each follows his own mode of life... as if each man knew certainly where reason and justice are. They find themselves continually deceived, and by a comical humility think it is their own fault, and not that of the art which they claim always to possess. But it is well that there are so many such people in the world, who are not sceptics for the glory of scepticism, in order to show that man is quite capable of the most extravagant opinions, since he is capable of believing that he is not in a state of natural and inevitable weakness, but, on the contrary, of natural wisdom.

Nothing fortifies scepticism more than that there are some who are not sceptics; if all were so, they would be wrong.

The sect derives more strength from its enemies than from its friends; for the weakness of man is far more evident in those who know it not than in those who know it. (1904: 101–2, nos. 374 and 376)

Pascal's point can be driven home by considering the nature of sceptical arguments. Properly understood, all such arguments are directed not against our beliefs but rather against attempts to prove or justify our beliefs. Properly understood, all such arguments conclude not that some belief is false but rather that it is uncertain. We glance into a room and declare 'There is a table'. The sceptic does not try to show that this statement is false by criticising it. Rather she tries to show that we cannot know for sure that the statement is true. We confidently expect the next piece of bread we eat to nourish us. The sceptic does not criticise this expectation and show it to be false. Rather she tries to show that we cannot know for sure that it is true. (The nature of sceptical criticism is often misunderstood. Some say sceptics make the mistake of arguing for the falsity of beliefs by showing that it is possible that they are false. But no sceptic takes the possibility of error to show error: rather, the possibility of error is taken to show lack of certainty.)

Now the fallibilist does not even attempt to prove or justify her beliefs. So it is obvious that sceptical arguments against such attempts will not hit the fallibilist. It is obvious, in other words, that traditional sceptical arguments against empiricism and rationalism are powerless against the fallibilist. Considering only those critical arguments, we must conclude that fallibilism is preferable to empiricism and rationalism.

NEW OBJECTIONS

Here is a new criticism of fallibilism: 'At the heart of fallibilism lies $R*$, the new theory of rational belief. But $R*$ is a very strange theory: it says we may be justified in believing things which, even though they happen to be true, we cannot prove to be true, cannot prove to be probably true, have no positive reason for at all. A theory that strange ought to be proved – or at least, we ought to be given some positive reason to accept it. But so far the fallibilist has done neither of these things: so far the fallibilist principle $R*$ is completely unjustified.'

How should the fallibilist respond here? It is true that (so far at least) we have no justification of $R*$. But the demand for one takes for granted precisely the view which the fallibilist rejects: that it is only reasonable to believe $R*$ if $R*$ can be proved or justified. So the consistent fallibilist should not try to justify $R*$. Instead the consistent fallibilist should try to show that we are justified in adopting $R*$ because it has withstood serious criticism. In fact, we have already started to show this, in showing that fallibilism withstands sceptical criticisms better than empiricism or rationalism. (Strictly speaking, that argument only shows that it is more reasonable to adopt fallibilism than empiricism or rationalism, not that it is reasonable to adopt fallibilism. But a plausible additional argument, which I will not pause to spell out, could lead us to the second, stronger conclusion.)

But this reply leads immediately to another objection. Suppose the fallibilist succeeds in showing that fallibilism withstands serious criticism or withstands it better than rival theories, and concludes that we are justified in adopting it. This is to show that fallibilism is reasonably believed by fallibilist standards. It is to argue in a circle.

I know of no convincing answer to this objection. At this level of abstraction circular reasoning is difficult to avoid. Nor are the alternatives to it any more palatable. One is to say that belief in fallibilism is reasonable by other then fallibilist standards. But this is to admit that fallibilism is not a comprehensive theory of rationality – and it is to be non-fallibilist about fallibilism. The only other alternative is to say that belief in fallibilism is not reasonable by any standards. But this is again to admit that fallibilism is not a comprehensive theory of rationality – and it is to be irrational about fallibilism itself. The latter is disastrous: the fallibilist was trying to defeat the irrationalist and you hardly do that if you admit to being irrational about your theory of rationality.

Of these three alternatives, the second is not really a genuine alternative. Suppose we show that belief in fallibilism is reasonable by some non-fallibilist standard S. (It does not matter what S might be.) The sceptic will ask us whether it is reasonable to believe S, and an infinite regress threatens. But we cannot ever come to the end of an infinite regress: there will come a point when we either argue in a circle (show that belief in S is reasonable by standard S^* and that belief in S^* is reasonable by standard S) or invoke some standard which is not reasonable by any standard. The only real alternatives in the matter are circular reasonings or irrationalism about your theory of rationality. I prefer the former – just.

Popper embraced the latter:

The rationalist's attitude is characterized by the importance it attaches to argument and experience. But neither argument nor experience can establish the rationalist attitude; for only those who are ready to consider argument or experience, and who have therefore adopted this attitude already, will be impressed by them. That is to say, a rationalist attitude must first be adopted if any argument or experience is to be effective, and it cannot therefore be based upon argument or experience ... We have to conclude from this that no rational argument will have a rational effect on a man who does not want to adopt a rational attitude. Thus a comprehensive rationalism is untenable.

But this means that whoever adopts the rationalist attitude does so because he has adopted ... an irrational *faith in reason*. So rationalism is necessarily far from comprehensive. (1945, II: 230–1)

Popper's concession to irrationalism was criticised by William Bartley (see Bartley 1962).

There Bartley argued that a comprehensive rationalism was possible and preferable, and proposed comprehensively critical rationalism (CCR). CCR was meant to be a theory which could be rational by its own standards (like our fallibilism or critical rationalism). Unfortunately, its account of rational belief seemed ludicrously weak: it seemed to say that a rational belief is a criticis*able* belief. On this view, it is rational to believe that the moon is made of green cheese, since this is eminently criticisable. (How do I know? Because it has been thoroughly criticis*ed*.) CCR is so weak that it is bound to be rational by its own standards. The adherent of CCR has a 'Heads I win, tails you lose' strategy. If no criticism of CCR is produced, it remains criticis*able* and hence rationally believed. And if an excellent criticism of CCR is produced, this gives further proof that it is criticisable, and hence rationally believed. (There is more on this in Radnitzky and Bartley 1987: Part II.) No similar objection can be levelled against fallibilism or critical rationalism because it incorporates a stronger account of rational belief: for a belief to be rational it must be criticisable and have withstood criticism. It is possible to be argued out of fallibilism – it is not possible to be argued out of CCR.

Bartley is right and Popper wrong, I think, that it is possible and preferable to have a comprehensive rationalism, a rationalism which is rational by its own lights. But Popper is clearly right that any argument showing that it is reasonable to believe fallibilism by fallibilist lights will fail to convince a person who is unimpressed by arguments. This would be like trying to justify the use of argument by argument. But it is even worse. When we show that it is reasonable to believe fallibilism, we argue thus:

(R^*) It is reasonable to believe P if and only if P has withstood serious criticism.

Principle (R^*) has itself withstood serious criticism.

Therefore, it is reasonable to believe principle (R^*).

Only someone who already accepts the conclusion of this argument will be prepared to accept both of its premises and be convinced by it. One need not be unimpressed by all arguments to be unimpressed by circular ones.

Popper's mistake was to go from the true premise that no argument will convince someone unimpressed by argument, to the false conclusion that no argument exists. The conclusion is false because there is an argument, albeit a circular one. My position differs slightly from both Popper's and Bartley's. It is that since any argument for critical rationalism is circular, no argument for critical rationalism will convince anyone who is unimpressed by circular arguments.

I said on p. 295, above, that having a circular argument for critical rationalism was marginally better than having no argument at all and confessing to irrationalism. Even so, the fallibilist's position is an uncomfortable one. All she can do is comfort herself that any other theory of rationality is in the same position. Any rationality theory is rationally acceptable by its own lights (circularity), or by other lights (potential infinite regress and actual circularity again), or is not rationally acceptable at all (irrationalism). So the criticism here being considered cannot discriminate against fallibilism and in favour of some rival theory.

One philosopher thinks that this kind of circularity is not a vice but a virtue:

Philosophers push or iterate a question, usually about justification, so far that they cannot find any acceptable deeper answer. Attempting to...justify the principle or position already reached, they fail, or covertly reintroduce the very result to be gotten. Whereupon a crisis for philosophy or reason is proclaimed: a surd has been reached which cannot be justified further. Reason has been forced to halt.

What did they expect? Either the chain...of justification...goes on indefinitely, or it goes in a circle, or it reaches an end-point, either a simple point or a self-subsuming loop. What result would *not* constitute a crisis? It seems plausible that philosophy should seek to uncover the deepest truths, to find...justificatory principles so deep that nothing else yields them, yet deep enough to subsume themselves. Reaching these should be a goal of philosophy, so when that situation occurs in some topic or area, instead of a crisis we should announce a triumph. (Robert Nozick 1981: 137–8)

I wish that Nozick were right but I fear that he is not. The trouble is that 'self-subsumption' is too easy to obtain. 'It is rational to believe anything written by Alan Musgrave' is a silly self-subsumptive principle and is certainly no 'triumph'.

CONJECTURAL KNOWLEDGE

Let us descend from these rather abstract regions, and consider a more down-to-earth objection to fallibilism. It is this: 'Fallibilism was introduced as a third positive solution to the problem of knowledge. That cannot be right. The fallibilist, like the sceptic, denies that we have any knowledge. For knowledge is justified true belief. And the fallibilist, like the sceptic, denies that we have any justified true beliefs.'

A fallibilist response to this objection has already been hinted at. It is to say that although (non-trivial) certain or justified beliefs are impossible, we may be said to have conjectural knowledge, defined thus:

A conjecturally knows that *P* if
(1) *A* believes that *P*;
(2) *P* is true; and
(3) *A* is justified in believing that *P*.

The fallibilist can point out that if we stick to the traditional justified true belief account of knowledge, then precious little can be known, and what can is pretty uninteresting ('I think therefore I am', 'Round red bulgy sense-datum here now' and such things). In particular, all of the interesting knowledge produced in the sciences will not count as genuine knowledge. John Locke admitted as much when he wrote (1690: IV, xii, 10) that 'natural philosophy [he meant science] is not capable of being made into a science [he meant a body of certain knowledge]'. The fallibilist might argue that if your theory of knowledge has the result that there is no scientific knowledge, it is time to amend that theory. And she might go on to point out that her amended theory leaves plenty of room for conjectural scientific knowledge.

This leads to another objection: '"Conjectural knowledge" is a contradiction in terms. "Knowledge" means "certain knowledge". To say "I know that *P* but I am not certain that *P*" is to contradict oneself. "I know that *P*" entails "I am certain that *P*" just as it entails "*P* is true". Fallibilists know

nothing, and fallibilism collapses into scepticism as before.'
(This objection, or something like it, is due to David Stove.)

This is an argument from ordinary English usage. There are
two ways one might respond to it: one might dispute the facts
about ordinary English usage; or one might say that ordinary
English usage is due for reform in the way suggested by the
fallibilist.

It is true 'I know that *P* but I am not certain that *P*' sounds
odd. This is because when one has specific reason to doubt *P*, a
specific reason for thinking *P* might be false, then one would not
say 'I know that *P*' but rather 'I think that *P*' or 'I believe that
P'. But when a fallibilist says 'I know that *P* but I am not
certain that *P*', it is not because of specific doubts about *P* but
rather because of general arguments against the possibility of
certain knowledge. Besides it is not clear that, as the word
'know' is ordinarily used, 'I know that *P*' does entail 'I am
certain that *P*'. If it did, then to say 'I know for certain that *P*'
would be redundant, like saying 'I am an unmarried bachelor'.
Yet the phrase 'We know for certain' does not seem redundant
in this way.

Suppose that in ordinary English 'know' does mean 'know
for certain'. The fallibilist could simply say that ordinary
English is infected with the epistemology of the Stone Age and
is due for reform (just as Bertrand Russell once remarked that it
was infected with the metaphysics of the Stone Age and was due
for reform). There is nothing sacrosanct about ordinary English
usage: philosophers might have good reason to reform it, just as
scientists sometimes have.

Here is an objection to the particular reform urged by the
fallibilist (supposing, for the sake of the argument, that it is a
reform): 'You want to change the meaning of the word
"know". But the change is quite unnecessary. Ordinary English
has the resources you need without messing it around at all: "I
believe that *P*", "I guess that *P*", "I conjecture that *P*". Why
not leave the word "know" alone, and recommend that people
abandon it in favour of such locutions. Why "conjectural
knowledge"? Why not just "conjectures"?'

The answer is plain: 'conjecturally know' means more than

'conjecture' or 'guess' or 'believe'. Conjectural knowledge requires truth: the fallibilist accepts that 'I know that P' entails 'P is true', accepts that 'false knowledge' is a contradiction in terms. Conjectural knowledge also requires that its possessor be justified in believing the thing conjecturally known. (This requirement is enough to exclude beliefs which are true by sheer fluke from counting as conjectural knowledge.) In short, the fallibilist (like everyone else) needs a concept of knowledge distinct from that of mere belief. And the concept of conjectural knowledge is close enough to the traditional concept of knowledge for both to be regarded as competing concepts of knowledge. (There is more on fallibilism or critical rationalism in Musgrave 1991a.)

References

Aristotle 1908. *The Works of Aristotle Translated into English*, ed. W. D. Ross, Volume VIII (*Metaphysica*). Oxford: Clarendon Press

Aubrey, J. 1898. *Brief Lives*, edited by A. Clark in two volumes. Oxford: Clarendon Press

Ayer, A. J. (ed.) 1959. *Logical Positivism*. Glencoe, Illinois: The Free Press

   1969. *Metaphysics and Common Sense*. London: Macmillan

Bacon, F. 1620. *Novum Organum*, in *The New Organon and Related Writings*, edited by F. H. Anderson. New York: The Liberal Arts Press (1960). References (e.g. 1, aphorism xlv) are to book and numbered aphorism.

Bartley, W. W. III 1962. *The Retreat to Commitment*. New York: Alfred A. Knopf

Berkeley, G. 1710. *A Treatise concerning the Principles of Human Knowledge*. In *The Works of George Berkeley, Bishop of Cloyne*, edited by A. A. Luce and T. E. Jessop, II. London: Nelson & Co. (1949). (References are to work, part, section and page numbers of the edition of 1949.)

   1713. *Three Dialogues between Hylas and Philonous*. In *The Works of George Berkeley, Bishop of Cloyne*, edited by A. A. Luce and T. E. Jessop, II. London: Nelson & Co. (1949). (References are to work and page number of this edition.)

Bonola, R. 1955. *Non-Euclidean Geometry: A Critical and Historical Study of its Developments*. New York: Dover Publications Inc.

Brown, G. M. 1972. *An Orkney Tapestry*. London: Gollancz

Bruner, J. S. and Postman, L. 1949. 'On the perception of incongruity: a paradigm', *Journal of Personality*, 18: 206–23

Carnap, R. 1966. *Philosophical Foundations of Physics*. New York and London: Basic Books Inc.

Carroll, L. 1865/71. *The Annotated Alice: Alice's Adventures in Wonderland and Through the Looking Glass*, with an introduction and notes by Martin Gardner (1965). Harmondsworth: Penguin Books

Chomsky, N. 1966. *Cartesian Linguistics*. New York: Harper & Row

Cohen, P. J. and Hersh, R. 1987. 'Non-Cantorian set theory', *Scientific American*, 217: 104–16

Cornman, J. W. and Lehrer, K. 1974. *Philosophical Problems and Arguments: An Introduction*. New York: Macmillan Publishing Co. (second edition)

Descartes, R. 1984. *The Philosophical Writings of Descartes*, translated by J. Cottingham, R. Stoothoff and D. Murdoch in two volumes. Cambridge University Press. (References are given by work, and volume and page number of this edition.)

Diogenes Laertius 1853. *The Lives and Opinions of Eminent Philosophers*, literally translated by C. D. Yonge. London: Henry G. Bohn

Eddington, A. S. 1939. *The Philosophy of Physical Science*. Cambridge University Press

Einstein, A. 1921. 'Geometry and experience', in his *Sidelights on Relativity*, pp. 25–56. New York: E. P. Dutton (1923)

1949. 'Autobiographical notes', in P. A. Schilpp (ed.), *Albert Einstein: Philosopher-Scientist*, pp. 1–95. New York: Harper & Brothers (1959)

Euclid 1956. *The Thirteen Books of Euclid's Elements*, translated with introduction and commentary by Sir Thomas L. Heath in three volumes. New York: Dover Publications Inc.

Field, H. 1980. *Science without Numbers: A Defense of Nominalism*. Oxford: Basil Blackwell, Princeton: Princeton University Press

1989. *Realism, Mathematics and Modality*. Oxford: Basil Blackwell

Flew, A. 1971. *An Introduction to Western Philosophy*. London: Thames and Hudson

Galileo Galilei 1957. *Discoveries and Opinions of Galileo*, translated with an introduction and notes by Stillman Drake. New York: Doubleday Anchor Books

Gettier, E. 1963. 'Is justified true belief knowledge', *Analysis*, 23: 121–3

Gödel, K. 1962. *On Formally Undecidable Propositions of Principia Mathematica And Related Systems*, translated by B. Meltzer. Edinburgh and London: Oliver and Boyd

Hanson, N. R. 1969. *Perception and Discovery*, edited by W. C. Humphreys. San Francisco: Freeman, Cooper and Company

Horwich, P. 1990. *Truth*. Oxford: Basil Blackwell

Hume, D. 1739–40. *A Treatise of Human Nature*. Edited, with an analytical index, by L. A. Selby-Bigge. Oxford: Clarendon Press (1888). (References are to work, book, part, section, and page number of this edition (e.g. *Treatise*, I, iv, 1; 1888: 186).)

1748. *An Enquiry Concerning Human Understanding*. Edited by L. A. Selby-Bigge. Oxford: Clarendon Press (1902)

1779. *Dialogues Concerning Natural Religion*, ed. H. D. Aiken. New York: Hafner Publishing Company (1948)

James, W. 1878. 'Brute and Human Intellect', in *Essays in Psychology*, ed. F. H. Burkhardt, F. Bowers and I. K. Skrupskelis, pp. 1–37. Cambridge, Mass.: Harvard University Press (1983)

1907. *Pragmatism: A New Name for Some Old Ways of Thinking*. London: Longmans, Green, and Co.

Joad, C. E. M. 1943. *A Guide to Modern Thought*. London: Pan Books

Kant, I. 1781. *Critique of Pure Reason*. Translated by N. Kemp-Smith. London: Macmillan & Co. (1929)

1783. *Prolegomena to any Future Metaphysic that will be able to present itself as a Science*. Translated with an introduction and notes by P. G. Lucas. Manchester University Press (1953)

Katz, D. 1953. *Animals and Men: Studies in Comparative Psychology*, translated by H. Steinberg and A. Summerfield. Harmondsworth: Penguin Books

Keller, H. 1904. *The World I Live In*. London: Hodder & Stoughton

Klibansky, R. and Mossner, E. C. (eds.) 1954. *New Letters of David Hume*. Oxford: Clarendon Press

Lakatos, I. (ed.) 1968. *The Problem of Inductive Logic*. Amsterdam: North-Holland Publishing Company

1976. *Proofs and Refutations: The Logic of Mathematical Discovery*, eds. J. Worrall and E. Zahar. Cambridge University Press

Laudan, L. 1977. *Progress and its Problems*. London: Routledge and Kegan Paul

Lettvin, J. Y., Maturana, H. R., McCulloch, W. S. and Pitts, W. H. 1959. 'What the frog's eye tells the frog's brain', *Proceedings of the Institute of Radio Engineers*, 11: 230–55

Levin, M. 1984. 'What kind of explanation is truth?', in J. Leplin (ed.), *Scientific Realism*, pp. 124–39. Berkeley and Los Angeles: University of California Press

Locke, J. 1690. *An Essay Concerning Human Understanding*. Collated and annotated by A. C. Fraser. New York: Dover Publications Inc. (1959). (References are to book, chapter and section (e.g. II, iv, 6).)

Lorenz, K. Z. 1952. *King Solomon's Ring*. London: Methuen

Mandelbaum, M. 1964. *Philosophy, Science and Sense Perception: Historical and Critical Studies*. Baltimore: The Johns Hopkins Press

Mill, J. S. 1843. *A System of Logic*. London: Longmans, Green, and Co. (eighth edition, 1872)

Moskowitz, B. A. 1978. 'The acquisition of language', *Scientific American*, 239: 82–96

Mossner, E. C. 1954. *The Life of David Hume*. Edinburgh: Thomas Nelson and Sons

Musgrave, A. 1977a. 'Explanation, description and scientific realism', *Scientia*, 112: 99–127

1977b. 'Logicism revisited', *British Journal for the Philosophy of Science*, 28: 99–127

1983. 'Theory and observation: Nola versus Popper', *Philosophica*, 31: 45–62

1988. 'The ultimate argument for scientific realism', in R. Nola (ed.), *Relativism and Realism in Science*, pp. 229–52. Dordrecht, Boston, London: Kluwer Academic Publishers

1989. 'Deductivism versus psychologism', in M. A. Nottorno (ed.), *Perspectives on Psychologism*, pp. 315–40. Leiden: E. J. Brill

1991a. 'What is critical rationalism?', in A. Bohnen and A. Musgrave (eds.), *Wege der Vernunft: Festschrift zum siebzigsten Gerburstag von Hans Albert*, pp. 17–30. Tübingen: J. C. B. Mohr (Paul Siebeck)

1991b. 'The myth of astronomical instrumentalism', in G. Munevar (ed.), *Beyond Reason: Essays on the Philosophy of Paul Feyerabend*, pp. 243–80. Dordrecht, Boston, London: Kluwer Academic Publishers

Naess, A. 1958. '"Truth" as conceived by those who are not professional philosophers', *Skrifter utgitt av Det Norske Videnscaps-Akademi i Oslo, II. Hist-Filos Klasse*, vol. IV. Oslo.

Neurath, O. 1959. 'Protocol sentences', in Ayer (ed.), 1959, pp. 199–208

Newton, I. 1730. *Opticks*. London: Dover Publications Inc. (1952)

Nozick, R. 1981. *Philosophical Explanations*. Oxford University Press

Pascal, B. 1904. *Pascal's 'Pensées'*, translated by W. F. Trotter. London and Toronto: J. M. Dent, New York: E. P. Dutton (1931)

Popkin, R. H. 1964. *The History of Scepticism from Erasmus to Descartes*. New York: Humanities Press (revised edition)

Popper, K. R. 1945. *The Open Society and Its Enemies*, two volumes. London: Routledge and Kegan Paul (fourth revised edition, 1962)

1959. *The Logic of Scientific Discovery*. London: Hutchinson

1962. *Conjectures and Refutations: The Growth of Scientific Knowledge*. London: Routledge and Kegan Paul

1972. *Objective Knowledge*. Oxford: Clarendon Press

Putnam, H. 1975. *Mathematics, Matter and Method (Philosophical Papers, Volume I)*. Cambridge University Press

1981. *Reason, Truth and History*. Cambridge University Press

Radnitzky, G. and Berkeley, W. W. III (eds.) 1987. *Evolutionary Epistemology, Rationality, and the Sociology of Knowledge*. La Salle, Illinois: Open Court Publishing Company

Ramsey, F. P. 1931. *The Foundations of Mathematics and other Logical Essays*, edited by R. B. Braithwaite. London: Routledge and Kegan Paul

Reid, T. 1764. *An Inquiry Into the Human Mind*, edited with an introduction by Timothy Duggan, Chicago and London: University of Chicago Press (1970)

Russell, B. 1912. *The Problems of Philosophy*. London: Oxford University Press

   1927. *An Outline of Philosophy*. London: George Allen & Unwin

   1935. *Sceptical Essays*. London: George Allen & Unwin

   1940. *An Inquiry into Meaning and Truth*. London: George Allen & Unwin

   1946. *History of Western Philosophy*. London: George Allen & Unwin

   1948. *Human Knowledge Its Scope and Limits*. London: George Allen & Unwin

Sextus Empiricus 1933–49. *Sextus Empiricus with an English translation by the Rev. R. G. Bury in Four Volumes*. London: William Heinemann Ltd. and Cambridge, Mass.: Harvard University Press

Singer, B. F. 1971. 'Towards a psychology of science', *American Psychologist*, 26: 1010–15

Sluckin, W. 1964. *Imprinting and Early Learning*. London: Methuen

Tarski, A. 1944. 'The semantic conception of truth and the foundations of semantics', *Philosophy and Phenomenological Research*, 4: 341–75

   1956. *Logic, Semantics, Metamathematics: Papers from 1923 to 1938*. Oxford: Clarendon Press

Tinbergen, N. 1953. *The Herring Gull's World*. London: Collins

Urbach, P. 1987. *Francis Bacon's Philosophy of Science*. Illinois: Open Court

van Fraassen, B. 1980. *The Scientific Image*. Oxford University Press

Watkins, J. W. N. 1968. 'Hume, Carnap and Popper', in Lakatos (ed.), 1968, pp. 271–82

   1984. *Science and Scepticism*. London: Hutchinson & Co.

Weiler, G. 1958. 'On Fritz Mauthner's critique of language', *Mind*, 67: 80–7

Wigner, E. 1967. *Symmetries and Reflections: Scientific Essays*. Bloomington, Indiana: Indiana University Press

Wittgenstein, L. 1922. *Tractatus Logico-Philosophicus*. London: Routledge and Kegan Paul

Wyndham, J. 1951. *The Day of the Triffids*. London: Michael Joseph

Index